PRAISE FOR
LEADING SIX SIGMA

"Six Sigma promises dramatic performance improvement and significant bottom-line results for businesses. So...why is there so much variation in the actual impact that the many businesses that are pursuing Six Sigma are experiencing? *Leading Six Sigma* reveals the root causes. Ron Snee and Roger Hoerl, two respected and seasoned practitioners, take readers beyond the technical 'methods-and-tools' view of Six Sigma and focus their practical insights on what leaders must do to unlock the transforming power of Six Sigma. Their advice is not theoretical but rather distilled to proven approaches based on their experiences as consultant and GE insider. Whether you are engaged in Six Sigma now or are tempted to launch the initiative, this book will help you do it right."

—Eric Mattenson
VP, Six Sigma, Quest Diagnostics
Formerly Six Sigma Process Leader for GE Capital

"*Leading Six Sigma* does an excellent job of explaining the value of using Six Sigma to drive business performance and giving practical guidance for implementation. Ron Snee and Roger Hoerl have made it simple, understandable, and compelling. The examples they use from different companies such as GE and Grace prove without question that Six Sigma works in companies of very different sizes and cultures. If you are interested in upgrading the capabilities of the people in your company, improving its performance quickly, and positioning it for better results in the future, read this book!"

—Paul J. Norris
Chairman, President, and CEO, W. R. Grace & Co.

"Ron Snee and Roger Hoerl are to be congratulated on writing a book that draws from their diverse firsthand experience with Six Sigma deployment. Much has been written about the DMAIC project implementation strategy, but Snee and Hoerl present a compelling, four-step initiative implementation strategy that goes beyond the boilerplate recommendations. They stand firm on the things that do and don't work, as well as offer options on things that may or may not work based on the implementing organization's current situation. This book is a invaluable resource for organizations in any stage of their deployment."

—Dr. Steven P. Bailey
Certified Master Black Belt DuPont Global Services
Past President American Society for Quality

"*Leading Six Sigma* is a good reference to compare your progress—from deployment through sustaining momentum to integration into your process-management system. Snee and Hoerl capture the essence of the leadership, commitment, and resource deployment necessary to make Six Sigma successful."

—Bill Schroer
VP of Operations and Manufacturing Strategy
Trane American Standard Companies

LEADING SIX SIGMA

ISBN 0-13-008457-3

FT Prentice Hall
FINANCIAL TIMES

In an increasingly competitive world, it is quality
of thinking that gives an edge—an idea that opens new
doors, a technique that solves a problem, or an insight
that simply helps make sense of it all.

We work with leading authors in the various arenas
of business and finance to bring cutting-edge thinking
and best learning practice to a global market.

It is our goal to create world-class print publications
and electronic products that give readers
knowledge and understanding which can then be
applied, whether studying or at work.

To find out more about our business
products, you can visit us at www.ft-ph.com

Pearson
Education

LEADING SIX SIGMA
A Step-by-Step Guide Based on Experience With GE and Other Six Sigma Companies

Ronald D. Snee
Roger W. Hoerl

FT Prentice Hall
FINANCIAL TIMES

An Imprint of PEARSON EDUCATION
Upper Saddle River, NJ • New York • London • San Francisco • Toronto • Sydney
Tokyo • Singapore • Hong Kong • Cape Town • Madrid
Paris • Milan • Munich • Amsterdam

www.ft-ph.com

Library of Congress Cataloging-in-Publication Data

A CIP catalog record of this book can be obtained from the Library of Congress

Production Supervisor: Wil Mara
Acquisitions Editor: Jim Boyd
Editorial Assistant: Kate Wolf
Marketing Manager: Bryan Gambrel
Manufacturing Manager: Alexis Heydt-Long
Cover Designer: Nina Scuderi

© 2003 Pearson Education, Inc.
Publishing as Financial Times Prentice Hall
Upper Saddle River, NJ 07458

Financial Times Prentice Hall books are widely used by corporations and government agencies for training, marketing, and resale.

For more information regarding corporate and government bulk discounts, please contact: Corporate and Government Sales, Prentice Hall PTR, One Lake Street, Upper Saddle River, NJ 07458. Phone: 800-382-3419; FAX: 201-236-7141; E-mail: corpsales@prenhall.com.

Company and product names mentioned herein are the trademarks or registered trademarks of their respective owners.

Printed in the United States of America

10 9 8 7 6 5 4

ISBN 0-13-008457-3

Pearson Education LTD.
Pearson Education Australia PTY, Limited
Pearson Education Singapore, Pte. Ltd
Pearson Education North Asia Ltd
Pearson Education Canada, Ltd.
Pearson Educación de Mexico, S.A. de C.V.
Pearson Education—Japan
Pearson Education Malaysia, Pte. Ltd
Pearson Education, Upper Saddle River, New Jersey

FINANCIAL TIMES PRENTICE HALL BOOKS

For more information, please go to www.ft-ph.com

Dr. Judith M. Bardwick
  Seeking the Calm in the Storm: Managing Chaos in Your Business Life
Gerald R. Baron
  Now Is Too Late: Survival in an Era of Instant News
Thomas L. Barton, William G. Shenkir, and Paul L. Walker
  Making Enterprise Risk Management Pay Off: How Leading Companies Implement Risk Management
Michael Basch
  CustomerCulture: How FedEx and Other Great Companies Put the Customer First Every Day
J. Stewart Black and Hal B. Gregersen
  Leading Strategic Change: Breaking Through the Brain Barrier
Deirdre Breakenridge
  Cyberbranding: Brand Building in the Digital Economy
William C. Byham, Audrey B. Smith, and Matthew J. Paese
  Grow Your Own Leaders: How to Identify, Develop, and Retain Leadership Talent
Jonathan Cagan and Craig M. Vogel
  Creating Breakthrough Products: Innovation from Product Planning to Program Approval
Subir Chowdhury
  Organization 21C: Someday All Organizations Will Lead this Way
Subir Chowdhury
  The Talent Era: Achieving a High Return on Talent
Sherry Cooper
  Ride the Wave: Taking Control in a Turbulent Financial Age
James W. Cortada
  21st Century Business: Managing and Working in the New Digital Economy
James W. Cortada
  Making the Information Society: Experience, Consequences, and Possibilities
Aswath Damodaran
  The Dark Side of Valuation: Valuing Old Tech, New Tech, and New Economy Companies
Henry A. Davis and William W. Sihler
  Financial Turnarounds: Preserving Enterprise Value
Ross Dawson
  Living Networks: Leading Your Company, Customers, and Partners in the Hyper-connected Economy

Robin Miller
The Online Rules of Successful Companies: The Fool-Proof Guide to Building Profits

D. Quinn Mills
Buy, Lie, and Sell High: How Investors Lost Out on Enron and the Internet Bubble

Dale Neef
E-procurement: From Strategy to Implementation

John R. Nofsinger
Investment Blunders (of the Rich and Famous)...And What You Can Learn from Them

John R. Nofsinger
Investment Madness: How Psychology Affects Your Investing...And What to Do About It

Erica Orloff and Kathy Levinson, Ph.D.
The 60-Second Commute: A Guide to Your 24/7 Home Office Life

Tom Osenton
Customer Share Marketing: How the World's Great Marketers Unlock Profits from Customer Loyalty

Richard W. Paul and Linda Elder
Critical Thinking: Tools for Taking Charge of Your Professional and Personal Life

Matthew Serbin Pittinsky, Editor
The Wired Tower: Perspectives on the Impact of the Internet on Higher Education

W. Alan Randolph and Barry Z. Posner
Checkered Flag Projects: 10 Rules for Creating and Managing Projects that Win, Second Edition

Stephen P. Robbins
The Truth About Managing People...And Nothing but the Truth

Fernando Robles, Françoise Simon, and Jerry Haar
Winning Strategies for the New Latin Markets

Jeff Saperstein and Daniel Rouach
Creating Regional Wealth in the Innovation Economy: Models, Perspectives, and Best Practices

Ronald Snee and Roger Hoerl
Leading Six Sigma: A Step-by-Step Guide Based on Experience with GE and Other Six Sigma Companies

Eric G. Stephan and Wayne R. Pace
Powerful Leadership: How to Unleash the Potential in Others and Simplify Your Own Life

Jonathan Wight
Saving Adam Smith: A Tale of Wealth, Transformation, and Virtue

Yoram J. Wind and Vijay Mahajan, with Robert Gunther
Convergence Marketing: Strategies for Reaching the New Hybrid Consumer

TABLE OF CONTENTS

Deployment Questions and Answers 223

Appendix Six Sigma Deployment Plan–An Example 255

GLOSSARY 267

ACRONYMS 271

INDEX 273

PREFACE

Six Sigma is about radically improving the performance of an organization—a pursuit to which we have collectively dedicated more than fifty-five years of our careers. We first worked together at DuPont in the early 1980s. We continued our professional relationship over the years and, in 1995, we both independently began our work in Six Sigma. Having been involved in improvement efforts most of our careers, we were both amazed at the tremendous financial results produced by Six Sigma. We continued our discussions of Six Sigma over the next several years as we deployed the method in different organizations.

While we began to see numerous books on Six Sigma, they tended to either be focused on the technical tools of Six Sigma, or were using hype and fanfare to sell the reader on implementation. Our colleagues and clients, on the other hand, were raising deeper issues about how to actually deploy Six Sigma and avoid potholes along the way. These questions highlighted to us the paucity of practical guidance on the deployment of Six Sigma. This book represents our attempt to fill this important void.

How This Book Can Help You

Six Sigma began at Motorola in the 1980s as a statistical measure of process performance. AlliedSignal and General Electric (GE) broadened and further popularized the approach in the 1990s. Their successes encouraged other companies such as DuPont, Dow Chemical, 3M, Ford, American Express, and companies in Europe and the Pacific Rim to undertake Six Sigma initiatives. The methodology has evolved significantly along the way, and today Six Sigma has grown into a holistic strategy and methodology for improving the performance of an organization. Six Sigma integrates the improvement tools that have proven effective over the years into a comprehensive approach that improves both customer satisfaction and the bottom line. As a result, Six Sigma builds on what has been successful in the past and takes performance improvement to a new level of effectiveness.

Although the theory is simple, many who implement Six Sigma struggle with the details of overall deployment. Being sold on Six Sigma is of little value if it cannot be successfully implemented. While most companies have experienced tremendous success with Six Sigma, some have not. Our research indicates there is a lack of literature on why this is so. We have examined both very successful and minimally successful organizations in order to understand the root causes for success or failure. We have found that successful companies have important similarities in deployment, as do the unsuccessful companies. Understanding these common success factors enables one to significantly enhance the probability of success, while understanding the commonalities of unsuccessful companies enables one to avoid the potholes.

Of course, each organization is different. You cannot blindly adopt the Six Sigma deployment models used by other companies and expect to be successful. It makes much more sense to understand what specifically led these companies to success, and *adapt* those approaches and methods to your own organization. Providing a roadmap to do just this is the focus of this book.

What's In This Book

We present a deployment roadmap that has worked in a number of different circumstances. It shows how to get started, manage the important aspects of the initiative, maintain the momentum over time, and eventually how to scale down the initiative and institutionalize Six Sigma. Specific advice is given in such areas as:

- Identifying your company's most promising Six Sigma opportunities and leaders
- Providing leadership, talent, and infrastructure for a successful launch
- Implementing systems, processes, and budgets for ongoing Six Sigma projects
- Measuring and maximizing the financial value of your Six Sigma initiative

Avoiding the subtle mistakes that can make Six Sigma fall short

Our guidance is based on a total of over fourteen years' experience deploying Six Sigma in large and small companies, manufacturing and research and development (R&D), and non-manufacturing organizations such as financial services. Indeed, we have found that Six Sigma can work everywhere—different cultures, countries, industries, functions, and processes—if you follow the process.

In Chapter 1 we provide an overview of Six Sigma, highlighting the difference between the deployment aspects of Six Sigma and the tools and methods used to conduct Six Sigma projects. To date the lion's share of literature has focused on the methods and tools and virtually ignored the critical subject of deployment. As a result there is precious little in the literature to guide executives as they deploy Six Sigma.

Chapter 2 provides four case studies—General Electric, W. R. Grace and two less successful deployments—highlighting what has worked and what hasn't. Unfortunately, implementing Six Sigma is no guarantee of success. The focus in the press has been on the successes, but there have certainly been failures. As you will see, you can learn from both.

In Chapter 3 we analyze the four case studies to identify success factors for the deployment of Six Sigma. You will see specific reasons why some companies succeeded and others didn't. These factors are identified and integrated into an overall strategy for deploying Six Sigma within an organization. The remainder of the book provides detailed advice on each step of this strategy.

The focus of Chapter 4 is on launching the initiative, probably the most important phase of Six Sigma. If Six Sigma is poorly launched, it will be difficult to reorganize and regain momentum. The pros and cons of full (across the company) and partial deployment are addressed. Particular focus is placed on selecting the right projects and the right people.

Chapter 5 focuses on managing the ongoing effort, highlighting the need for supportive managerial processes and systems. After Six Sigma has been launched, there is often a loss of momentum as other priorities take center stage. It's these management systems that enable Six Sigma to continue to work and change the culture.

Chapter 6 introduces ways to sustain momentum and growth longer term. Using a sports analogy, it focuses on the defensive effort needed to hold the line and the offensive effort needed to score more points. Issues such as system reviews, ongoing training systems, and expanding Six Sigma throughout the enterprise and to suppliers and customers are addressed. The use of Six Sigma as a leadership development tool is also discussed.

Bringing Six Sigma to the level of day-to-day work is the focus of Chapter 7. This includes the integration of Six Sigma with operational and managerial processes as well as developing an overall organizational improvement system. The integration of Six Sigma with ISO 9000, Baldrige assessment criteria and lean manufacturing is also discussed.

Chapter 8 provides additional guidance for leaders: deepening understanding of Six Sigma, ensuring success of individual improvement projects and the overall initiative. Particular attention is placed on helping managers understand what actually goes on in Six Sigma projects without getting buried in the details of the Six Sigma tools.

The concluding section focuses on answers to more than thirty frequently asked questions, and references that will help deepen your knowledge of Six Sigma. These questions have been the most critical that we have been asked by a variety of organizations implementing Six Sigma. They concern issues that almost all those deploying Six Sigma encounter at one time or another. An example deployment plan is shown in the appendix.

How to Use This Book

Using this book as a guide, you can get your Six Sigma deployment process off to a solid start and help assure its continuing success. A body of knowledge of how to properly deploy Six Sigma, as well as the pitfalls to avoid, is provided. You can speed up the deployment and success of Six Sigma if you utilize what those who have gone before you have learned; as such you don't have to reinvent the wheel. Each element of Six Sigma is relatively simple. However, putting it all together is the hard part. This book not only provides a roadmap for deploying Six Sigma but also highlights the keys to successful deployment, and a way to maintain the gains—putting it all together in a single document. By reading this book you will learn what works and what doesn't, learn effective deployment strategies and become fluent in the language of Six Sigma. Of course, a roadmap is not a cookbook—each organization will still need to customize its approach based on its own unique situation.

All those involved in Six Sigma can benefit from this book. Executives will learn how to design and lead the deployment process and how to focus on critical improvement areas. Champions will learn how to select and charter projects and how to select and guide Black Belts and Green Belts. Master Black Belts will learn the deployment process, a knowledge that is needed to work effectively with management, Champions and the Black Belts and Green Belts. Black Belts and Green Belts will learn more about the Six Sigma deployment process which will deepen their understanding of their role.

It is becoming increasingly recognized that Six Sigma is not only an effective process improvement methodology, but also an effective strategy for culture change and leadership development. Six Sigma obviously emphasizes the use of facts and data to guide the decision making process. But the improvement project selection and review, recognition and reward, and communication processes used to support Six Sigma are also effective culture change vehicles. Increasingly, companies are seeing Six Sigma as an effective leadership development methodology with companies such as GE, Honeywell, 3M and DuPont requiring Six Sigma Black Belt and Green Belt experience for managerial advancement.

ACKNOWLEDGEMENTS

We are pleased to acknowledge the numerous individuals who provided insights, suggestions and constructive criticism in the development of this book. These include Bill Rodebaugh, Joe Ficalora, Steve Bailey, Linda Bankowski and Jacque Thompson.

We also express our sincere gratitude to Jim Boyd, Wil Mara, and the other members of the Financial Times Prentice Hall publication team for their guidance and assistance in making this book a reality.

Our sincere appreciation goes also to our spouses, Marjorie and Senecca, whose support and understanding went well beyond what was reasonable to expect.

1

So You Want to Do Six Sigma?

"The significant problems we face cannot be solved at the same level of thinking we were at when we created them."

—Albert Einstein

You may have learned about Six Sigma from colleagues, customers, or suppliers. You may have read about how much money Motorola, AlliedSignal, General Electric (GE), or others made after implementing Six Sigma. And, because success breeds success, you may have decided to deploy Six Sigma within your own company. We certainly encourage you along this path, but with one caveat: proceed with caution.

Six Sigma is definitely not a get-rich-quick scheme; it is a business strategy and methodology that can help your organization create real and lasting improvement in performance that leads to increased customer satisfaction and an improved bottom line.

This book provides a detailed strategy for Six Sigma deployment and helps you develop a step-by-step approach, guidance that has been lacking, despite the volumes of Six Sigma literature. To set the stage, some basic background of Six Sigma is provided, along with a brief discussion of the roles managers and employees play in the process. This book assumes a basic knowledge of Six Sigma. To study Six Sigma history or tools in greater detail see the references provided. For example, Harry and Schroeder (2000), Pande, et al. (2000), and Eckes (2001) provide sound descriptions of, and convincing arguments for, Six Sigma. Similarly, Breyfogle (1999) provides a detailed treatise of the Six Sigma tools–the statistical and problem-solving methods that are applied in Six Sigma projects.

Why You Need This Book

Motorola developed Six Sigma around 1987 and other companies, large and small, embraced the theory in the 1990's.

Although the theory is simple, many who implement Six Sigma often struggle with the details of overall deployment. Your company is not GE or AlliedSignal; therefore, you cannot simply adopt their Six Sigma deployment models. But it makes sense to take what has worked successfully in other organizations and adapt those approaches and methods and that is the focus of this book.

To use an initial public offering (IPO) analogy, when a small private company decides to go public, there are legal, financial, investor relations, and other issues to be addressed. If this book were on IPOs, it would not attempt to convince the reader to go public. Nor would it focus on the details of corporate law, public accounting rules, or the history of investor relations policy. Rather, it would provide a step-by-step strategy for going public, and give details on how to succeed. It would answer questions commonly asked by executives of the company going public, and point out pitfalls to avoid, based on a careful study of successful—and unsuccessful—IPOs.

We focus on overall deployment strategy and step-by-step guidance for two reasons:

- First, our research indicates there is a lack of literature on these critical topics. Being sold on Six Sigma is of little value if it cannot be successfully implemented.

- Our second reason is that this focus coincides with our collective experience. Neither of us invented Six Sigma, but each has over seven years experience deploying it in large and small companies, manufacturing and research and development (R&D), and non-manufacturing organizations such as financial services.

As you will see in Chapter 2, implementing Six Sigma is no guarantee of success. The focus in the press has been on the successes, but there have certainly been failures. In Chapters 2 and 3 you will see specific reasons why some companies succeeded and others didn't. This book will highlight these factors, and integrate them into an overall strategy for deploying Six Sigma within an organization.   The focus of Chapter 4 is on launching the initiative, probably the most important phase of Six Sigma. If Six Sigma is poorly launched, it will be difficult to reorganize and regain momentum.

Chapter 5 changes from the launch stage to the manage stage, keying in on putting systems into place. After Six Sigma has been implemented, however, there is often a loss of momentum as other priorities take center stage. Chapter 6 introduces ways to sustain momentum and growth. Like a good coach, it focuses on the defensive effort needed to hold the line and the offensive effort needed to score more points.

Bringing Six Sigma to the level of day-to-day work is the focus of Chapter 7. Chapter 8 covers final thoughts for leaders: understanding Six Sigma tools, ensuring success for the project and the overall initiative. Answers to frequently asked questions and references will help clear the air further. An example of a deployment plan is shown in the appendix.

Using this book as a guide, you can get your Six Sigma deployment process off to a solid start and help assure its continuing success. A body of knowledge of how to properly deploy Six Sigma is now available, as well as the pitfalls to avoid. You can speed up the deployment and success of Six Sigma if you utilize what those who have gone before you have learned; as such you don't have to reinvent the wheel. Each element of Six Sigma is relatively simple. However, putting it all together is the hard part. This book not only provides a roadmap for deploying Six Sigma, but also the key elements of successful deployment and a "way to maintain the gains," putting it all together in a single document. By reading this book you will:

- Learn what works and what doesn't

- Learn effective deployment strategies

- Become fluent in the language of Six Sigma

Of course, a roadmap is not a cookbook—each organization will still need to customize its approach based on its own unique situation.

An Overview

After Motorola's creation of Six Sigma, AlliedSignal and GE popularized it in the 1990s. Today it has become widely recognized as an effective method for improving business performance. These successes have encouraged many other companies such as Ford, DuPont, 3M, Dow Chemical, and American Express, as well as companies in the Pacific Rim and in Europe to undertake Six Sigma initiatives. Many small and mid-size companies such as W. R. Grace, Crompton, Cummins and Lincoln Electric are also using the Six Sigma approach. Six Sigma has been found to be effective in all types of companies including manufacturing, service, financial, and health care. Six Sigma also applies in all parts of the organization, including manufacturing, new product development, and transactional and administrative processes. In short, Six Sigma provides an overall strategy and methodology for improving the performance of the organization. As such, it is also applicable to government, academic, and not-for-profit organizations.

Staying Power

Executives of AlliedSignal and GE who have left to become CEOs of other companies, including 3M, Home Depot, Raytheon, W. R. Grace, Great Lakes Chemical, Huber Chemical, and American Standard, have started Six Sigma improvement initiatives shortly after taking over their new companies. It is unlikely that these CEOs would have initiated the use of Six Sigma if they saw it only as a management fad with a short life.

Six Sigma helps employees grow into effective and knowledgeable managers having the ability to understand the business from a cost, quality, and delivery point of view as well as understand the role of improvement from a practical perspective.

The meaning of Six Sigma has evolved since Motorola introduced the concept in the 1980's. From a statistical viewpoint, a Six Sigma process has a defect level of 3.4 per million opportunities. Six Sigma is also used to define a philosophy of improvement focused on reducing defects and improving customer satisfaction. Most companies today, however, view Six Sigma as a business strategy and methodology for improving process performance in such a way that customer satisfaction is increased and the bottom line ($$) is improved. The bottom line focus attracts the attention and support of corporate executives and financial analysts, and makes Six Sigma different from many earlier improvement approaches, such as statistical process control (SPC), total quality management (TQM), and ISO 9000, none of which have the explicit bottom line focus.

The Essence of Six Sigma

Table 1-1 summarizes the key elements of Six Sigma. The approach can be broken into two key aspects: a managerial initiative and a set of methods and tools. Let us discuss the mangement initiative first.

Breakthrough Improvement. Six Sigma is about business improvement; it is not about culture change per se, although it will radically change culture. The strategy is to get the improvements, then create the infrastructure and systems (culture) that will grow and maintain the gains. Six Sigma is not about quality—at least not in the traditional sense of the word—although it results in improved quality. It is not about training, although training is used to build the skills needed to deploy it. Viewing Six Sigma as a massive training initiative is a low-yield strategy. Six Sigma is about breakthrough business improvement, not incremental improvement. Six Sigma projects are defined to produce major improvements (30%, 40%, 50%, 60% and more) in process performance in less than 4-6 months with a significant bottom line impact. Such changes greatly change how business is conducted day-to-day.

TABLE 1-1   Two Key Aspects of Six Sigma

Initiative	Methods and Tools
• Improvement	• Process Thinking
• Breakthrough	• Process Variation
• Systematic, Focused Approach	• Facts, Figures, Data
• Right Projects	• Define, Measure, Analyze, Improve,
—Linked to Business Goals	Control
• Right People	• 8 Key Tools
—Selected and Trained	—Sequenced and Linked
• Project Management	• Statistical Tools
—Management Reviews	• Statistical Software
• Sustain the Gains	• Critical Few Variables
—New Projects	
• Results	
—Process and Financial ($$)	

Six Sigma Uses a Systematic and Focused Approach. Not all executives are used to the discipline that such an approach requires. There are road maps and step-by-step procedures for the managerial and technical aspects of Six Sigma. These processes and systems enable the key players in the initiative, such as Champions, Black Belts, and Green Belts to move up the learning curve more quickly and keep the organization focused on rapid improvement. (These and other titles are defined in the "Roles of Six Sigma Leaders" section later in this chapter.) Six Sigma is not an art, although experience, good judgment, and creativity are certainly required.

Right Projects. Six Sigma is about working on the right projects; those that support the business strategy. Six Sigma projects are linked to the goals of the business and to key problems that must be solved if the organization is to be successful (e.g., critical customer complaints, process downtime producing stock outs, major accounts receivables issues, etc.). As you will see in later chapters, project selection is often where the battle is won or lost. Even top talent cannot salvage a poorly selected project. Black Belts and Green Belts work on important projects during as well as after the training. The specific roles of the Black Belts and Green Belts, who lead the improvement projects and are the primary "doers" in Six Sigma, will be discussed later in this chapter and in Chapter 4. Working on the right projects obviously requires careful business planning and coordination. Having Black Belts and Green Belts pick their own project is not a good strategy in our experience. It is important, however, that the goals of the Black Belt and Green Belt projects are realistic and achievable so that the projects will be successful and the Black Belts and Green Belts—and organization as a whole—will build confidence that Six Sigma will work "here."

Right People. Six Sigma is about selecting and training the right people to fill the key roles. Successful organizations select their best people to fill the key Six Sigma positions (Champions, Master Black Belts (MBBs), Black Belts, and Green Belts). Most companies consider these people to be their future leaders. After those selected complete their Six Sigma assignments they move into leadership positions and utilize their Six Sigma experience to guide others in improving the organization using the same approach. In this way, the cycle of continuous improvement is ingrained into the culture of the organization, and the company is assured of having "enlightened" leaders in the future.

Project Management and Reviews. Six Sigma is about effective project management, including project selection, planning, and management reviews.   Proper planning is important to ensure success. Such planning helps to avoid "scope creep" (project size and definition slowly growing beyond what is reasonable to accomplish considering the allotted time and resources), misalignment with management, resource issues, projects that move at glacial speed, and other common project pitfalls. Management reviews are critical to success. Projects should be reviewed weekly and monthly (different types of reviews), and the overall Six Sigma system should be reviewed quarterly and annually. Management reviews are critical to success. The lack of management reviews significantly reduces the impact of the Six Sigma effort. The reviews keep the Black Belt and managers focused on the project and emphasize the long-term commitment of management to improve the performance of the organization ensuring it will be a long-term source of products, services, and employment.

Sustaining the Gains. A methodology for sustaining the gains is an integral part of the Six Sigma approach. This methodology is usually called the "control plan," and is one of the unique aspects of Six Sigma. The control plan can be viewed at both a tactical and strategic level. At the tactical level it sustains the gains of individual projects, and at the strategic level it sustains and broadens the gains of the Six Sigma initiative overall. A key element of the strategic control plan is the continual identification of new projects and the placing of those projects in the project hopper. As the Black Belts complete their projects they are assigned new projects that have been taken from the hopper.

Right Results. Six Sigma is about getting the right results—improvements in process performance that are linked to the bottom line. The team estimates what a project is worth, typically with the help of the finance organization, before work is initiated. After the project has been completed, the team calculates the bottom line savings. Many organizations, such as GE, require a sign-off from the finance organization verifying the financial impact, and identifying where in the income statement it will show up. In this way you will know exactly what the bottom line impact of the project has been. Surprisingly, many previous improvement initiatives discouraged focus on the financials when identifying or evaluating projects.

Six Sigma Methods and Tools

Now let us turn to the methods and tools of Six Sigma.

Process Thinking. The first key method is process thinking—taking the view that all work is a process. All work in all parts of the organization, whether it is in manufacturing, new product development, finance, logistics, or procurement, is accomplished by a series of interconnected steps. When you view problems from the framework of a process with inputs, processing steps, and outputs, a common approach to improving processes and solving problems can be applied. Since Six Sigma had its roots in electronics manufacturing, there is a common misunderstanding that Six Sigma can only help in this one activity. This mistake is analogous to assuming that the Internet can only be useful in the defense industry (where it originated).

A schematic of a generic process is shown in Figure 1-1. Examples of the process inputs, controlled variables, uncontrolled variables, and process outputs for manufacturing and non-manufacturing processes are shown in Tables 1-2 and 1-3, respectively. These tables illustrate that the process inputs include those things that are used to produce the process outputs. The controlled variables are those that run the process and, as the name implies, can be controlled ("knobs" on the process). The uncontrolled variables are those that affect the output of the process but that there is limited control over. Obviously, the inputs come from suppliers, which could be the person down the hall or another process or raw mate-

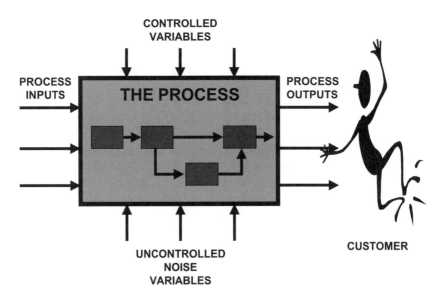

FIGURE 1-1   Schematic of a Process and Its Variables

TABLE 1-2   Manufacturing Process Variables

Process Input Variables
• Raw materials
• Water
• Energy

Controlled Process Variables
• Temperature
• Pressure
• Flow rate
• Catalyst concentration

Uncontrolled (Noise) Process Variables
• Ambient conditions—temperature and humidity
• Shift
• Team
• Operators
• Machines
• Raw material lot

Process Output Variables
• Yield
• Waste
• Capacity
• Downtime
• Production rate

---

rial supplier, and the outputs go to customers, either internal or external to the organization. Viewing processes this way produces the SIPOC model (suppliers, inputs, process, outputs, customers). In the SIPOC model, all processes, no matter the source, begin to look similar in nature.

Process Variation. Variation is present in all processes and every aspect of the workday. It reduces process performance, decreases customer satisfaction, and has a negative impact on the bottom line. Customers want a consistent product or service—one that they can count on to provide the same value all the time. Products need to work as anticipated, and be delivered and serviced on time, just as financial transactions need to proceed smoothly with minimal disruptions. Six Sigma is focused on reducing the negative effects of process variation in two major ways: (1) it shifts the process average to the desired target level and (2) it reduces the variation around the process average. This results in a process performing at the right average level with minimal variation from product to product or transaction to transaction. The need to address variation is the primary reason for including so many statistical tools in the Six Sigma toolkit. Statistics is the only science focused on identifying, measuring, and understanding variation, thereby being able to adjust process variables to reduce variation.

Facts, Figures and Data. Six Sigma is about facts, figures, and data—in other words, data-based decision making versus reliance on gut feel and intuition. The approach requires that data are available on all key process and input variables (see Tables 1-2 and 1-3). The project doesn't proceed until adequate data are available. The focus on the use of data along with process thinking and variation helps integrate the scientific method into the Six Sigma methodology. The integration of process thinking, understanding of variation, and data-based decision making is often referred to as statistical thinking (see Hoerl and Snee [2002]).

DMAIC Improvement Methodology. The primary improvement methodology of Six Sigma is a standard improvement process that has five key phases: define, measure, analyze, improve, and control (DMAIC). All improvement projects touch on these phases in one way or another (new design projects use a different process called Design for Six Sigma). The tools of Six Sigma are integrated into these phases. This is a strength and uniqueness of Six Sigma. All projects utilize the same improvement process, although the individual applications may be quite different. In contrast to most statistics training that throws a lot of tools on the table and lets practitioners fend for themselves, the DMAIC framework shows practitioners how to integrate and sequence the tools into an overall improvement strategy. This enables practitioners to attack virtually any problem in a systematic manner.

Eight Key Tools. Six Sigma utilizes many individual tools, but eight are most frequently applied. These eight key tools are linked and sequenced in the DMAIC framework. This relatively small number of improvement tools helps the Black Belts and Green Belts move up the learning curve more quickly. They learn the order in which to use the tools and how the output of one tool becomes the input for another tool. You will learn how to think about the tools in Chapter 8, but this book is not a

TABLE 1-3   Customer Order (Non-Manufacturing) Process Variables

Process Inputs
- Email, fax, phone, and postal service reliability
- Completeness of customer orders
- Accuracy of customer orders

Controlled Process Variables
- Customer service representative training
- Inventory level
- Shipment method
- Promise date

Uncontrolled (Noise) Process Variables
- Customer service representative attitude
- Day of week
- Season of year
- Customer required date
- Shift
- Team

Process Output Variables
- Order correctness
- Delivery time
- Package quality

reference book on the tools. For such a tools reference, we recommend Breyfogle (1999).

Statistical Tools. Some, but not all, of these tools are statistical tools. As noted earlier, statistical tools are required so that process variation can be effectively dealt with. Six Sigma has effectively integrated statistical tools with those from other disciplines, such as industrial engineering, quality management, operations research, mechanical and electrical design, and reliability. The result is a toolkit much broader and more powerful than available within any one discipline. Because the toolkit is diverse and flexible, and because the focus is on a limited set of core tools, Black Belts and Green Belts do not need to become professional statisticians to be successful. Black Belts and Green Belts are trained to use statistical thinking and methods and data to improve processes

User-Friendly Statistical Software. Another reason Six Sigma has been effective is the general availability of user-friendly statistical software that enables effective and broad utilization of the statistical tools. The statistical software package most widely used in Six Sigma is probably Minitab™. Prior to the availability of such user-friendly software, statistical methods were often the domain of professional statisticians, who had access to, and specialized training in, proprietary statistical software. Specialists in statistical methods have an important role to play in Six Sigma, but practitioners who are not professional statisticians do the vast majority of statistical applications.

Critical Few Variables. The final key methodology of Six Sigma is its focus on the identification of the critical few input and process variables. Most processes, from extruding a plastic to closing the books for a global conglomerate, involve a large number of potentially important input and process variables. Studying each in-depth, and then managing them on an ongoing basis would be time consuming and prohibitively expensive. Fortunately, there are often three to six critical input and process variables that drive the process output variables. Identification of these variables can lead to effective ways to optimize and control the process in a parsimonious and cost-effective way. Six Sigma finds, and then focuses attention on, these few key variables. This principle of focusing attention on a few key things is consistent with general principles of good management. The ultimate goal is to move from measuring outputs and making process adjustments as the primary way to control the process to measuring and then adjusting process inputs to control the process and achieve the desired process performance.

Roles of Six Sigma Leaders

Six Sigma has well-defined leadership roles, and success depends on each of the roles fulfilling its unique responsibilities. Some of the key players involved in a Six Sigma initiative are shown in Figure 1-2.

For this discussion we will define the organization as the unit that has responsibility for identifying the improvement opportunities and chartering the Six Sigma projects. This could be a corporation, a division, a facility, or a function. The leadership team (often called the Six Sigma Council) leads the overall effort and has responsibility for approving the projects undertaken by the Black Belts.

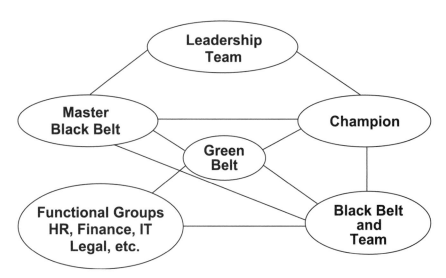

FIGURE 1-2   Roles of Leaders

In the case of a manufacturing facility, the leadership team is typically the plant manager and selected members of his or her staff. In the case of a finance function, the leadership team might be the chief financial officer (CFO) and selected members of his or her staff.

Each project has a Champion who serves as its business and political leader. (Some organizations use the term Champion to refer to the overall leader of the Six Sigma effort.) The project Champion is typically a member of the leadership team and has responsibility for:

- Facilitating the selection of projects
- Drafting the initial project charters
- Selecting Black Belts and other resources needed to conduct the project
- Removing barriers to the successful completion of the project
- Holding short weekly progress reviews with the Black Belt

The Black Belt leads the team that does the actual work on the project. Black Belts are hands-on workers, devote work full time to their projects, and do much of the detailed work. The Black Belt also leads the team, acts as project manager, and assigns work (e.g., data collection) to the team members as appropriate.

Black Belt projects are defined so that they can be completed in less than four to six months, are focused on high priority business issues, and are targeted to produce $175,000 to $250,000 per year to the bottom line. The team that works with the Black Belt is typically four to six members who may spend as much as 25 percent of their time on the project. The amount of time spent by each team member will vary depending on the person's role. The team may also include consultants and specialists as well as suppliers and customers. Black Belts also act as mentors for Green Belts, as do MBBs.

Green Belts may lead a project under the direction of a Champion or MBB, or they may work on a portion of a Black Belt project under the direction of the Black Belt. Green Belt projects are typically less strategic and more locally focused than are Black Belt projects.   A Green Belt project is typically worth $50,000 to $75,000 per year to the bottom line and should be completed in less than 4-6 months. Green Belts do not work full time on improvement projects, and typically have less intensive training. Green Belts work on improvement projects in addition to their existing job responsibilities. Several companies (such as GE) have recognized the value of Six Sigma as a leadership development tool and have the objective of all members of the professional staff being at least a Green Belt.

The MBBs are the technical leaders and enable the organization to integrate Six Sigma within its operations. The MBBs have typically completed several Black Belt projects and two to five weeks of training beyond the four weeks of Black Belt training. They help the champions select projects and review their progress. They provide training and mentoring for Black Belts and in some instances training for Green Belts. They are also responsible for leading mission critical projects as needed. In essence, they are intended to combine technical skills beyond that of a Black Belt with managerial and leadership skills similar to a Champion.

The functional support groups, such as Human Resources, Finance, Information Technology, and Legal, assist the Six Sigma effort in four key ways, beyond improving their own processes through Six Sigma projects. (1) They provide specialized data as needed by the Black Belt and the team. (2) They provide expertise associated with their functional responsibilities. (3) They provide members for the Black Belt project teams when appropriate. (4) They help identify improvement opportunities for the organization to pursue. Functional groups are typically involved in more aspects of the organizations' work than other groups. They interact across the organization, and as a result they see where improvements are needed in cross-functional processes operated by the organization. For example, the finance organization interacts with procurement, manufacturing, marketing, logistics, sales, and research and development, and therefore can more easily pinpoint cross-functional issues that need to be addressed.

There are two other types of Champions in addition to the Project Champion. As noted earlier an organization typically names a Corporate Six Sigma Champion who reports to the president or CEO and has overall responsibility for developing the Six Sigma infrastructure. In large organizations it is not unusual for each business and each functional unit (Human Resources, Finance, IT, Engineering) to name what they will call a business or functional Champion. Different organizations have used different titles for such roles, such as Quality Leader, Six Sigma Leader, or Six Sigma Champion, but the role is basically the same. It is essentially to oversee the implementation of Six Sigma in that unit. It is more prudent to focus on the actual role, and not get hung up on the title.

Summary

This chapter has provided a general overview of Six Sigma—the key elements of the initiative and the key concepts, methods and tools. An overview of the roles in Six Sigma was also included. Now that you have a general idea of what Six Sigma is, its uniqueness, and the roles of the players involved, you are ready to review case studies that show how Six Sigma has been deployed by different organizations. The case studies in Chapter 2 will demonstrate how Six Sigma should and should not be implemented. Comparing the successful with the less-successful case studies will enable us to highlight the key success factors for Six Sigma deployment (Chapter 3). The details of the resulting deployment strategy and methodology will be the focus of the remainder of the book.

References

Breyfogle, Forest W. III. (1999). *Implementing Six Sigma—Smarter Solutions Using Statistical Methods.* Wiley-Interscience, John Wiley and Sons, New York.

Eckes, George. (2001). *The Six Sigma Revolution.* John Wiley and Sons, New York.

Harry, Mikel, and Richard Schroeder. (2000). *Six Sigma: The Breakthrough Management Strategy Revolutionizing the World's Top Corporations.* Currency Doubleday, New York.

Hoerl, Roger W., and Ronald D. Snee. (2002). *Statistical Thinking—Improving Business Performance*. Duxbury Press, Pacific Grove, CA.

Pande, P., R. Neuman, and R. R. Cavanagh. (2000). *The Six Sigma Way*. McGraw-Hill, New York.

2

FOUR CASE STUDIES: WHAT WORKS AND WHAT DOESN'T

"Those who remain ignorant of history are doomed to repeat it."

—George Santayana

Now that we know what Six Sigma is and why leaders need to be very careful in how they implement it, it's time to look at how it works. Two case studies in this chapter illustrate very successful implementations. However, because Six Sigma is not a silver bullet—there are no guarantees of success—two other case studies show much less successful efforts.

In Chapter 3 we will compare and contrast the very successful implementations with the less successful ones, showing the key implementation factors that ultimately determine how successful an organization will be with Six Sigma. We then incorporate these factors into an overall implementation strategy that can be used by virtually any organization.

As noted, later chapters will provide more detailed practical advice on how to succeed in each step of this strategy, including key pitfalls and answers to questions commonly asked by leaders implementing Six Sigma.

Our first case study will be that of GE. A great deal has already been written about GE's Six Sigma initiative, so we will not cover all the details. However, while some of the published material on GE's Six Sigma experiences has been accurate, much has been written from second- or third-hand sources. In addition, virtually none of this published material provides insight into what it was really like within GE during the time that Six Sigma was originally implemented. We'll highlight GE's experiences with Six Sigma, and provide a more personal viewpoint on the implementation. Next, we'll review the implementation and results at a less publicized company, W.R. Grace. Finally, we present two less successful Six Sigma implementation cases.

Inside GE's Experiences

The story of GE's Six Sigma implementation has been pretty much beaten to death in the media so, rather than reiterating the highlights of the financial results, we'll provide a more personal, first-hand account of what it was like to be at GE at the time. What follows are the personal experiences of Roger Hoerl in the midst of this implementation, with some key points clarified. All views expressed are the personal opinions of this author, and should not be construed as representing GE.

The Beginnings—Jack Never Bluffs!

Within two months of starting at GE's Research and Development Center in Schenectady, NY, in September 1995, I was informed that all employees at the Center were to come to the auditorium for an important video presentation. Having just left Scott Paper Company, which had been downsized, dismantled, and eventually sold to Kimberly Clark by Al Dunlap (nicknamed "Chainsaw" by the media for his expertise in dismantling hostile takeovers), I had low expectations of such meetings. No one knew what to expect when we were informed that Jack (CEO Jack Welch) had made a video that he wanted shared with every employee of the company. (Within GE, the CEO is commonly referred to by his/her first name—a symbol of informality, not disrespect.)

The video lasted only a few minutes. It consisted of a brief statement from Jack explaining that GE was about to embark on a major new initiative called Six Sigma. Jack noted that there were a number of quality-related issues in the company, and that he felt Six Sigma was the solution. He made his famous statement that this initiative would be the most important priority of the company for the next five years, and that we would be a totally different company at the end of that time because of it. He was particularly proud that GE had not invented Six Sigma, but had been mature enough to overcome the NIH Syndrome (not invented here), and adopt a proven methodology pioneered by others, such as Motorola and AlliedSignal. More details were to follow from our individual business leaders.

Being somewhat skeptical of grandiose managerial pronouncements, and perhaps tainted by my recent experiences with Al Dunlap, I commented to a colleague as we stepped outside the auditorium: "That sounds great, *if* he's really serious."

The colleague, aware that I was new to GE, shot back: "There's one thing you need to understand about GE. Jack never bluffs."

"What does that mean?" I asked.

"It means that if Jack says he's going to do something, he's going to do it. You can take it to the bank."

That pretty much summarized my experiences over the next five years with Six Sigma. Jack wasn't bluffing.

No Second Guessing

Within a few weeks, I was attending the first MBB (Master Black Belt) training session being held at GE's executive development center in Crotonville, NY. The session was led by Mikel Harry of the Six Sigma Academy. I found Harry to be part Six Sigma guru, part good old boy, and part P.T. Barnum-type showman. However, what struck me most as I sat with newly appointed MBBs from the various GE businesses was the degree of focus everyone had on what needed to be done. There was no debating the merits of Six Sigma: were the reported results from AlliedSignal or Motorola real? Would it apply to GE? Was this just a repackaging of TQM? Rather than debating these questions, virtually all the MBBs were asking about how to implement Six Sigma as quickly and effectively as possible.

This was another unique aspect of GE culture; there is a lot of debate over important decisions, but once the decision has been made, there is very little ongoing debate as to whether or not this was the correct decision. This was definitely not the culture I was used to.

When my two colleagues and I got back to the R&D center, we were extremely excited about this initiative. We could see the tremendous potential of getting armies of talented people trained in a sound improvement methodology, with full management support and commitment, systematically attacking the company's biggest issues. An open debriefing meeting was held where we reported what we had learned at this session.

The vast majority of people shared our enthusiasm, although there was some isolated skepticism.

Unfortunately, both at the Research Center and across GE, such rare skepticism led to some leaders leaving GE. While such reactions may seem extreme, they go back to a statement made by Jack that if executives could not support Six Sigma 100 percent, GE was not the right company for them. While it was acceptable to debate the merits of Six Sigma while the issue was still being considered, once the decision had been made there was no time to continue the debate—we had to focus totally on implementation. Leaders had to lead.

The First Year—1996

This turned out to be a year of learning for both GE and me (see Figure 2-1). The major focus was on improvement of manufacturing processes using the MAIC (measure, analyze, improve, control) process. GE Capital (the financial services business of GE) subsequently added the define stage, wherein one ensures that an appropriate project has been selected, and that it is properly defined, scoped, and planned. This would turn out to be one of several major enhancements to Six Sigma made by GE, and would change the standard acronym to DMAIC. Each business in GE began its own separate initiative, but there was a lot of interaction and sharing of best practices, utilizing the Corporate Executive Council (CEC), and newly created councils for MBBs and Quality Leaders (Champions). The opportunity to learn from others' successes and failures within GE turned out to be a major advantage.

We certainly made a number of mistakes along the way, each of which became a test of leadership's commitment. For example, some businesses named part-time MBBs and Black Belts. Leaders wanted people to be change agents and focus on breakthrough improvements, while continuing to do their regular jobs. Of course, this is a recipe for disaster, at least at the start-up of the initiative.

Fortunately, when businesses began reporting large numbers of assigned MBBs and Black Belts to corporate headquarters in Fairfield, CT, senior management asked them to revise their numbers to include only dedicated, full-time Black Belts and MBBs. The numbers dropped dramatically, and these businesses realized that they were going to have to bite the bullet and dedicate their Six Sigma resources.

There was suspicion that some businesses were assigning people to the Six Sigma effort based on availability. One of the common problems with business improvement initiatives is that those who are available, or

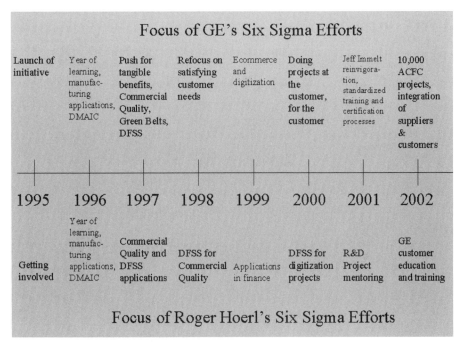

FIGURE 2-1   Six Sigma Deployment Timeline

perhaps those who can't do anything else well, are often assigned to work on these initiatives, while the best people are off doing the "really important" stuff. After corporate began asking to see previous performance appraisals for those who were put into Black Belt and MBB roles, top performers started appearing in Six Sigma roles.

This ties to another very important point—GE never viewed the MBB or Black Belt as a permanent role for technically oriented people. This was intended to be a temporary developmental role for future leaders of the company. If this critical work had been delegated to techies, there would never be a fundamental shift in the company's "genetic code," as Jack referred to it.

We needed future leaders who had the experience of being dedicated to process improvement work. This important point was later reinforced in the 2000 Annual Report, which stated:

"It is a reasonable guess that the next CEO of this Company, decades down the road, is probably a Six Sigma Black Belt or Master Black Belt somewhere in GE right now, or on the verge of being offered—as all our early-career (3-5 years) top 20% performers will be—a two-to-three-year Black Belt assignment. The generic nature of a

Black Belt assignment, in addition to its rigorous process discipline and relentless custom-er focus, makes Six Sigma the perfect training for growing 21st century GE leadership."

(Note that Jeff Immelt had already been named Jack's successor as CEO, hence the "next CEO" mentioned will be Jeff's successor.)

The use of Six Sigma as a developmental role for future leaders does not appear to have been copied by many other companies. It appears that the assumption in such companies is that "Leadership is OK, we just need to improve things in operations." Fortunately, despite its success GE did not have an arrogant culture (and still doesn't). Senior management re-alized that even they had to continuously learn and improve.

Financially, businesses started reporting huge savings from their initial projects. Were people stretching the truth to make their business look better than it really was? Leadership's response was to require that someone in the finance department personally sign off on each project, verifying that the claimed savings were real, and noting specifically where they would show up on the bottom line. Corporate auditors would period-ically audit these evaluations. The size of the reported savings from Six Sig-ma projects decreased dramatically once the audits were put into place. It also became impossible to get credit for intangible benefits, such as cus-tomer satisfaction, impact of one process improvement on other processes in the same system, and so on.

Despite some published healthy skepticism (e.g., Paton 2001 and Last Word 2001), I am confident that the publicly reported savings from Six Sigma at GE have been *underestimated*, as a result of these financial con-trols and audits.

As will be explained, this conservative estimation of benefits has been even greater in Design for Six Sigma (DFSS) projects. Interestingly, the net payoff from Six Sigma that first year was negative: $200 million invested, $170 million saved. GE leadership accepted this, realizing that there would be significant start-up costs. In this first year, the businesses were pushed for activity, not necessarily for tangible results. This would change in 1997.

The Push for Tangible Benefits

Jack had given the businesses investment money to backfill MBBs and Black Belts, conduct training, and so on, and by 1997 he was expecting a payoff. To reinforce the point, he announced that 40 percent of bonuses paid to managers would be tied to Six Sigma results. This certainly got peo-ple's attention, and the money began to roll in seriously in 1997. The offi-cial numbers for 1997 were $400 million invested, $700 million saved.

Recall that all of these numbers were rigorously audited—no creative accounting was involved.

In 1997, GE also began to place heavier focus on three initiatives that had begun in 1996: commercial quality (CQ) applications, creation of Green Belts (GBs), and Design for Six Sigma (DFSS). As noted, the initial applications of Six Sigma had been focused on improvements in manufacturing. However, GE Capital, a large financial services conglomerate in itself, accounted for approximately 40 percent of GE's profits. Focusing on manufacturing would miss at least 40 percent of the potential benefits to the company.

Similarly, even in an engineering company like GE Aircraft Engines or GE Power Systems, a very small percentage of the people or work processes are directly associated with manufacturing. For example, manufacturing businesses have accounts payable and accounts receivable processes, inventory management processes, pricing processes, and so on, each of which involve large sums of money. We gradually discovered that there is often more money to be found, and obtained more easily, in these processes than there is in manufacturing. We referred to these processes originally as transactional quality, and later changed it to commercial quality, or CQ.

GE had to pretty much pioneer the field. We weren't able to find anyone who had done CQ deployment in a holistic, systematic way, or who knew a lot about it. This was also a learning experience for me, as most of my previous experience had been in manufacturing and engineering improvements.

In 1997 I was asked to focus on CQ, and took it on a leap of faith that Six Sigma would apply equally well here. At the time I admittedly had no idea how. One project in credit card collections that resulted in annual savings of $2.9 million (see Hahn, Doganaksoy, and Hoerl [2000]) solidified my convictions that Six Sigma would apply anywhere. Surprisingly, most other corporations continue to focus on manufacturing in their Six Sigma efforts. There are a couple of showcase non-manufacturing examples, but based on the published literature, the vast majority of the effort appears to be stuck in manufacturing.

DFSS and a Critical Mass of Green Belts

The second big push in 1997 was DFSS. We were discovering that there were limits to the level of improvement you could obtain with existing processes. At some point, you needed a new design to reach a breakthrough level of improvement. This was equally true of soft processes, such as manual account reconciliation, as it was of hard processes, such as running antiquated manufacturing equipment. As with CQ applications, there was no pat solution. We enlisted the assistance of consultant Maurice Berryman, who brought valuable additional tools, and a framework on which to integrate them.

Combining these tools and this framework with what we already had, we developed an overall process for DFSS analogous to DMAIC: define, measure, analyze, design, verify (DMADV). Rolling out this process across GE became a focal point for corporate R&D, and led to success stories such as the LightSpeed CT scanner from GE Medical Systems, which reduced full body CT scans from about 3 minutes to less than 30 seconds, and brought $60 million in orders in the first 90 days of release (see 1998 GE Annual Report). Growing the business through DFSS-designed new products and services remains a key objective.

The third big push in 1997 was creating a critical mass of Green Belts to complement the MBBs and Black Belts. Businesses were putting their best people into MBB and Black Belt roles, and those chosen were receiving intangible rewards like recognition and visibility, and would soon start receiving tangible rewards, including bonuses and stock option grants.

Understandably, many of those not selected for MBB or Black Belt roles, especially those who wanted to be, began to feel left out. A we-they mindset between those who were directly involved in Six Sigma and those who weren't began to develop, which could have caused serious problems if not addressed promptly. Obviously, nothing less than getting everyone in the game would be required to completely transform the company. This is a lot easier said than done.

The creation of the Green Belt role had been announced previously, but now it was receiving major emphasis. These Green Belts would be people trained in the methodology of Six Sigma who applied it to their work part time. They would still be accountable for their regular duties, but would also conduct Six Sigma projects. With dedicated MBBs and Black Belts maintaining momentum, this move turned out to be an excellent way of ensuring that everyone could get into the Six Sigma game. And just about everyone did.

It was first announced that Green Belt status would be a prerequisite for promotions to management, and for the receipt of stock option grants. Later it was announced that being Green Belt trained (and on the way to certification) by the end of 1997 would be a condition of employment for all professionals. Jack definitely wasn't bluffing!

A Refocus on Customers

The focus of Six Sigma changed again in 1998. While ecstatic with the bottom-line impact Six Sigma was having on the company, senior management was disturbed with feedback from key customers. The quote that appeared in the 1998 Annual Report was: "When do I get the benefits of Six Sigma? When does my company get to experience the GE I read about in the GE Annual Report?"

Up until this point most projects had been focused on opportunities for GE to generate internal savings. While many of these process improvements ultimately affected customers positively, at that time it was certainly fair to say that Six Sigma had done more for GE's stockholders than for its customers.

In 1998 the direction was to focus more projects on direct customer issues, such as product delivery processes. In addition, primary emphasis was placed on reducing variation in such processes, not just fixing the average. The 1998 Annual Report is one of very few instances of a Fortune 500 CEO providing a detailed explanation of why focus on the average is insufficient, and why one must reduce process variation as well.

Application to Finance

In November 1998 I became the Quality Leader of the corporate audit staff (CAS), a part of corporate finance. While maintaining a core competency in financial auditing, CAS devotes considerable effort to driving corporate initiatives (e.g., Six Sigma, globalization, services growth, eCommerce), compliance issues, acquisitions, and other critical business issues. It obtains additional influence from the fact that it is a key leadership development program in GE, with a number of key business leaders being graduates of CAS.

The head of CAS wished to accelerate the staff's Six Sigma efforts, and make sure that they were in a position to be true Six Sigma leaders, particularly in financial applications. I admittedly knew virtually nothing about finance, but had a core belief that Six Sigma could (and should) be applied everywhere. Personally this was somewhat of a challenge to prove my belief.

While some auditors initially balked, both the leader of CAS and his replacement made it clear that Six Sigma would be implemented in a way to ensure success.

This leadership commitment won 80 percent of the battle. I was able to focus entirely on deployment, without wasting any time trying to win people over. This reinforced my belief that there is no substitute for leadership!

Details of CAS's Six Sigma efforts have been well documented (see Agrawal and Hoerl 1999, and Hoerl 2001). Suffice it to say that Six Sigma went from being added work to being a means to do better finance. CAS (in partnership with GE businesses) pioneered use of Six Sigma in a variety of application areas, such as digitization (eCommerce), cash flow, collections, product delivery, reserves, the auditing process, hedging of foreign currencies, compliance, acquisition integration, and many others. The list given here illustrates some financial applications of CAS's Six Sigma projects.

The best news was that we were reaching people early in their careers, which meant that they would be carrying this continuous process improvement mindset to each of their subsequent positions within the company, perhaps to senior management. By the time I left CAS in 2000 I was wondering why I had spent so many years in manufacturing and engineering.

1. Reducing average and variation in days outstanding of accounts receivable (collecting money faster).

2. Optimizing timing of invoice payment in accounts payable (paying in time to collect discounts, but otherwise holding on to the money as long as the terms allow).

3. Managing costs of public accounting firms (investigating why we sometimes pay more per hour than other times, and why we sometimes have highly paid accounting people, i.e., partners, doing lower level work).

4. Skip tracing in collections (determining financially optimal strategies for finding consumers who have skipped on accounts [credit cards, leases, etc.]).

5. Determining the best way to factor inventory (pay a third party to hold it on their books), taking into account several criteria, such as net income, cash flow, and so on.

6. Determining the best way to factor accounts receivable (selling our accounts receivable to a third party to enhance cash flow, while maintaining profitability).

7. Closing the books faster (frees up time of finance resources).

8. Improving the audit process to be more accurate (fewer missed issues) and faster.

9. Reducing the number of manual account reconciliations (relates to several other applications).

10. Improving the acquisition process (faster, fewer resources, fewer mistakes).

11. Realizing revenue from long-term service agreements faster (accounting rules require equal revenue realization over the life of the contract unless you can provide evidence that your costs will not be equal).

12. Hedging foreign currencies (improving the manner in which we convert foreign currencies to U.S. dollars). Since all financial measures are generally reported in dollars, this can have a huge impact on the bottom line for international companies.

13. Reducing variation in cash flow (sometimes cash flow follows profitability, sometimes it doesn't. Why?). Because of so much creative accounting today, analysts often want explanations if cash flow is not increasing at the same rate as earnings.

14. Credit scoring (improving our ability to predict which individuals or businesses are good credit risks, and which aren't).

15. Journal entry accuracy (a rule of thumb suggests that most businesses have a 3–4% error rate in journal entries, resulting in a lot of rework later).

16. Financial forecasting accuracy (enough said!).

17. Improving accuracy and reducing cycle time of standard financial reports (cycle time relates to freeing up finance resources, as well as getting more timely info).

18. Filing federal, state, and local taxes (typically to reduce cycle time, and ensure that we are not overpaying).

19. Managing the pension fund better; i.e., obtaining higher rates of return (the federal government requires certain reserves, but if we manage the pension fund well, we can take the amount overfunded to the bottom line).

20. Payroll accuracy, including deductions for taxes and benefits (enough said!).

Digitization and Six Sigma

In 1999 the dotcoms were all the rage, and there was a general belief that small startups were in a much better position to succeed in eCommerce than large conglomerates. Blue chips were seen as too slow to change, and stuck in a traditional business paradigm. GE took the Internet very seriously, however, and began pushing web-based business, as well as internal digitization, very hard. Many businesses started putting their Quality Leaders and MBBs into eCommerce roles. Part of the rationale was that these employees tended to be the top talent in the company, and part was due to a desire to put those with a Six Sigma mindset into eCommerce.

At the Research Center, which I was to return to shortly, we took a DFSS approach to digitizing business processes, such as cash application, deal approval, new product development, and so on. Six Sigma's rigor forced us to take a holistic approach, and avoid the rush to get websites online without thinking through the overall business process. This enabled us to avoid the fulfillment trap that plagued many dotcoms; they were great at putting up websites and taking orders, but had poorly designed fulfillment processes. While I have only anecdotal evidence that Six Sigma significantly impacted our eCommerce efforts, it seems a strange coincidence that a huge conglomerate like GE has subsequently been named the eCommerce company of the year by business publications such as *Internetweek* (June 2000).

At the Customer, For the Customer

The focus in 2000 was primarily on making Six Sigma work for customers, and on institutionalizing it into the GE culture. The push to enable customers to feel the benefits of Six Sigma had begun some time ago, but we were now taking it to a new level. We progressed from doing projects that would benefit customers, to partnering with customers on joint projects, to having GE Black Belts go into customer operations and do projects solely for the benefit of the customer. This type of project was referred to as "at the customer, for the customer."

The vast majority of these projects done for customers have been completed at GE expense with no direct monetary reward for GE. The primary motivation is improved customer relationships and loyalty. The competition can always cut its prices to match ours, and may be able to provide similar product features—in some cases—but none can offer the same level of Six Sigma expertise. This unique benefit gives GE a significant advantage in wooing major customers. Over 2,000 at the customer, for the customer projects were documented in the first year.

In terms of institutionalizing Six Sigma into the GE culture, GE actually has a successful track record of doing this with major initiatives. For example, it had an informal team problem-solving initiative in the 1980s called "Work Out." While this is no longer a formal initiative, both the term "Work Out" and the use of informal team problem solving are still commonly used in GE.

One specific example of institutionalizing Six Sigma was its inclusion in the 2000 update to the GE values (see the 2000 Annual Report), and in the 2002 update (see www.GE.com). Within GE, employees are formally evaluated on the degree to which they demonstrate the GE values as part of their annual performance appraisal. This has a significant impact on their overall evaluation, so the values are taken quite seriously. Similarly, it was announced that all early career (3-5 years) top performers would be offered Black Belt assignments.

A Reinvigoration

In 2001, new CEO Jeff Immelt announced a reinvigoration of Six Sigma. This was an important step symbolically, since there was some concern that the emphasis on Six Sigma might decline once Jack Welch retired. The reinvigoration included a push to further increase the percentage of senior executives with dedicated Six Sigma experience, acceleration of at the customer, for the customer projects (over 10,000 planned for 2002), and standardization of Black Belt course material and certification criteria across the company. As the manager of the Applied Statistics Lab at the Research Center, my primary Six Sigma role at this time was mentoring of R&D projects.

Looking into the near-term future, one could anticipate further integration of Six Sigma into the supply chain, working more with customers and suppliers on joint training and applications. It also appears that Six Sigma will remain a cornerstone of GE's executive development system. There has been speculation that GE will get into the Six Sigma consulting business, but there has been no indication of this being planned. Going forward, perhaps the greatest challenge will be ensuring that the focus remains on tangible results, and does not regress into the bureaucratic ticket-punching exercise that many companies have experienced with various improvement initiatives.

The following lists key attributes of GE's Six Sigma deployment–

General Electric	W.R. Grace
■ GE was already one of the world's most respected companies, and doing quite well financially, when it embarked on Six Sigma. Its efforts were not directed at solving an immediate business crisis.	■ The company had strong leadership. Leadership set clear direction, and stayed actively involved throughout Six Sigma implementation.
■ Senior Executives, especially Jack Welch, provided unyielding leadership to get the initiative going, and ensure its continued success.	■ It had a regular "drumbeat" of project reviews. As noted by CEO Norris, "Just schedule the reviews and show up. You don't even have to say anything for the reviews to be effective."
■ Six Sigma was directed towards specific, tangible objectives, including financial objectives.	■ Grace put top talent into the MBB and Black Belt roles, and freed them up to work on Six Sigma full time.
■ Some of the best people in the company, in virtually all business functions, were freed up from their normal duties to focus on Six Sigma.	■ It selected good projects, which had full leadership support.
■ GE used a very formal and structured deployment plan, including the required infrastructure (the Six Sigma organization, project selection systems, benefit verification systems, and so on).	■ It put an emphasis on obtaining hard financial results.
	■ Business leaders had direct involvement in reviews and project selection. This allowed for continuous alignment of Six Sigma projects in the business environment.
	■ Grace used a rigorous project completion process with appropriate documentation to close out projects.
	■ The company's philosophy was that Green Belts should also deliver positive financial results. Everyone trained was expected to complete a project that would be the first in a continuing list of completed projects.

The W. R. Grace Story

W. R. Grace presents an interesting contrast to GE in terms of Six Sigma success. While GE is a massive (about $130 billion in revenue), internationally known company, Grace is a much smaller and lower profile company. Some analysts have hypothesized that size is a key component to Six Sigma success; that it is an initiative that only works for large companies. As we shall see more clearly, this is not the case, and Grace provides an excellent illustration.

Grace is an international specialty chemical and materials company with about $2 billion in revenues. Its main businesses are catalysts, construction chemicals (fireproofing, waterproofing, concrete admixtures, etc.), coatings/sealants, and silicas/adsorbents. While it entered Chapter 11 protection in April 2001 because of previous asbestos-related lawsuits, the financial performance from operations has been good. The primary reason Grace adopted Six Sigma was that CEO Paul Norris had been involved in the Six Sigma effort at AlliedSignal, prior to coming to Grace. Norris had seen what Six Sigma could do, and was determined to achieve similar improvements at Grace.

Grace began its Six Sigma initiative in 1999, shortly after Norris arrived, utilizing Sigma Breakthrough Technologies Incorporated (SBTI) as its provider. The company held its first executive workshop in August 1999, quickly followed by three waves of Champion workshops (for each major business), two of which were held in Europe. The Grace leadership team developed a deployment plan at an executive workshop, and identified critical projects at the Champion workshops. These projects were selected primarily because of their anticipated financial payoff. Grace named a Six Sigma leader for each business, with overall accountability for implementation.

The Six Sigma leader put the deployment plan into effect, which led to three waves of Black Belt training, in 1999, 2000, and 2001. The Black Belts, which were in both the U.S. and European operations, initially implemented the projects selected during the Champion workshops. Champions held weekly project reviews, and business VPs held monthly reviews. CEO Paul Norris held quarterly reviews to monitor the overall progress of the implementation. Initially one MBB supported the company, and this has evolved into one MBB for the catalyst and silicas/adsorbents business and three MBBs in the construction products business. All the MBBs and Black Belts were freed up to work on Six Sigma full time.

The people put into these roles were generally viewed as top performers. Grace put a reward and recognition system in place early in the initiative to reinforce the contributions of the Black Belts, Green Belts, and project team members. In early 2001, an Internet-based project tracker was developed to better monitor the status and impact of each project. As per the deployment plan, Grace added additional training and types of projects over time, as depicted in the following list—

- Began six waves of DFSS training in November 2000 in Europe and the US, to bring Six Sigma to the R&D function. The program was aligned with the current Grace development system, linking specific tools to the various stage gates.

- Began holding waves of Green Belt training for non-manufacturing operations in February of 2001

- Held an advanced Black Belt workshop in February 2001.

- Began holding waves of "Yellow Belt" training for process operators, primarily focused on the measure phase, in June 2001.

- Held the first Green Belt course in Asia in July 2001.

- Began Green Belt training tailored to Finance in October 2001.

- Developed specific in-house training for Catalyst Technical Service professionals, who work throughout refineries and chemical plants around the world, in the first quarter of 2002.

- Developed in-house analytical Green Belt training that focuses on running and evaluating measurement systems in 2002

At the end of 2000, Grace had formally completed about 80 projects. It had about 40 Black Belts and 80 Green Belts. The company documented a financial impact of $26 million in hard savings, and another $7 million in cost avoidance. While $26 million may not sound like a lot relative to the numbers published by GE, it represents a higher percentage of both total revenues and profits than GE's published savings in any year to date! Clearly, Six Sigma was working quite well for a much smaller company.

By the end of 2001, the catalysts and silicas/adsorbents business alone had about 50 Black Belts, almost 200 Green Belts, and almost 500 Yellow Belts (process operators trained primarily in the measure phase methods). By the first quarter of 2002 this business had completed over 100 projects, with many more than this in progress. Grace's 2001 results came in even better than 2000 with $50 million in hard savings, and $9 million in cost and capital avoidance.

Less Successful Six Sigma Deployments

To preserve confidentiality, some details of the companies discussed in this segment have been changed. The names (Royal Chemicals and Diversified Paper) are fictitious, and any resemblance to real company names is coincidental. Our intent is to show how Six Sigma can fail to achieve the desired results if not properly deployed, rather than criticizing any particularly company. We emphasize, however, that all the facts pertaining to Six Sigma deployment and results are accurate, and are taken from sources involved with the actual implementation efforts.

Royal Chemicals

Royal Chemicals (remember, the name is fictitious) is a chemical food additives company with approximately $1 billion in annual sales. It has a small number of large production facilities, as well as an R&D Center. The CEO of this company heard about what Six Sigma had done for others, and was curious to learn more. He attended a trade conference for the food additives business that had Six Sigma as a theme, and, based on the positive testimonials he heard, he returned with the intent of suggesting a major Six Sigma initiative at Royal Chemicals.

A year passed before he made the case for Six Sigma to his leadership team, and there was considerable resistance. Royal was rumored to be looking for a buyer, and some felt that the primary motivation for Six Sigma implementation was to make the company appear more attractive. Others felt that since the company was already using statistical process control (SPC) and design of experiments (DOE), it was already doing Six Sigma. Another argument was that Six Sigma was a repackaging of TQM, which had been tried before and which many felt had never achieved its promise. The naysayers pointed out that Royal was in the chemical food additives business, which was different from other manufacturing businesses in which Six Sigma had been deployed. There was widespread skepticism as to whether Six Sigma could work in such a business.

A compromise was finally reached. The company would pilot the application of Six Sigma in one area of the business to see whether it worked. If it worked, they would expand it, if not, they would drop it. The senior management team was to attend a two-day leadership-training course, prior to having others attend technical training. The leadership team decided that two days was too much of a time commitment, and had the training reduced to one day. Several leaders were unable to clear their calendars, and did not make even this one-day event.

In the sector of the business selected for the pilot, a handful of Black Belts were identified, as well as a couple of Champions (one for each site). Site leadership workshops were held. The rank-and-file employees viewed some, but not all, of the Black Belts as top talent. Royal designated no MBBs. The Black Belts attended public Six Sigma training, which was not oriented toward the chemical food additives business. When they returned from training, their leaders asked them to continue with their current jobs, and lead Six Sigma projects in addition to these duties. Finance was not involved in the project selection or evaluation process. It was not clear to many people what the project selection process actually was, or what the criteria were.

Local Champions held occasional project reviews, but the site managers did not (only one review in nine months), nor did senior corporate leadership. Some Black Belts felt that many of the projects did not actually follow the standard Six Sigma solution process (DMAIC), but rather utilized various statistical tools to try to solve a problem. The Champions did not have in-depth training, and there were no MBBs, so there was no one in authority to point out this fact to the rest of the Black Belts.

At the end of nine months management reviewed the status of implementation, especially results achieved. Amazingly, only one project had been completed in nine months, although many others were in progress! The completed project was a success, and had achieved a $300,000 impact to the bottom line. However, there was certainly no fundamental change in the way the company operated or was managed. It was not clear that the projects would actually cover the implementation expenses.

At this point Six Sigma stalled, as many in senior leadership felt that they had enough evidence to conclude that it did not fit their business, despite the one successful project. The following lists some key attributes of Royal Chemicals' Six Sigma deployment—

Royal Chemicals	Diversified Paper
■ The CEO did not provide strong leadership for Six Sigma, and was not clear regarding the value of Six Sigma to the company. ■ Senior management had a lack of confidence from the very beginning, leading to a tentative implementation strategy. Some were looking for the pilot to show that Six Sigma worked, others were looking for evidence that it didn't. ■ Senior management failed to become directly involved in a significant way. ■ Royal utilized generic Black Belt training, even though their applications were in a specialized area (food additives). ■ Royal designated no MBBs, used part-time Black Belts, and gave minimal training to Champions and company leaders. ■ Employees did not view all Black Belts as top talent.	■ There was minimal leadership shown at the corporate level. ■ There was minimal leadership shown at the business unit level. ■ Diversified used a questionable MBB and Black Belt selection process. ■ The MBBs and Black Belts were part time resources. ■ The project selection process was poorly designed. ■ The allocation of resources to projects and root cause solutions was inadequate. ■ Diversified lacked a reward and recognition system to support the work of the MBBs and Black Belts.

Diversified Paper

Diversified Paper (a fictitious name) is an international paper company with annual sales of about $3 billion. It manufactures a wide range of paper products for both consumer and commercial applications. Its facilities are located throughout the world, with concentrations in North America, Europe, and Asia. Implementing Six Sigma was a natural step for Diversified, since its CEO sat on the board of another company implementing Six Sigma. In addition, the leader of one of its business units had recently come from a company that had implemented Six Sigma, and she was a strong proponent for the initiative.

Despite these advantages, upon discussing the possibility of implementing Six Sigma, corporate leaders expressed a great deal of resistance. After some internal haggling, they decided to let each business unit decide when and how to deploy Six Sigma. They chose not to select an overall corporate Six Sigma leader, so no consistent deployment direction was given to the individual businesses. Not surprisingly, some made significant progress, while others made minimal progress. At the corporate level, leadership training consisted of only one day. In addition, leaders did not widely disseminate the original corporate deployment plan once the decision was made to implement Six Sigma on a business unit by business unit basis.

While each business unit followed its own path, some common issues began to emerge. For example, the CEO directed that implementation be limited to manufacturing operations. As often happens, this led to a victimization attitude from manufacturing. Those who work in manufacturing often feel that all improvement or cost-cutting initiatives focus solely on them, implying that the only source of problems in the company is manufacturing. Obviously, manufacturing is only one function and cannot be the root cause of all problems in corporations.

Such a narrow focus often prevents leaders from improving all aspects of their organizations.

These leaders also had a difficult time identifying top talent that could be freed from their regular duties to serve as MBBs or Black Belts so they decided to primarily utilize the Quality organization in manufacturing plants for these key roles. Of course, the message conveyed by this action was that Six Sigma was delegated to the Quality organization, and not the responsibility of other leaders.

Champions were identified, but were generally inactive. The CEO did a few visible project reviews, but did not review overall implementation status. No special reward and recognition system was put in place to support the work of the Black Belts or MBBs. Business unit leaders decided that the existing reward and recognition system was adequate to support the Six Sigma initiative.

The MBBs and Black Belts worked on their existing job duties in addition to Six Sigma, slowing the implementation effort. As a result, only a small number of projects were initiated. Even these tended to be aimed at lower savings than what is generally recommended. Without a formal project selection system, Diversified struggled to identify good projects, resulting in some Black Belts being trained without having a project on which to apply their learning.

In addition, most MBBs only received Black Belt training. This hampered project execution, because Black Belts had difficulty getting the needed support, not to mention team participation. When projects identified root causes of problems, the Black Belts also had difficulty obtaining the required resources to fix the root causes.

The business unit whose leader had come from a Six Sigma company did report significant progress, and corresponding financial benefits. However, there was no system in place to validate claimed financial benefits, therefore the other business units were skeptical of this leader's claims.

Energy was spent on debating the accuracy of the financial measurement system, rather than on transferring the successes and lessons learned to other business units. Finally, after about two years of slow and painful progress and minimal financial impact, the Six Sigma initiative was restarted with the appointment of a corporate Six Sigma leader. At the time of this writing, it is not clear whether or not this restart will be successful. The list on page 35 illustrates some key attributes of Diversified Paper's Six Sigma deployment.

Summary

We have seen that while Six Sigma brought huge tangible benefits to GE and Grace, other companies have failed to achieve the same level of success. Deciding to implement Six Sigma does not guarantee success; organizations must deploy it wisely to achieve the full benefits. There are obvious contrasts between the very successful and less successful Six Sigma deployments. These can be easily seen by comparing the lists on pages 30 and 35.

In the next chapter we will further compare and contrast these cases to clarify the key success factors for deployment. We will then integrate these keys to success into a recommended process for overall deployment.

Subsequent chapters will provide step-by-step advice for each phase of this overall deployment process.

References

Agrawal, R., and R. W. Hoerl. (1999). "Commercial Quality: The Next Wave in Statistical Thinking." *Proceedings of the Section on Physical and Engineering Sciences*, American Statistical Association, Alexandria, VA.

Hahn, G.J., N. Doganaksoy, and R. W. Hoerl. (2000). "The Evolution of Six Sigma," *Quality Engineering*, 12, 3, 317-326.

Hoerl, R.W. (2001). "Six Sigma Black Belts, What Do They Need to Know?" (with discussion), *Journal of Quality Technology*: 33, 4, 391-434.

"Last Word," *Quality Digest*, 21, 8 (August 2001): 80.

Paton, S.M. (2001). "First Word," *Quality Digest* (August): 21,8: 4.

3

HOW TO SUCCESSFULLY DEPLOY SIX SIGMA

"If you don't know where you are going any road will get you there."
—from *Alice in Wonderland*

A key point to remember from previous chapters is that jumping on the Six Sigma bandwagon is no guarantee of success.

We will take another look at the case studies in Chapter 2 to elaborate on the key factors that led to significant—or minimal—success in Six Sigma. We will show how to analyze the keys to a successful Six Sigma deployment and how they can be integrated into an overall, step-by-step process. In subsequent chapters we will provide more detail and specifics on how to effectively move through each deployment phase.

Why Were GE and Grace Successful?

On the surface, GE and Grace are as different as two companies might be.

GE is a name recognized throughout the world, and its 2001 revenues were about $130 billion. Both the giant conglomerate and its previous

CEO, Jack Welch, have been studied and reported on by business schools and journals for 20 years.

Grace is a small company focused in a few niche markets. Many consumers, not to mention business scholars, are likely to be unfamiliar with it.

Yet, both firms achieved remarkable financial results from Six Sigma. In fact, on some metrics Grace might be considered even more successful than GE. What did they have in common that led to such success?

Some Common Misconceptions

We should first note what the two companies do not have in common:

- They are at opposite ends of the size spectrum
- They are not in the same industry
- They did not use the same Six Sigma deployment provider

The myth that Six Sigma works only for large companies like GE ($130 billion in revenue) has likely persisted because business journals, books, and articles tend to focus on large companies like GE or AlliedSignal, so the successes of small companies, like Grace ($2 billion in revenue), are not visible to the general public. In reality, big companies have more layers of middle management, which may make it more difficult to implement Six Sigma effectively. Change is often easier to introduce in smaller companies.

Another misconception is that Six Sigma applies to only certain industries, such as electronics. This theory is also inconsistent with the available evidence. As of this writing, successful implementations have occurred in all major areas of the economy, from electronics to health care to insurance to power generation to consumer credit, and so on.

Six Sigma is a methodology for improving processes, to make them more efficient internally (bottom-line benefits), and more effective at satisfying customers (top-line growth). All businesses need to improve their processes to achieve, maintain, and enhance competitiveness. In fact, non-profit organizations and government agencies also need to improve their processes to better achieve their objectives. Who would want to invest time or money in an organization that says it has no desire to improve?

GE and Grace also used different Six Sigma providers who recommended slightly different paths to deployment. Providers of Six Sigma training and consulting services often argue over which is the "true" Six Sigma methodology. Trade journals are full of ads from providers claiming that only their unique approach will lead to success. The evidence does not validate these claims. GE and Grace used different providers, but both flourished. Several providers have a long list of successful and very satisfied clients; clearly, no single provider can claim to have a monopoly on winning with Six Sigma.

That said, there are certainly differences between providers, and some are clearly better than others. Tips on selecting a provider are offered in Chapter 4 and in the frequently asked questions at the back of the book. This is an important decision, and needs to be given careful consideration.

Success Starts at the Top

If company size, type of industry, and provider were not the determining success factors at GE and Grace, what were? The most obvious commonality in their cases is that in both companies success started at the top. Just as Jack Welch led GE's Six Sigma charge with relentless energy and passion, CEO Paul Norris had seen what Six Sigma could do at AlliedSignal and was totally committed to making it work at Grace. These CEOs' commitments should not be measured in speeches or quotes from the annual report, but rather in such things as the time, attention, and money they gave to the effort.

In both cases, the senior leaders personally drove Six Sigma implementation:

- They ensured that their leadership team was fully on board, and that there was a well thought out game plan for implementation.
- They provided resources, in terms of people and funding, to properly support the effort.
- They expected, even demanded, results from the effort.
- They were willing to change internal policies and procedures to support implementation.

Beyond the CEOs, leadership was evident in the designation of overall Six Sigma leaders, and from the active participation of the rest of the corporate executive teams. In short, one could argue that getting effective leadership from the top, not just buy-in or support, was the most critical success factor. Many other case studies would help validate this hypothesis (see Harry and Schroeder [2000]).

Six Sigma Requires Top Talent

Another similarity that helps explain GE and Grace's successes is both put top talent into the Six Sigma initiative. One might be able to fool market analysts with an impressive PowerPoint™ presentation, but once the names of individuals going into Six Sigma roles are announced, it is impossible to fool the rank and file employees. Since people generally know their peers well, they can immediately see the level of staffing of the Six Sigma effort: top talent, whoever was available, or people who couldn't do anything else. Many improvement initiatives have failed not because they weren't technically valid, but because they weren't viewed as business critical, and therefore didn't get the organization's top talent.

An Infrastructure to Support the Effort

Both companies developed an appropriate supporting infrastructure—the network of processes, systems, and organizational structure required to support Six Sigma. This network includes designation of a leader, identification of specific roles and responsibilities for those involved, formal systems to obtain and utilize human and financial resources, formal processes for project selection and review, and so on. This support network is often formalized by creating a function called the Six Sigma Organization, but it does not have to be.

Any new initiative is likely to die on the vine if it continues to be extra work for everyone involved. Creating the appropriate infrastructure supports the effort in the long term because the organization has legitimatized it, and ensured that it will be able to obtain the needed resources and attention. Lack of a supporting infrastructure is often pointed to as a key reason for the failure of many TQM initiatives in the late 1980s and early 1990s. Some key actions taken by GE and Grace to create the supporting infrastructure are shown here—

- Designated an overall leader for the effort.
- Developed formal implementation plans, which were reviewed with senior management.
- Designated Champions and full time MBBs and Black Belts.
- Introduced formal project selection and review mechanisms.
- Formally integrated Six Sigma into the budgeting process, both in terms of including the costs as well as the anticipated savings.
- Implemented focused training systems for key roles.
- Modified HR, reward and recognition, business planning, financial, and other business systems to support Six Sigma implementation.

Proper project selection and regular managerial reviews are particularly important. Both GE and Grace avoided the common problem plaguing many improvement initiatives—huge projects that begin with great intentions, spend large amounts of money, but months or even years later have little tangible benefit to show for the effort.

Senior management tends to lose faith in such projects, resulting in disenchantment with the initiative, and eventual failure. Both companies implemented formal processes that ensured selected projects:

- Were strategically important

- Were tied directly to the bottom line or to key customer issues

- Could be completed in a reasonable timeframe (4-6 months)

- Had the resources to succeed

Similarly, project review processes were set up at different organizational levels. These reviews ensured that appropriate progress was being made, and that any barriers to success were identified quickly so they could be addressed by the project Champion. Such project selection and review processes minimize the possibility of projects dragging on indefinitely with no tangible results to show for the effort. These common attributes of the very successful case studies are summarized in Figure 3-1.

Very Successful Case Studies	**Less Successful Case Studies**

• Committed leadership
• Use of top talent
• Supporting infrastructure
  • Formal project selection process
  • Formal project review process
  • Dedicated resources
  • Financial system integration
	• Supportive leadership
	• Use of whoever was available
	• No supporting infrastructure
	  • No formal project selection process
	  • No formal project review process
	  • Part time resources
	  • Not integrated with financial system

Same Issues!

FIGURE 3-1   Common Attributes of Very Successful and Less Successful Case Studies

Why Were Others Less Successful?

Remember the keys to Six Sigma success at GE and Grace: Leadership, top talent, and infrastructure. Specifically, senior leadership:

- Ensured that the leadership team was fully on board, and that there was a well thought out game plan for implementation.

- Provided resources, in terms of people and funding, to properly support the effort.

- Expected, even demanded, results from the effort.

- Were willing to change internal policies and procedures to support implementation.

Using these same criteria, let's look at the less successful efforts at Royal Chemicals and Diversified Paper (remember, these are fictitious company names).

How Committed Was Senior Leadership?

The answer should be obvious. Royal Chemicals and Diversified Paper did not share the key attributes of GE and Grace. Neither company had committed leadership; at best they were supportive. At Royal Chemicals, there was open skepticism as to whether Six Sigma would work for them. Similarly, there was no clear corporate leadership in Diversified Paper's efforts.

Now that Six Sigma has achieved a great deal of notoriety, there may be some belief that it is a silver bullet, and that once a company announces a Six Sigma initiative, positive results will immediately begin to occur. Such perceptions may lead to companies jumping on the bandwagon without carefully considering the commitment required to be successful.

Many employees questioned Royal Chemicals' motivation for selecting Six Sigma in the first place. Some felt that it was only a ploy to make Royal a more attractive buyout opportunity. Using a pilot implementation to see if Six Sigma worked clearly demonstrated a lack of confidence on the part of leadership. When the leadership team determined that they were too busy for a two-day leadership training session, and then several leaders didn't attend the reduced one-day session, one could have safely predicted that this implementation would meet with minimal success.

Similarly, Diversified Paper's decision to allow each business unit to decide whether and when it would deploy Six Sigma tells most of the story. Optional initiatives are not business critical by definition. The leadership decision to restrict Six Sigma to manufacturing operations suggested a lack of understanding of what Six Sigma is all about. Unfortunately, there is no substitute for strong leadership!

Who Was Selected for Key Six Sigma Roles?

Another common problem with these two companies' initiatives was that they did not consistently utilize top talent in their Six Sigma efforts. Certainly they had some top talent in the Black Belt ranks. However, both Royal Chemicals and Diversified Paper also assigned people to key roles, including Black Belts, who were not viewed as top talent. Diversified Paper generally restricted MBBs and Black Belts to members of the Quality organization. There may well be top talent in the Quality organization, but it is highly unlikely that *all* the top talent in the company is in the Quality organization.

These companies missed the important point that Six Sigma results happen through people.

A Lack of Support

As noted, any new initiative needs new supporting infrastructure to maintain momentum until it has been institutionalized. This infrastructure of systems, processes, and organizational structure was quite visible and effective at GE and Grace. However, those trying to implement Six Sigma at Royal Chemicals and Diversified Paper were left to fend for themselves. For example, there was no formal process for selecting projects. This led to selection of some poor projects, as well as a lack of organizational alignment and support for the projects that were selected. If leadership has not agreed on the logic for each project selected, they are that much less likely to provide ongoing support to these projects. This lack of support was particularly debilitating at Diversified Paper, when Black Belts were unable to obtain the resources needed to address the root causes of problems that were uncovered by their projects.

Neither was there a formal, consistent, project review system. When this system breaks down or is never implemented, as in these cases, the project momentum slows, and projects drag on indefinitely. In the case of Royal Chemicals, lack of appropriate project reviews led to many projects that didn't follow the Six Sigma process. In addition, after nine months of effort, only one project had been completed!

Another piece of infrastructure missing in the efforts at Royal Chemicals and Diversified Paper was a well-designed training system for each role. Each role (Black Belts, MBBs, Champions, senior leaders, and, eventually, Green Belts) must receive the appropriate training, and there must be an ongoing system to provide refresher courses and advanced or specialized training, and to bring new resources on board.

Royal Chemicals was clearly in need of specialized training for continuous processes, but went with generic training because it was cheaper. MBBs at Diversified Paper did not receive MBB training, but only Black Belt training. Neither leadership team received the level of training that is required. Both companies viewed training as a one-time event, rather than an ongoing process of capability development. Of course, any job is difficult if you have not received the training and development required, even more so with a radical change initiative like Six Sigma.

The appropriate training system required to support Six Sigma deployment will be discussed in greater detail in Chapter 7.

The financial system for estimating and measuring benefits from projects was another important system missing in the less successful case studies. For example, Diversified Paper did not have a standardized financial system to measure project benefits, so other business units did not believe the savings claimed from successful projects. This prevented them from taking notice and getting on board.

Another infrastructure failure was that neither organization named a corporate Six Sigma Leader; i.e., an overall Corporate Champion. A leaderless initiative is like a rudderless ship; it goes wherever the prevailing winds and currents take it. There is a reason that virtually every major corporation has an overall financial leader (CFO), an overall legal leader (CLO or general counsel), an overall human resources leader, and so on. Such infrastructure is critically important to developing and deploying strategic direction in these areas. The common attributes of the less successful case studies are summarized in Figure 3-1.

The Keys to Successful Six Sigma Deployment

By comparing the successful case studies to the unsuccessful ones, the keys to successful deployment are readily apparent. While we have only discussed four companies' experiences here, these conclusions are corroborated by many other companies' experiences, not to mention current research in organizational change. (See for example Harry and Schroeder [2000], and Weisbord [1989]).

The keys to success can be grouped into the three broad, overlapping categories:

- Committed leadership
- Top talent
- Supporting infrastructure

Let's take a closer look at each of these categories.

Committed Leadership

By committed leadership we mean leaders who have the conviction to make a difficult decision, and then personally lead the organization in the chosen direction without wavering. Such commitment goes well beyond being supportive or in favor of Six Sigma. In addition to the leadership of GE and Grace in their Six Sigma efforts, history provides many examples of committed leadership.

For example, historians tell us that when Hernán Cortez landed in Mexico in 1519 to begin the Spanish conquest of the Aztecs, there was considerable dissension in the Spanish ranks as to whether it was possible for 500 soldiers to defeat the entire Aztec Empire. Most soldiers, and even Cortez's senior officers, felt that the more prudent course of action would be to sail back to Cuba to obtain more troops.

Cortez's solution to this dilemma was not to hold a prolonged debate, but rather to burn and sink his own ships! With the Spanish ships destroyed, there was no choice but to go forward toward the Aztec Empire; there would be no more debate or indecision.

While the authors do not find Cortez's mission of conquest and destruction praiseworthy, he did provide a classic example of leadership commitment. In his mind there was no alternative to conquest, and no thought of ever turning back. Senior leaders should realize that this is the level of commitment required to make Six Sigma successful.

The following is a checklist for measuring leadership commitment. As discussed, if there is not a clear commitment for Six Sigma, the effort will gradually be sabotaged until it loses all momentum. If the financial and human resources are not provided, it will never get off the ground. Similarly, lack of a strategic deployment plan is an indication that senior leadership does not view Six Sigma as being strategically important.

- ☑ Clear, unwavering direction on deploying Six Sigma.
- ☑ Commitment of required resources, including personnel.

☑ Development of a strategy for deployment, i.e., a "game plan," including tangible goals and objectives.

☑ Frequent and clear communications to the organization.

☑ Personal involvement.

☑ Willingness to revise company policies and procedures to be supportive (e.g., management bonus plans).

☑ Reward, recognition, and celebration of successes.

☑ Insistence on tangible results.

The issue of personal involvement is a critical one. Many feel that dollars measure senior leadership's commitment; i.e., the more funding they provide, the more committed they are. While there is some truth to this, we have found that personal time is an even better barometer of leadership commitment.

Leaders can always get more money. However, even CEOs only have 24 hours in a day; they can't get any more time than that. Given the many demands on their time they are forced to prioritize, and only the most critical issues receive their commitment. Six Sigma either makes the grade or it doesn't.

GE and other companies have found that some systems and policies need to be revised to be consistent with the direction on Six Sigma. One obvious example is GE revising its reward and recognition system so that management bonuses would be heavily weighted by Six Sigma results.

Other examples include allowing additional headcount to backfill for Black Belts and MBBs, rethinking career progression paths, incorporating Six Sigma as a criterion in performance evaluations at all levels, and adding Six Sigma as a line item in budgets. This last point also relates to the last item in the previous list.

Just as financial resources need to be provided to properly implement Six Sigma, financial benefits also need to be expected as a return. Having financial savings from the Six Sigma effort as a line item in the budget sets clear direction that to whom much is given, much is expected. Conversely, if leadership does not demand financial benefits, the organization will quickly see that this is an optional initiative. Why worry about Six Sigma if there are other things that you might actually get fired for not delivering on?

Top Talent

There are three major reasons why top talent is so important to the Six Sigma effort:

- The better the talent the better the results
- Top talent attracts more top talent
- Top talent becomes the next organizational leaders

The first on the list is fairly obvious—the better the talent involved, the better results we will achieve with the effort. This is true in any initiative; e.g., sports teams with the best records tend to have the most talented players. If this is obviously true, why don't improvement efforts tend to obtain the top talent in general?

One answer is that assigning top talent to Six Sigma causes significant stress to the system, because these folks have to stop what they are currently doing, their work needs to be reprioritized, and many replacements have to be found. Naturally, the replacements will often not perform as well as the top talent on these important projects.

Weak leaders will generally follow the path of least resistance, even if it is not the path to success. It takes committed leaders to choose the more difficult and stressful path. Our experience has been that only companies that have taken the more difficult path have fully benefited from Six Sigma. Certainly GE and Grace followed this path, and accepted the additional stress and difficulties it required. Note also that obtaining top talent applies to filling not only the full time roles, such as MBBs and Black Belts, but also the roles of other members of the Black Belt project teams, and to finding functional support needed to address root causes identified by the team.

The second reason that selection of top talent is so critical is somewhat subtler. If top talent is selected for key roles, this sends a very clear message to the organization that management is serious about Six Sigma, and it will create suction for the initiative. By suction we mean that people will naturally be drawn to Six Sigma, will want to be involved with it, and may even start to compete with one another for MBB and Black Belt positions.

We are not fans of internal competition, but we do think it is healthy to have more people vying for Six Sigma roles than there are positions to fill. We need to repeat our earlier point that the organization knows the talent, so no words leadership may say here make a difference. Once the names are announced, the organization will immediately know whether or not top talent has been selected. The names will speak for themselves.

The third reason for selecting top talent for Six Sigma roles is to utilize the effort to develop the future leaders of the company. Today's top talent will likely become tomorrow's leaders, and we need to ensure that these leaders fully understand and embrace Six Sigma. Having ex-Black Belts and MBBs in senior leadership positions will help ensure that the culture change is permanent, and is a major element of making the transition from an initiative to the way we work (see Chapter 7).

Further, the experience of being dedicated to disciplined continuous improvement work will make them better leaders.

As Jack Welch writes in his autobiography (Welch [2001] p. 339):

> "We've always had great functional training programs over the years, particularly in finance. But the diversity of the company has made it difficult to have a universal training program. Six Sigma gives us just the tool we need for generic management training since it applies as much in a customer service center as it does in a manufacturing environment."

Supporting Infrastructure

As noted, the presence of a supporting infrastructure was a key reason that GE and Grace achieved major success, and the lack of one was a key cause that Royal Chemicals and Diversified Paper achieved minimal success. Even committed leaders and top talent will have difficulty succeeding without a proper infrastructure.

In practice, of course, these items tend to go together, since committed leaders will ensure that the required supporting infrastructure is developed; uncommitted leaders won't. The infrastructure elements that we feel are most critical are listed here—

- An organizational structure for Six Sigma deployment that includes overall leadership of the effort, a Six Sigma Council, and dedicated positions for key roles (MBBs, Black Belts, etc.).

- Six Sigma planning systems; i.e., development and managerial review of implementation plans, budgets, human resources plans, and so on, on at least an annual basis. This is nothing more than what is typically done for each business unit in a major corporation, but often overlooked for improvement initiatives.

- Project selection and review processes.
- Training systems for key roles.
- Modification of human resources, reward and recognition, business planning, financial, and other business systems to support Six Sigma implementation, as needed.

Relative to the first bullet point, there need to be formal roles, assigned leadership, and dedicated resources to get the initiative going, overcome inertia, and maintain momentum. No major corporation operates its finance department without a designated leader or a finance committee, with unclear roles, or with resources doing finance in their spare time. If such a disorganized approach fails for finance, why would we expect it to work for Six Sigma?

When Six Sigma becomes ingrained into the organization, it will be possible to scale down the level of dedicated resources, similar to the safety department in a well-managed company, which typically has few full-time resources since everyone in the company works on safety every day.

The second item addresses the need to have Six Sigma formally managed like any other activity of the company. The Six Sigma effort needs to plan, to develop a budget, to have clear objectives, to obtain resources, and so on. Similarly, if leadership takes Six Sigma seriously, they will want to review and potentially revise these plans. Good companies spend a lot of time planning, which in turn means less time has to be spent fighting fires and solving crises. As UCLA basketball coaching legend John Wooden noted, "Failing to plan is planning to fail." The same principle holds for Six Sigma.

As we have seen, project selection is a critical component of success. Often the battle is lost before we have even begun due to selection of poor projects.

We also need a formal project review process. The review process ensures that the projects are continuing to move in the right direction at an appropriate pace. As noted, without a regular drumbeat of reviews, projects often get bogged down, and move at a glacial pace. The reviews also give leadership an opportunity to make midcourse corrections, and to quickly learn of barriers getting in the way. Also, the reviews provide a visible symbol that leadership is personally involved.

In later chapters we will provide more detailed advice about project selection and the different types of reviews required, and their appropriate timing.

Training systems may at first glance seem obvious. Everyone who gets involved with Six Sigma receives training. However, there is a big difference between establishing a formal training system and doing a wave of mass training. A training system is not a one-time event, but rather an ongoing set of interconnected processes. It will evaluate and document the business needs, develop or obtain tailored training courses to meet those needs, and then deliver the appropriate type and depth of training to those that need it, at the most appropriate time. This may require a more complex curriculum with several courses of varying breadth and depth, rather than a single one-size-fits-all course. It will also require that new people joining the organization be trained promptly. Development of the required training system is discussed in detail in Chapter 7.

We have commented previously on the need to modify systems, policies, and procedures to be consistent with Six Sigma direction. For example, in order to attract top talent to the effort, career progression paths will need to be modified so that MBB and Black Belt roles are clearly seen as accelerators, rather than hindrances, to career advancement. Similarly, managerial bonus programs, annual performance appraisal systems, communication processes, and the like will need to be modified to help drive Six Sigma. These points illustrate why the three key success factors of leadership, top talent, and supportive infrastructure must be tightly linked.

A High-Level Roadmap For Six Sigma Deployment

Now that we have identified the key factors that separate very successful from less successful deployments of Six Sigma, we can use them to develop a high-level roadmap for deployment to maximize success.

By high-level we mean that at this point we provide only the major steps and their objectives. Subsequent chapters will provide much more detailed, step-by-step advice for succeeding in each step. The overall deployment process, and the individual steps, are intended to be flexible enough that they can apply to organizations of different sizes, industries, cultures, and so on. The recommended deployment process is illustrated in Figure 3-2. This roadmap is certainly not the only possible means of deploying Six Sigma, but it takes into account the experiences of many companies, including lessons learned about the key success factors.

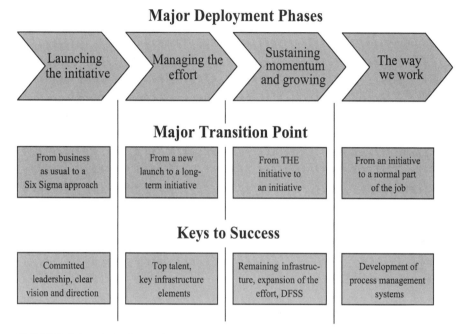

FIGURE 3-2   A High Level Deployment Process for Six Sigma

Figure 3-2 shows that this deployment process consists of four macro steps or phases:

- Launching the initiative,
- Managing the effort,
- Sustaining momentum and growing,
- Being the way we work.

Our experience has been that all organizations deploying Six Sigma go through each phase, although each will progress through the phases differently. Each phase has unique challenges and issues, and, of course, there may be overlap. In some cases organizations may have to recycle through previous phases if they have not been properly addressed. So while we have found these steps to be common to all companies implementing Six Sigma, each organization is likely to experience them in a unique way.

A good analogy would be child development; all children go through some common stages as they develop from infants, to toddlers, to children, to teenagers, to adults, but each child's experience with these stages is unique.

These four steps have been carefully chosen to align with the major transition points in Six Sigma deployment. Unfortunately, no one has gone immediately from being a non-Six Sigma company to being a Six Sigma company in one large step. Everyone has had to go through an evolutionary deployment over several years, resulting in several transitions. Organizational transitions often provide major opportunities for breakthroughs, as well as for pitfalls.

During transitions direction changes, roles change, often circumstances change, and there is always some level of anxiety in the organization, if not confusion and fear. It is therefore very important that the transitions in Six Sigma deployment be planned properly, and take into account the key success factors discussed previously. Without proper planning, these transitions could turn out to be full of landmines, and derail deployment.

Our four deployment steps are intended to guide organizations through these transitions successfully. Let's take a closer look at each of them.

Launching the Initiative

The first transition occurs when the organization makes the decision to implement Six Sigma. This transition corresponds to our launching the initiative step.

Implementing Six Sigma will cause significant change to the status quo of the organization. There may be current managers who are philosophically opposed to Six Sigma, or who want to jockey for position based on political motivations. Individual contributors in the organization will no doubt have a lot of serious questions. Opinions at this point may be based on hearsay, or sound bites from the media that may or may not be accurate. The organization will be looking for clear vision and direction at all levels.

Some of the key issues that will need to be addressed in the launching the initiative step are:

- Setting of the overall vision and justification for deployment of Six Sigma.

- Selecting an external Six Sigma provider, if needed.

- Developing a long-term deployment plan, including objectives.

- Developing a short-term implementation plan, based on the long-term deployment plan. This task includes selection of initial resources and projects.

- Writing a clear communication plan to explain this direction to the entire organization (As explained in Chapter 5, this is sometimes done in the second phase).

Of the key success factors discussed earlier, committed leadership is particularly relevant during this step. Committed leaders will provide the compelling vision and strong leadership required to ensure that each of the issues is properly addressed, while supportive leaders will likely hope that someone else takes care of these issues while they focus on whatever they consider to be critically important to the organization. It is very important that everyone in the organization understands why the organization is deploying Six Sigma, and has a clear understanding of the long-term vision. Understanding the rationale for change, and seeing where the organization is headed, are crucial to any change initiative (Weisbord [1989]).

Managing the Effort

After the Six Sigma initiative has been formally implemented, the next key transition occurs when the first set of projects are being completed, and people start wondering where we go from here. If Six Sigma is properly implemented, there will likely be a wave of enthusiasm that will carry the effort through the first set of projects. It is at this crucial transition point that Six Sigma will either fizzle out as just another short-lived fad, or it will be properly managed as a long-term business priority.

To successfully move through this transition, you will need the involvement of the organization's top talent (change is tough!), as well as initial elements of the supporting infrastructure. These are the most critical success factors for this phase.

Key requirements at this step are:

- Strong leaders in Six Sigma roles

- An effective project selection system

- A multitiered project review system

- An approved Six Sigma budget

- Good communication processes

- Formal recruitment and career progression processes for MBBs and Black Belts

- Reward and recognition systems

Sustaining Momentum and Growing

Even after a successful introduction of Six Sigma, and a good transition to ongoing management of the effort, there is still a tendency to lose steam after a couple of years. Virtually all organizations implementing Six Sigma have experienced such difficulties. The reasons for this phenomenon are based on business realities and human nature.

One of the realities of business is that the environment is constantly changing due to economic fluctuations, new government regulations, technological breakthroughs (e.g., the Internet), or even world political events, such as the fall of the Berlin Wall, and the subsequent opening of Eastern Europe and Russia.

With Six Sigma progressing well, leadership's attention will naturally be distracted toward emerging trends and opportunities in the marketplace. For example, Internet commerce exploded on to the business scene in the middle of Six Sigma deployment at Grace and GE. Similarly, it is only human nature to be attracted to the latest hot topic in the business world, even at the expense of successful initiatives that may be viewed as yesterday's news.

These reasons help explain why so many corporations go through a series of flavor-of-the-month fads without reaping sustained benefits from any of them. If these natural impulses are not checked, Six Sigma will gradually slip in organizational importance. The participation of leadership will fade, Six Sigma will struggle to attract top talent, and it will slowly become a second tier or back burner initiative. After the leadership presence, top talent, and infrastructure fade away, so will the benefits. Analysts will eventually ask, "Whatever happened to Six Sigma?" An embarrassed leadership team will likely either claim that the organization is still driving Six Sigma, or that it has been successfully integrated into daily operations. Customers and employees will know better.

There is an alternative to this scenario. Certainly business leaders will have to respond to multiple issues and various crises in the marketplace. They do not have the luxury of having only one thing to worry about. The tragic attacks of September 11, 2001, and the subsequent economic impact, are unfortunate examples of an unexpected crisis that management must respond to. Even under the best of circumstances, the organization will have to transition from Six Sigma being *the* initiative to *an* initiative. The key to maintaining momentum and growing Six Sigma during this transition is the proper functioning of the rest of the supporting infrastructure.

A good infrastructure will ensure that Six Sigma gets the nourishment it needs when the organization must focus attention on other issues as well. To grow, we will also have to continually expand the effort to include all aspects of the organization, including using Six Sigma to grow the top line. DFSS is critical to doing this.

In order to successfully get to this point organizations will have already implemented several infrastructure elements such as good project selection and review systems.

Other components of the supporting infrastructure that become key in this step are:

- Well-defined organizational structure, especially a functioning Six Sigma Council. The Council will develop annual objectives and budgets, manage the Six Sigma systems and processes, and provide leadership for the overall effort.

- A training system that provides the required skills to new employees, as well as continuing education and training for experienced MBBs, Black Belts, and Green Belts.

- A system of audits to ensure that previously closed projects are continuing to reap benefits (the purpose of the Control phase in the DMAIC process).

- Quarterly management reviews of the Six Sigma system at the business and corporate levels to make sure that the system is performing as desired.

The Way We Work

The last transition point in deploying Six Sigma is perhaps the most difficult. This is the point at which we need to move Six Sigma from being an initiative to being the way we work. In other words, the concepts and methodologies of Six Sigma must become standard operating procedures, rather than a separate initiative.

Organizations can't go on indefinitely with Six Sigma being their primary focus-nor should they! If Six Sigma is deployed properly, it will fundamentally change the way leaders lead, and the way work is done. If it can be effectively institutionalized, the organization can continue its benefits without maintaining a separate Six Sigma infrastructure, or continuing the significant demands on leadership's time and energy. This allows leadership to focus on other strategically important issues, such as its eCommerce strategy, or rethinking safety and security systems after the September 11, 2001 terrorist attacks.

We believe this is the most difficult transition phase. First of all, it is rarely addressed well in the corporate world, for any initiative, not just Six Sigma. Business journals and textbooks are full of case studies where a variety of methodologies have been introduced and produced significant savings. In most companies, however, there are few traces of the initiative (or the benefits) after about five years. Examples include TQM, reengineering, activity-based costing (ABC), benchmarking, lean enterprise, and so on. Contrary to some commentators' opinions, this fact does not indicate a deficiency in any of these methodologies. In reality, each of these initiatives can reap huge benefits for organizations that deploy them properly.

The deficiency that generally causes this phenomenon is the organization's inability to successfully integrate the key concepts and methodologies of the initiative into its normal mode of operation; i.e., to make it the way we work. If this is not done, as soon as the separate infrastructure is dismantled, and leadership moves on to other issues (which they need to do), the initiative dissolves.

In fact, given the relative newness of Six Sigma, we do not feel that any organization has successfully made this transition. GE is perhaps the furthest along, but would likely admit that it has not yet fully institutionalized Six Sigma. Based on conversations we have had with Six Sigma resources at Motorola, it does not appear to us that they succeeded in this transition. Fortunately, there are some positive counter-examples from other initiatives. For example, GE launched an initiative called Work Out almost 20 years ago. This involved a series of "town meetings" where rank and file employees could get together to address bureaucracy and other issues in the workplace.

This initiative was hugely successful, and helped GE get through a key transition early in Jack Welch's tenure as CEO. There is no longer a Work Out initiative at GE, nor is there a Work Out infrastructure with dedicated resources, budget allocations, and so on. However, Work Out is still very much part of the GE culture, and the term is used on a regular basis when teams get together to tackle routine problems. The safety management system at DuPont is another outstanding example of a major initiative being successfully institutionalized for long-term benefit.

The key to such successes has been the ability to integrate the initiative into the culture of the organization, so that it is no longer seen as a separate initiative. How can this be done with Six Sigma? The best way that we know of is to migrate the Six Sigma improvement effort into an ongoing process management system. Six Sigma relies on formal projects and the allocation of dedicated, trained resources. When the separate infrastructure of Six Sigma matures, we need to integrate these key components into the existing infrastructure to create a new way of working, as shown in Figure 3-3.

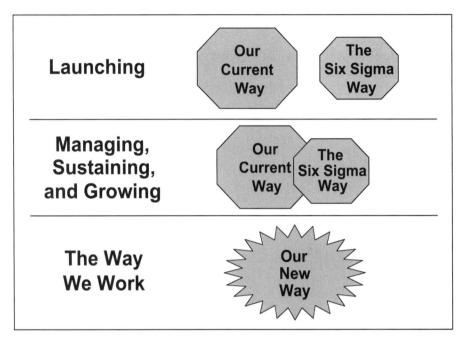

FIGURE 3-3   Stages of Integration of Six Sigma

We use the term process management system to refer to an enrichment of the existing infrastructure that incorporates measurement of key process metrics, response to out-of-control conditions, identification of key improvement opportunities, and assignment of resources to capture these opportunities. A key point is that this system is part of normal operations; i.e., people just doing their jobs, not a separate initiative. By making it a formal business system we minimize the need for a separate infrastructure. Process management systems will be discussed in greater detail in Chapter 7.

Summary

There are three common root causes that explain why some businesses achieve significant success with Six Sigma, and others achieve minimal success. These key success factors are committed leadership, involvement of top talent, and supporting infrastructure. By integrating these three key success factors we can identify a deployment roadmap that maximizes the probability of success. This roadmap has been successfully followed by numerous organizations of various sizes and business application areas.

The next four chapters will provide detailed guidance on how to succeed in each of the steps of this deployment roadmap. We begin with the first step, launching the initiative, in Chapter 4. The other three phases will be discussed in Chapters 5-7. Chapter 8 will provide summary advice to achieve success and avoid pitfalls. Commonly asked questions about deployment, and our answers to them, are presented after Chapter 8.

References

Harry, Mikel, and Richard Schroeder. (2000). *Six Sigma: The Breakthrough Strategy Revolutionizing the World's Top Corporations*. Doubleday, New York.

Weisbord, M.R. (1989). *Productive Workplaces*. Jossey-Bass, San Francisco.

Welch, J.F. (2001). *Jack: Straight From the Gut*. Warner Books, New York.

4

LAUNCHING THE INITIATIVE

"A journey of a thousand miles must begin with a single step."

—Lao Tzu

Chapter 3 provided an overall deployment process for Six Sigma, based on the case studies from Chapter 2. We will now delve into the first phase of the deployment process, a step referred to as launching the initiative. This is probably the most important phase. If Six Sigma is poorly launched it will be very difficult to reorganize and regain momentum. People will have already become skeptical, and resisters will have ammunition. Taking into full consideration the key points discussed in the chapter will help organizations hit the ground running on their initial implementation.

We define the launch phase of Six Sigma to be roughly the period between making the decision to deploy Six Sigma, and completion of the initial wave of Black Belt training. At the end of this phase you should have in place:

- An overall deployment plan (strategy)
- The initial wave of projects
- Trained Black Belts, and other key players

These are the key "deliverables" for the launch phase and they should be considered in that order. Before developing the deployment plan most organizations need to address the key preliminary question of which major deployment strategy to utilize. This decision will affect virtually every aspect of the deployment plan, so it will be addressed first, followed by the three main launch topics. The chapter will be completed with an overall summary of the launching the initiative phase.

Full or Partial Deployment?

Once organizations have decided to implement Six Sigma they are faced with the question of "how do I get started?" The most obvious answer is to adopt the approach of companies like GE and W. R. Grace and institute a CEO-led, company wide, top priority initiative. We believe that this kind of "full deployment" is the best strategy. The advantages and disadvantages of a full deployment approach are listed in Table 4-1.

Unfortunately, many business leaders below the CEO level are not in a position to take the full deployment approach. Another option is for

TABLE 4-1   Full Versus Partial Deployment

Full Deployment	Partial Deployment
Strengths	**Strengths**
• The organization knows what is going on	• Requires limited resources
• Vision and direction are clear	• Requires limited management attention
• Resources are more easily assigned	• Can be started by middle management
• Returns are large and come in the first 6-8 months	Easy to get started
Limitations	**Limitations**
• Top management commitment is required up front to get started	• Difficult to get:
	• BB assigned full time
• Priorities have to be redefined to include the Six Sigma work	• Functional resources to support BB
	• Tough to get management attention
• Management will have to change how they work	• Organization doesn't believe management is committed to Six Sigma
	• Returns are small because only a few BB are involved

leaders to deploy Six Sigma in their own realm of responsibility. This could be a division, business unit, or even a single plant. We refer to deployment on such a reduced scale as partial deployment. While this is not our first option, it may be the only practical one. Keep in mind, however, that Six Sigma will only flourish in the long term if it becomes a full deployment process. Sooner or later someone will squash a partial deployment if it does not spread to the rest of the organization. For that reason, the main objective of a partial deployment must be to make a convincing case for full deployment.

Partial deployment usually involves training one to five Black Belts and using their tangible results to make the case for full deployment. It takes little to get started, but if proper planning is not done and adequate resources are not assigned the effort can quickly run into trouble.

The result in the case of Royal Chemicals is discussed in Chapter 2. The strengths and limitations of partial deployment are also summarized in Table 4-1. Snee and Parikh (2001) report on one successful partial deployment of Six Sigma at Crompton Corporation, a chemical company based in Greenwich, CT. In the first wave seven Black Belts were trained and were given good support. One Black Belt was reassigned and his project postponed. The other six projects were completed, returning an average of $360,000 in savings per project.

These results encouraged a key business unit of Crompton Corporation to pursue a partial deployment on a much larger scale. This deployment was supported with Executive, Champion, and Site Leadership training and produced project savings similar to those of the initial six projects. Building on this success, the whole Crompton Corporation began a full Six Sigma deployment. The process of moving from partial deployment to full corporate deployment took approximately 18 months. Recall that the ultimate measure of success for partial deployment is that it leads to a successful full deployment. Contrary to popular belief, partial deployment requires more than just good Black Belt training to be successful. Executive, Champion, and Leadership training, as well as good project and people selection are also needed.

Those selecting the partial deployment route should be aware of the problems that they can expect to encounter. The biggest problems include identifying good projects for the Black Belts, getting Black Belts assigned full time, and assigning Champions who will provide good guidance for the Black Belts, including weekly reviews of the projects. It is sometimes difficult to get functional group support for the projects when the organization is not pursuing full deployment of Six Sigma. The completion of the Executive, Champion, and Leadership training helps ensure that these problems are minimized.

The partial deployment approach is most likely to succeed when all of the deployment plan elements for the full deployment are addressed. In other words, success is most likely when partial deployment is essentially a full deployment in one area, and looks just like a full deployment to those working in this area. This considered, many feel that to do the partial deployment well takes almost as much effort as doing a full deployment with not nearly the return. This leads some, including the authors, to conclude that full deployment is overall a better use of resources, and also increases the probability of success.

Developing the Deployment Plan

While there is usually a strong desire to launch Six Sigma as quickly as possible once the decision to deploy has been made, there is significant risk in taking a ready, fire, aim approach if proper planning is not done up front. Our experience is that one truly needs to begin with the end in mind when deploying Six Sigma. In other words, before you launch you should have a good idea of the long-term direction. Once the long-term strategy is set, it will be much easier to develop a short-term implementation process that will take you in the right direction. The long-term strategy is referred to as the deployment plan. Of course, this does not need to be developed in minute detail. You will simply need enough specificity to guide implementation. You will continually reevaluate, update, and add detail to this deployment plan as you move through the four phases of Six Sigma deployment.

The deployment plan should cover, at a minimum, all the elements listed on the following page. A real example of a typical (not necessarily best practice) deployment plan is given in the appendix. As noted, these elements are implemented not all at once, but rather in a phased approach. Think of the deployment plan as a work in progress. The key elements of the deployment plan during the launch phase are:

- Executive and Business Leadership workshops
- Champion workshop
- Selection of initial projects
- Selection of initial Black Belts and other key roles
- Finance personnel training
- Black Belt and Green Belt training

We consider these elements of the deployment plan to comprise an implementation or launch process, which is the focus of this chapter. Other elements of the deployment plan will be documented at a strategic level now, but details and actual implementation will come during the subsequent phases of deployment.

Our experience has been that most organizations are not ready to develop a proper deployment plan without more detailed understanding of Six Sigma, and facilitation from someone experienced in Six Sigma. For this reason we strongly recommend leadership workshops to develop this more detailed understanding, and to begin development of the deployment plan. Interestingly, the first draft of the deployment plan will be developed during the Executive and Business Leadership workshops, and then be used to guide development of the other elements of the implementation process. So there is somewhat of a chicken and egg relationship between the implementation process and the deployment plan. The implementation process is needed to develop the deployment plan, but in reality the implementation process is a subset of the deployment plan.

Required Deployment Plan Elements

- Strategy and Goals for Six Sigma
- Process Performance Measures
- Project Selection Criteria
- Project Identification/Prioritization System
- Deployment Processes for Champions, MBBs, BBs, etc.
- Roles of Management, Champions, MBBs, BBs and Functional Groups
- Curricula and Training System
- Project and Six Sigma Initiative Review Schedule
- Project Reporting and Tracking System
- Audit System for Previously Closed Projects
- Reward and Recognition Plan
- Communication Plan

This chapter will focus on how to organize and conduct the workshops that develop the first draft of the deployment plan with emphasis on elements that are critical to the initial launch of Six Sigma. The other aspects of this plan will be discussed in detail in Chapters 5 and 6, since they become critical in the later stages of Six Sigma deployment.

The Executive workshop should include all members of the executive team since they all have a role to play in Six Sigma deployment. This holds even if the initiative will involve manufacturing or operations only in the beginning of a partial deployment. All parties are needed to make Six Sigma successful regardless of the initial focus of the effort. In particular it is important that the heads of the finance, human resources (HR), and information technology (IT) organizations participate in the Executive workshop and subsequent Six Sigma deployment.

These are three new players not typically involved in previous improvement approaches, such as TQM or quality circles. Finance has the responsibility for determining the bottom line impact of the projects and creating the project tracking system that will be used to monitor the tangible results of the effort. HR is responsible for the career development paths of the Champions, Master Black Belts (MBBs), Black Belts, and Green Belts, as well as reward and recognition systems, communication vehicles, and performance management systems. IT will be needed to develop computer systems that collect key process measurement data identified by the Black Belt projects, to improve the cycle time and accuracy of manual systems through digitization, or to automate improvements as part of the project control plan.

While some data acquisition systems may already be in place, Six Sigma projects often uncover other process measurements that are needed to improve and effectively control the process. Quite frequently information systems have been put in place for financial (accounting) purposes, rather than to aid continuous improvement. Achieving this new purpose often requires new data acquisition systems.

The Executive workshop is typically two days in length and has as its products:

- More in-depth understanding of Six Sigma
- Defined roles of the members of the management team
- Identification of targeted areas for improvement
- Champions for these targeted areas
- A draft deployment plan

The first version of the deployment plan is finalized in the following weeks by the management team as a regular part of their management meetings. A key part of this work is the refinement of the list of project areas and associated Champions. In large organizations it is often appropriate to give the two-day Executive workshop not only for the corporate executives, but also for the leaders of the different strategic business units (SBUs). In such cases the focus of these additional workshops is on the Six Sigma deployment plan within each SBU.

The SBU leaders often attend the original Executive workshop to learn about the process, and then assume leadership roles in the SBU-specific workshops. Similarly, it is important to do Site or Functional Leadership training for the management teams in the areas (plant site, functional group, etc.) that are targeted for the initial projects. This ensures that the Black Belts get the support that they need to complete their projects in a timely fashion. The Site or Functional Leadership training should be completed prior to the first week of Black Belt training.

The Executive workshop is followed in approximately one month by a three-to-five day Champion workshop for the Champions identified during the Executive workshop. This workshop uses as input the initial deployment plan and the project areas that were outputs of the Executive workshop, and refined in subsequent weeks. The outputs of the Champion workshop include deeper understanding of Six Sigma and the roles of the players, a list of chartered projects, and assigned Black Belts. Special attention is focused on the role of the Champion and the way the Champion interfaces with the Black Belts and Green Belts.

This workshop is particularly important because inactive or ineffective Champions are often identified as the root cause of project failures. If this role is not taken seriously, or not properly understood, the Champions can become the weak link in the Six Sigma organization, with devastating consequences.

After their Champion workshop, the Champions meet with the Black Belts to discuss the projects and make any needed refinements. Such refinements are often needed because the Black Belts have detailed data and insights that were not available when the project charters were developed. Project charters will be discussed in greater detail shortly. The Black Belts are now ready to attend their training, which usually follows the Champion workshop by approximately one month. The Black Belts are expected to bring their project charters to the training, and work on their actual projects as part of the training. They will learn and deliver results at the same time. Such an approach is consistent with the principles of adult learning. We will now take a short detour to look at the elements of the deployment plan, and then come back to Black Belt training and the rest of the implementation process.

Deployment Plan Elements

The deployment plan elements shown on page 65 must be addressed whether a partial or full deployment approach is utilized. However, the elements are not all implemented at the same time. Some are critical at launch, others in the second phase of deployment (managing the effort), and others in the third phase (sustaining momentum and growing). At this point the launch elements need to be covered in detail, but the other elements can be defined at a high, strategic level. Details of these elements will be added at the appropriate time.

While seasoned planners may feel the need to define all deployment elements in detail from the very beginning, our experience is that trying to do so delays implementation, and can result in paralysis by analysis as you try to cross every "t" and dot every "i."

We will briefly describe each deployment plan element, and then go into detail on the critical launch phase items. We provide additional detail on the other elements in Chapters 5 and 6.

Strategy and Goals

Strategy and goals make up the first key element. This element is the responsibility of senior management, and sets the overall vision for Six Sigma deployment. A key element of the strategy is choosing the place where Six Sigma will start and what the rollout sequence and timing will be. Obviously, Six Sigma cannot be rolled out everywhere at once. A typical industrial rollout starts in manufacturing, and then when success is demonstrated, management initiates projects in the other areas of the business and new product development (DFSS—Design for Six Sigma).

Service businesses, such as insurance or consumer credit companies, would typically begin Six Sigma in operations. General business projects and DFSS typically begin six to eight months and one year after manufacturing, respectively.

There are two reasons for starting in manufacturing (operations in service companies)—both related to the fact that manufacturing tends to have the best measurement systems. First, it is much easier to achieve quick hits if you begin with a good measurement system, rather than having to take time to create one. Second, the existence of good measurements usually means that everyone is aware of the huge potential savings available in manufacturing, and anxious to go after them.

Conversely, many people will need to be convinced that huge savings are available in the finance department. Starting Six Sigma in manufacturing/operations sets the initiative up for success. Success in manufacturing/operations builds confidence that Six Sigma will work, as well as producing bottom line results that help "pay as you go," thereby enabling deployment throughout the organization.

Another decision is when to start Green Belt training—typically initiated eight to ten months after Black Belt training starts. Black Belts, dedicated to Six Sigma projects 100% of their time, are needed to get the initiative moving quickly. Some companies have a goal of training the entire professional staff as Green Belts (part time) as soon as it can be managed.

It is also important that one to two year goals for Six Sigma be developed and broadly communicated in the Executive workshop. The goals, which generally include financial targets, should be communicated for the organization as a whole and reinforced within each major part of the organization.

A goal not stated in financial terms is a clear indication that management is not serious about making Six Sigma successful. A financial goal tells the organization's members what is expected of them. For example, in the case of a $1 billion revenue company, a goal of $2 million to the bottom line from Six Sigma communicates a far different message than a goal of $10 million or $20 million. At $250,000 per project, $2 million translates into eight projects while $10 million and $20 million translate to 40 and 80 projects, respectively. Clearly, much more effort (people, time, and money) will be required to complete 40-80 projects than to complete eight. The financial goals will be revised over the course of several years of deployment.

Process Performance Measures

Process performance measures define what's important for success and are used to select projects. A pitfall to be avoided is selecting each project independently. This is analogous to spending five minutes starting to clean 10 different rooms in a house, versus spending 50 minutes to completely clean one room. In the first case, it is difficult to see what impact the effort has had; in the second case there is a visible, tangible success that will now be ready to be leveraged elsewhere. It is preferable to launch Six Sigma by focusing on a few strategic areas, rather than 10 or 20. The process performance measures determined by senior leadership help everyone focus the initial projects strategically.

One model for key measures is quality, delivery, and cost (QDC). This model provides three strategic focus areas for the initial projects. Capacity is added when additional capacity is needed for the market or to run a more efficient operation (e.g., moving from a six- to seven-day operation to a five-day operation).

If all the projects affect one of these three areas, you will have significant tangible results when they are completed. Quality obviously relates to customer satisfaction, and an emphasis on it will almost always have the fringe benefit of saving money because you will reduce the costs of rejecting or reworking defective finished products, dealing with customer returns, shouldering warranty costs, and so on. The only exception is likely to be the case where delivering the desired quality level requires significant upgrade to equipment or materials. Surprisingly, this is rarely the case. See the discussion of process entitlement later in this chapter.

Delivery relates to the procurement, inventory, and logistics systems. Again, improvement here almost always enhances customer satisfaction, while reducing internal costs (excess inventory, loss of sales due to out-of-stock conditions, return of damaged or spoiled product, etc.) Reducing cost means reducing internal sources of waste or rework, regardless of whether this effort directly affects the customer. Improving the internal processes almost always results in better products and services, which ultimately benefits the customer.

In the case of service or transactional processes, the key process metrics are usually some form of accuracy or cycle time measures. Accuracy includes defects in information such as account numbers or financial figures, and directly relates to both customer satisfaction and rework costs. Cycle time of business processes is a productivity measure, so it also relates directly to costs and, of course, to customer satisfaction (e.g., time to approve mortgage loan applications). Interestingly, in the vast majority of cases, attempts to define customer satisfaction or internal cost metrics result in some measure of accuracy or cycle time.

Project Selection Criteria

The process metrics are also used to develop a set of more specific criteria to select projects. The project selection criteria used by one company are summarized in the following list—

- Areas to improve
  - Waste reduction
  - Capacity improvement
  - Downtime reduction
  - Resource consumption (labor and raw materials)
- Effect on Customer Satisfaction
  - On-time delivery in full
  - Defect levels
- Effect on the bottom-line
  - >$250k per project
  - Doable in 4-6 months
  - Benefit realized in < 1 year

These criteria define areas that are important to improve and will produce significant bottom-line results. Note that the areas to improve are those that directly affect the customer satisfaction measurements. Project selection criteria also communicate what types of improvements are important to the organization. By communicating these criteria you alert the organization as to what your objectives are and the kinds of projects on which you want to focus. This increases the probability that large numbers of people in the organization will be involved in identifying opportunities for improvement. As noted, you will want to select projects strategically, rather than haphazardly.

Project Identification and Prioritization System

These project selection criteria are used in the Champion work-shop to develop a set of initial candidate projects. The projects are put in the project hopper and prioritized for assignment to a Black Belt or Green Belt. Project selection will be discussed in greater detail later in this chapter. In later deployment phases organizations develop an ongoing system to identify potential projects, rank them, and place them in the project hopper, so that there is a continuously refreshed list of good projects.

Deployment Processes for Leaders

Lists of the Champions, Black Belts, MBBs, and Green Belts are also part of the deployment plan. In later deployment phases these lists will be expanded to become a system for selection, deployment, and advancement for each of these roles. The list of initial Champions will be developed at the Executive workshop. At the Champion workshop, the Champions will develop the list of initial projects, and based on this, develop a list of candidate Black Belts to lead these projects.

In Chapter 1 you learned that Six Sigma is about improvement—not training. It is strongly recommended that the projects be selected first and then the Black Belts for these projects. The Champions should be selected at the Executive workshop based on the areas targeted for improvement. Selecting the Champions and Black Belts before identifying specific projects increases the risk that important projects will be overlooked. This critical issue is discussed in-depth later in the chapter.

Roles of Management and Others

While there are generic job descriptions for Six Sigma titles, such as Champion, MBB, Black Belt, Green Belt, and so on, there is considerable variation in the actual role that these people play in different organizations.

Organizations should take the time to consider the specific roles that each of these will play in their deployment. Within reasonable boundaries, management can tailor the roles to a specific organization. The roles of the leadership team, Champions, MBBs, Black Belts, and functional groups should be defined in the Executive workshop and communicated to the organization. Discussion of guidelines for each of these roles is located later in this chapter.

Curricula and Training System

An overall training system for each of the Six Sigma roles is a key element of the deployment plan. At launch, a training schedule is needed only for the initial wave of Black Belts. As more and more people in various roles are involved in Six Sigma, new employees are hired, and the need is found for advanced training in certain areas (DFSS in engineering), a functioning training system with diverse curricula will need to be developed. A wave of mass training does not make a training system; mass training is an event that usually has no lasting impact. What is needed is a well thought out system that identifies all the training needs of all the roles, and puts together a sustained, ongoing system to continuously satisfy these needs in the most efficient way possible. This will be a tremendous amount of work, but fortunately the complete training system is not needed at the launch of Six Sigma.

Project and Six Sigma Initiative Review Schedule

A project review schedule is key for the deployment plan. Experience has shown that an effective schedule involves short (30-minute) weekly reviews by the Champion, and monthly reviews with the Plant Manager, functional leader, or SBU leader, as appropriate. These will be needed soon after the kick-off of the initial projects, and will be discussed in more detail in Chapter 5.

A review of the Six Sigma deployment should be done quarterly by the corporate or SBU leader as appropriate. All the elements of the deployment plan, and the associated goals, are appropriate agenda items for the quarterly reviews. This review is focused on how well the overall initiative is going; it does not focus on a review of individual projects. This review is critical to sustaining momentum of the Six Sigma effort long term, and is discussed in more detail in Chapter 6.

Project Reporting and Tracking System

This system documents the results of the projects, and provides valuable managerial information. Development of a formal system is not required in initial deployment, and is typically emphasized later in the deployment process, such as in the managing the effort phase discussed in Chapter 5. The project reporting and tracking system will keep a record of all the Six Sigma projects, providing a corporate memory of what has been accomplished to date. The system will generate managerial reports at several levels to keep management informed of progress.

This includes financial results from the tracking system, as well as non-financial information, such as number of projects completed or in progress, time to completion of projects, status reports, and so on. The tracking part of this system is intended to document the financial benefits of closed projects. Obviously, this system needs to be designed with rigor so that the claimed financial benefits are accurate and credible. For small organizations, or to get started, a simple Excel™ spreadsheet will do the trick. Dedicated computer systems are eventually needed for larger organizations. More details on this system are given in Chapter 5.

Audit System for Previously Closed Projects

When your organization gets to the sustaining momentum and growing phase (Chapter 6) there will be a large number of completed projects, many of which will claim perpetual benefits; that is, benefits that will recur year after year. For example, if waste levels drop from 10 percent to 5 percent, and this improvement is maintained, cost savings from lower waste will be reaped every year. Unfortunately, in many improvement efforts these lower costs begin to creep up over time, much like weight lost on a diet. To some degree this is to be expected, since it is human nature to revert to old habits once the additional resources and focus brought by Six Sigma move on to other priorities.

Of course, you will need to preempt the natural digression back to old ways and rework levels if your efforts are to have lasting impact. Six Sigma has the advantage of a formal step in the DMAIC process, the control phase, which is specifically targeted to implement controls that prevent backsliding to the previous performance. As a second layer of protection, an audit system for previously closed projects needs to be implemented. This is not primarily a financial audit system to ensure that claimed benefits are real—financial controls need to be implemented from the very beginning. Rather, this audit system is intended to audit the control plan of previously closed projects and ensure that it is working. In other words, the audit system will check to make sure the benefits of this project are still being received. If not, action will be initiated to revisit the project, regain the benefits, and institute an effective control plan. This system is discussed at greater length in Chapter 6.

Reward and Recognition Plan

HR needs to develop a reward and recognition plan to ensure that the organization is able to obtain (and eventually promote) the best possible candidates for Six Sigma roles. We believe in the power of "intrinsic motivation" (the idea that people do something because they really want to do it), rather than solely relying on "extrinsic motivation" (people do something because they are coerced or "bribed" to do it). Therefore, those that have a fire in the belly for improvement will likely perform better in Six Sigma roles than those solely looking for money or promotion.

However, it must be recognized that a total lack of extrinsic rewards for involvement in Six Sigma is essentially a disincentive, therefore, consider rewarding these roles in such a way that top performers will be drawn to Six Sigma. This plan, which will be discussed in greater detail in Chapter 5, should be reviewed and revised as needed over time to ensure that the Champions, Black Belts, MBBs, Green Belts, and team members are properly recognized for their contributions. Most successful Six Sigma companies have revised their reward and recognition systems to more effectively support the Six Sigma initiative. A balance of both intrinsic and extrinsic motivation is encouraged.

Communication Plan

A communication plan has to be developed to support the Six Sigma initiative. This will be a very important part of the deployment plan because it will significantly affect the impression that rank and file employees have of Six Sigma.

Communication about Six Sigma typically utilizes existing media, but sometimes new media have to be developed. It is important to use a variety of media because people take in information and learn in different ways. There is variation in people as well as in processes. Some prefer personal contacts, either one-on-one or in groups. Others prefer to read newsletters or memos, while still others respond well to videos, webcasts, or emails. Leadership needs to carefully communicate why they chose to deploy Six Sigma, what they hope to get out of it, and where it will take the organization. One example of such a communication plan was the video that Jack Welch made (see Chapter 2), and which each exempt employee at GE was expected to watch. This was followed up with frequent emails to all employees with updates on progress of the initiative.

In some cases, such as GE and AlliedSignal, the CEO will make a bold statement about Six Sigma at the very beginning. However, we have also worked with organizations that did not feel comfortable making such bold statements. There is often a concern that if too big a deal is made of Six Sigma at the very beginning, unrealistic expectations will be set. Every employee might expect to begin Six Sigma training the next week. Customers may expect better products and services immediately. Confidence in the initiative may fade if people's unrealistic expectations are not fully met. Therefore, many organizations choose to begin the initiative in a fairly low-key manner, without hoopla.

Once actual projects are begun, and results are starting to flow in, the initiative will be more formally and broadly communicated. Leadership will be able to point to tangible savings that have already been accomplished, and can communicate the sequenced rollout of projects and training. The decision of when to begin implementing the communication plan needs to be made at the Executive workshop. The communication plan is discussed more fully in Chapter 5.

Experience and surveys have shown that every item on this list is important. Moreover all are needed for success; none are optional. Not paying attention to any of these items can seriously limit the effectiveness of the Six Sigma initiative. As previously noted, however, not all items need to be developed to the same degree of detail in the launch phase. The items that comprise the implementation process are the most critical initially.

Selecting the Right Projects

As noted earlier, the project selection process is started in the Executive workshop where areas for improvement are identified. Initial projects are selected in the Champion workshop based on the improvement areas identified by the executives, project selection criteria, and the project chartering process. This section discusses the characteristics of a good project and how to select one (see Snee [2001], Snee and Rodebaugh [2002]). Project selection is one of the key success factors for the launch phase.

What is a Six Sigma Project?

Six Sigma is about solving business problems by improving processes. Typical problems fall into two major categories: solution known, and solution unknown. Six Sigma is aimed at solving the problem in which the solution is not known.

Such problems include decreasing errors in invoices, increasing the yield of a chemical process, decreasing the defect rate of an assembled project, and decreasing the days outstanding in accounts receivables. In 1989, J.M. Juran pointed out that "a project is a problem scheduled for solution." We define a Six Sigma project as a problem scheduled for solution that uses a set of metrics to set project goals and monitor progress.

The second category of problems frequently encountered is that in which the solution is known at the outset. Implementing a new computer network to conform to corporate guidelines, installing a new piece of equipment in manufacturing, or building a new plant are examples of known-solution projects. Most capital projects also fall into this category.

In each of these situations it is known what has to be done. The project is completed by assigning a project manager to the project, providing the needed resources, and using good project management techniques. Six Sigma techniques are usually not needed here, although project management can benefit from the process thinking, measurement, and monitoring techniques used by Six Sigma.

An organization's improvement plan typically includes projects of both types: solution known and solution unknown. Both types of projects are important and are needed to improve the performance of an organization. Solution-unknown projects are led by Black Belts or Green Belts. Solution-known projects are lead by project managers.

It is also essential that you carefully identify and document the process that contains the problem. The process provides the focus and context for the Six Sigma improvement work. Process identification is usually easy in manufacturing where you can simply follow the pipes, but it is much less obvious in finance or marketing. A Black Belt or Green Belt who utilizes the Six Sigma methodology then completes the project. Of course, there is no guarantee that every problem will be successfully solved, but with proper project and people selection we can expect a very high (80 to 90%) success rate.

To use Six Sigma, you also need one or more measurements that quantify the magnitude of the problem and can be used to set project goals and monitor progress. These measurements are usually called critical to quality (CTQ) measures. Six Sigma takes a disciplined, rigorous approach to problem identification, diagnosis, analysis, and solution. It is well suited for problems that do not have a known solution.

Selecting Good Six Sigma Projects

Now we turn our attention to selecting a Six Sigma project. The characteristics of a good Six Sigma project are—

- Clearly connected to business priorities
  - Linked to strategic and annual operating plans
- Problem is of major importance to the organization
  - Major improvement in process performance (e.g. >50%)
  - Major financial improvement (e.g. >$250K/yr)
- Reasonable scope—doable in 4-6 months
  - Support for project often decreases after 6 months
  - Project scope too large is a common problem
- Clear quantitative measures of success
  - Baseline, goals, and entitlement well-defined
- Importance is clear to the organization
  - People will support a project that they understand and see as important
- Project has the support and approval of management
  - Needed to get resources, remove barriers, and sustain over time

Projects should be clearly linked to business priorities, as reflected by the strategic and annual operating plans. It is also important to include projects addressing critical problems that must be solved in order for the organization to be successful in the next year.

A project should represent a breakthrough in terms of major improvements in both process performance (e.g., greater than 50%) and significant bottom-line results (e.g., greater than $250,000). The determination of project impact is the responsibility of the financial organization working in cooperation with the Black Belt and Champion.

This approach to measuring project impact sets Six Sigma apart from most other improvement approaches, because the financial impact is identified for each Six Sigma project by the finance department. Finance should know what the project is worth to the bottom line before work begins. This makes it an active participant in the improvement of the organization. This will be a new role for Finance in many organizations. Of course, Finance and other functions will still have their own projects, in order to improve their own processes.

The projects should be doable in four to six months. As pointed out by Bill Gates (1999), it is critical that projects be completed in this time frame in order to keep the organization and resources focused on the project. Organizations typically lose interest in projects that run longer than six months. Projects requiring more than six months of effort can usually be divided into subprojects of shorter duration, with the projects being conducted sequentially or in parallel. For this approach to work there needs to be strong project management to coordinate the set of projects.

There should also be clear quantitative measures of success, the importance of the project to the organization should be clear, and the project should have the full support and approval of management. These three characteristics are needed so that the organization sees the importance of the project, provides the needed support and resources, and removes barriers to the success of the project. People are more likely to support a project that they can see is clearly important to the organization.

Of course, these are generic attributes of a good project. Organizations still need to develop their own specific project selection criteria. Compare the generic attributes on page 78 to the more specific project selection criteria from one company listed on page 71.

The criteria on page 71 defined areas that were important to improve for this company, and projects based on these criteria did, in turn, produce significant bottom-line results. Note also that the areas to improve included customer satisfaction measurements. Project selection criteria communicate what types of improvements are important to the organization.

Project ideas can come from any source such as process assessments, customer and employee surveys and suggestions, benchmarking studies, extensions of existing projects, and so on. Many organizations struggle with how to find high-impact projects. Some sources that we recommend are:

- Rework and scrapping activities
- Overtime, warranty, and other obvious sources of waste
- Products with major backlogs—need for more capacity
- High volume products (small improvements can have huge impact)
- Problems needing solutions to meet annual operating plan
- Major problems with financial impact (customer or environmental crises)
- Large budget items, receivables, payables, treasury, taxes (follow the money)

Collectively these ideas are focused on major sources of waste, major problems (customer and environmental), major opportunities (capacity limitations in sold-out markets), and places where the money is going. Budget statements and cost of quality studies are also good sources for identifying opportunities (Conway [1992, 1994]).

Experience has also identified some characteristics of projects to avoid, or at least to further refine. Briefly stated, you should avoid, or redefine, projects that fall into any of these classifications:

- Fuzzy objectives
- Poor metrics
- No tie to financials
- Too broad a scope
- No connection to strategic or annual plans
- Solution already identified
- Too many objectives

For example, for the project to be successful the objectives need to be very clear. Such clarity is usually reflected in the process performance metrics and goals associated with the project. The process metrics should be clearly defined, and have baseline and entitlement values identified. In the case of non-manufacturing projects, the most useful process performance metrics are typically accuracy, cycle time, and cost. Cost is usually directly related to accuracy and cycle time metrics.

The project must be tied to the bottom line in some way. The project scope should be for improvements that are attainable in the four to six month time frame. An unrealistic scope (often referred to as a "boiling the ocean" project) is probably the most commonly encountered cause of project failure. Projects that are not connected to business priorities or that have too many objectives also need further refinement. Projects with an "identified solution" should be handled by a project manager instead of Six Sigma, or as mentioned earlier, be redefined to omit the specified solution in favor of allowing the Six Sigma methodology to identify the best solution.

The Concept of Process Entitlement

Entitlement is one of the most important concepts in process improvement, and is particularly useful in project selection. It is defined as the best performance that you can reasonably expect to get from a process (Harry and Schroeder [2000]). As the term implies, leadership is essentially entitled to this level of performance based on the investments they have already made.

Knowing the process entitlement defines what's possible. If entitlement is 500 units per day and the baseline performance is 250 units/day, you can easily see that there is a lot of room for improving this process. On the other hand, if current baseline performance is 480 units/day there is little room for improvement. If higher production rates are needed, a search for a totally new process may be in order (i.e., reengineering or DFSS).

As an analogy, the concept of par for a golf hole is intended to represent the entitlement for a very good golfer. That is, for such a golfer par represents what score is possible and reasonable to expect. On one hole a golfer may score less than par, but it is unrealistic to expect such performance on every hole, or even on average. Of course, all golfers have their own unique capability, so the official par doesn't represent process entitlement for the average duffer. Proper analysis and/or calculations would reveal the appropriate individual entitlement, which for professionals would be better than par, and for most golfers much worse. Note that standard golfing handicaps are usually based on average performance, which is not the same concept as entitlement.

It is not uncommon to learn in situations where capital is being requested to increase capacity that baseline production is not near entitlement, once it is carefully calculated. Six Sigma projects are subsequently instituted to increase the capacity of the current process with solutions that don't require capital. Most companies deploying Six Sigma have been able to cancel existing capital expansion plans because of capacity that has been freed up through Six Sigma with no capital expenditures. For example, if a chemical plant with six production lines is running at a 25 percent waste level, reducing the waste levels to 10 percent (60 percent reduction) creates additional capacity of 6 x 15% = 90% of a production line, or essentially creates a new line with no capital expense.

Entitlement should be determined for all key process performance measures (yield, cost of poor quality, capacity, downtime, waste, etc.). It may be the performance predicted by engineering and scientific fundamentals, nameplate capacity provided by the equipment manufacturer, or simply the best, prolonged performance observed to date.

Entitlement can also be predicted from empirical relationships. In one instance it was observed that a process operating at a cost of $0.36/unit had at one time operated at $0.16/unit (correcting for inflation). This suggests that the process entitlement (as determined by best prolonged performance) should be $0.16/unit. On further investigation it was observed that there was a linear relationship between defects and cost/unit of the form:

$$\text{Cost} = \$0.12 + 3(\text{defects})/1{,}000{,}000.$$

Therefore if defects could be reduced to very low levels (essentially zero) the true process entitlement may be as low as $0.12/unit.

Entitlement is used in project selection as follows:

- Look at the gap between baseline performance (current state) and entitlement (desired state).
- Identify a project scope that will close the gap and can be completed in less than 4-6 months.
- Assess the bottom line impact of the project and compare it to other potential projects. A Black Belt or a Green Belt is assigned as priority dictates.

The gap between baseline and entitlement is rarely closed in the course of a single project. It is not uncommon for several projects to be required. In each instance the business case for the project is determined, the project is prioritized relative to the other potential projects, and a Black Belt or Green Belt is assigned as business priorities dictate.

Entitlement defines the performance level it is possible for a process to attain. It provides a vision of possible process performance, thereby providing a performance level for which to aim. It tells you how close current performance (baseline) is to the best possible performance. It also provides a benchmark that you can use to compare your process to other processes in your company or to processes in other companies. It is prudent to compute process entitlement values before doing any benchmarking studies to provide a basis of comparison.

Keep in mind that process entitlement can, and often does, change as you learn more about it. In most cases, the process entitlement calculations are simply estimates of the true entitlement, and you can update and enhance them over time. After a few Six Sigma projects, it is not uncommon for a process to be performing beyond the entitlement level initially determined for the process. Changing the value of process entitlement as you better understand the process is a natural result of Six Sigma projects, and the need to do so should not come as a surprise.

Developing the Project Charter

The project charter has a critical impact on project success. This one-page document summarizes the key aspects of the project, in effect, defines what management wants done and what the Black Belt and Champion have agreed to accomplish. It forms a contract between all parties involved in the project.

Experience has shown that many continuous improvement projects fail because of misunderstandings among the team, the project leader, the customer, or management. For example, a team may proudly present a completed project that developed a web-based system for underwriting U.S. commercial credit lines for a leasing company. Management may have expected an internationalized version, however, and view the project as inadequate because it cannot be used in either Europe or Asia. A clear, concise, project charter avoids such misunderstandings and helps protect the project team from being second-guessed.

The charter is drafted by the Project Champion, refined by the Project Champion and Black Belt, and approved by the leadership team. It is not unusual for the charter to be revised a few times as the problem is better understood and data become available. Somewhere near the end of the measure phase the charter should define the scope of work that the project will accomplish. If such commitment is not made it will be hard for the project to satisfy expectations. It will be like trying to hit a moving target if the expectations, as defined by the charter, are constantly changing.

Figure 4-1 shows a template we have used for project charters that is similar to the template of Harry and Schroeder (2000). It is important that all the information required by the project charter be reported in the template. Blank entries are not acceptable. There are some potential problems for which you should be on the lookout.

Product or Service Impacted		Expected Project Savings($)	
BlackBelt/GreenBelt		Business Unit	
Champion		Start Date	
MBB		Target Completion Date	

Element	Description					
1. Process:	Process in which opportunity exists.					
2. Project Description:	Problem and goal statement (project s purpose)					
3. Objective:	Key process metrics impacted by the project	Process Metric	Baseline	**Goal**	Entitlement	Units
		Metric 1				
		Metric 2				
		Metric 3				
4. Business Case:	Expected financial improvement, or other justification					
5. Team members:	Names and roles of team members					
6. Project Scope:	Which are the dimensions of the project? What will be excluded?					
7. Benefit to External Customers:	Who are the final customers, what are their key measures, and what benefits will they see?					
8. Schedule:	Key completion dates.	**Project Start**				
	M- Measurement	**"M" Complete**				
	A- Analysis	**"A" Complete**				
	I- Improvement	**"I" Complete**				
	C- Control	**"C" Complete**				
	Other milestones					
		Project Complete				
9. Support Required:	Will any special capabilities, hardware, etc. be needed?					

FIGURE 4-1 Six Sigma Project Charter Template

It should be clear what process you are trying to improve (Charter Element 1). The process provides the focus and context for the work. A clear process definition helps the Black Belt see where the work will focus and what needs to be accomplished. Identifying the process is often difficult for those persons and organizations that are not skilled in thinking about their work as a series of interconnected processes.

The scope should be clear and attainable in less than a four to six month period (Charter Elements 2 and 6). Many projects fail because the scope is too big for the allotted time. Answering the question "Can we get this work done in less than four to six months (or whatever the required time frame)?" is a very effective way to test whether the project is properly scoped.

Keen attention should be paid to the process metrics (Charter Element 3). These measurements focus the Black Belt on the aspects of process performance that need to be improved, and the quantitative goals for the project. They are also used to calculate the financial impact of the project.

Leaving this section of the charter blank is not acceptable because the project will not be successful without the metrics, and should not proceed until data are available to properly define the project and allow you to calculate business impact.

The baseline, goal, and entitlement values for each of the key process metrics should be entered in the charter. You should include the metrics you want to improve as well as the metrics you don't want to negatively influence. For example, if the project is a capacity improvement project, and it is particularly important that product quality doesn't deteriorate, then both capacity and quality metrics should be addressed in the charter.

It is important that the business impact of the project is determined (Charter Element 4). This should identify both hard dollars (cost savings and profits from increased sales) that flow to the bottom line, as well as any soft dollar benefits such as cost avoidance. Many organizations deploying Six Sigma, including GE, only consider the hard benefits when publishing savings from the effort. Even when only hard benefits are reported, you should also document planned soft benefits in the charter. Leaving this section blank is unacceptable because without quantitative knowledge there will be no way of knowing what the project is worth and whether it is the right project on which to be working.

The project team should be small and not have more than four to six members (Charter Element 5). It is important that the team members be identified by name in the charter to ensure that each is available to work on the project. The team can include specialists and technical experts as needed. All core team members should be available for at least 25% of their time. A common pitfall is having team members that are overloaded and not available to work on the project.

Another key item is the project schedule (Charter Element 8). As noted earlier the project should be scheduled for completion in less than 4-6 months. Some will try to resist such an aggressive schedule. Projects scheduled for competition in more than six months is another way a project can fail. The scope of projects taking longer than six months should be reduced, or serious consideration should be given to dividing the work into more than one project.

Once the project charter has been developed you are in a position to select the Black Belt and Champion who will be responsible for doing the project. The critical step of selecting the right people for your Six Sigma initiative is addressed in the next section.

Selecting the Right People

Finding the right people for the key Six Sigma roles is another ingredient for success in the launch phase, and is part of the implementation process. Leadership is the key characteristic to keep in mind when selecting the people who are to be involved in Six Sigma.

Achieving the desired results will require changing the way you work, and that means changing how you think about your work. Leaders are required in order to move everyone successfully from the old way of working to making Six Sigma an integral part of your new way of working. Everyone involved in Six Sigma is a leader (Champions, MBBs, Black Belts, Green Belts). To be successful select your top talent—your best performers—those persons that are capable of providing the needed leadership. Deploying Six Sigma is not an easy task; breakthrough improvement is the goal. For the longer-term you will want Six Sigma to be the driver of your improvement process. You want your senior managers to be skilled in using Six Sigma to help run your business. It is a serious mistake to place only technical specialists (engineers, statisticians, quality professionals, and so on) in key Six Sigma roles. Such major culture change requires persons experienced and skilled in leadership.

The need for leadership is evident in the roles of corporate and unit leadership, Project Champion, Black Belt, and MBB, summarized in Table 4-2.

TABLE 4-2   Six Sigma Roles

Corporate Leadership	Unit Leadership	Project Champions	Black Belts	Master Black Belts	Functional Support Groups
Create and deploy strategy and goals	Establish project selection criteria	Facilitate project selection	Learn and use the Six Sigma methodology and tools	Develop and deliver Six Sigma training	Provide data and aid in data collection
Define boundaries—what's in and what's out	Approve projects—ensure linkage to strategy and key needs	Create project charter	Develop and maintain project work plan	Assist in the selection of projects	Provide team members
Communicate purpose and progress	Select Project Champions	Facilitate identification of resources—BB, team, $$, functional resources	Provide leadership for the team	Coach and council Black Belts	Support with expertise in the department such as financial value of projects
Provide resources—people, time, and $$	Provide needed resources and training	Remove barriers	Meet weekly with the Project Champion	Ensure the success of "mission critical" projects	Identify opportunities for Six Sigma projects
Ensure training plan is in place	Review Black Belt and Green Belt projects monthly	Review projects weekly	Communicate support needs to functional groups	Support the efforts of Champions and leadership team	Help with benchmarking
Ensure recognition plan is in place	Establish and use communication process	Verify project deliverables for each phase of DMAIC	Ensure that the right data are collected and properly analyzed		Set boundaries (legal, company policy, environmental)
Quarterly review of overall initiative	Review the entire process every 3-6 months	Communicate purpose and progress of projects	Identify and communicate barriers to Champion		Provide reality check, diversity of ideas, perspective
Periodic reviews of plant and business initiatives	Establish reward and recognition structure	Approve project closure	Provide monthly updates to Champion and Master Black Belt		

(continued on next page)

TABLE 4-2   Six Sigma Roles *(continued)*

Corporate Leadership	Unit Leadership	Project Champions	Black Belts	Master Black Belts	Functional Support Groups
Support initiative with rewards and recognition	Link rewards to performance	Identify next project for the BB/GB	Be responsible for delivering results ($$)		
Publicly celebrate successes	Be accountable for the success of the effort	Celebrate, recognize, and reward BB and team			
		Be accountable for project results			

The role of the leadership team depends on the size of the company. In large companies there should be a leadership team at the corporate level as well as a leadership team for each of the business units and functions. The key elements of the corporate leadership role are:

- Providing strategy and direction

- Communicating purpose and progress

- Enabling and providing resources

- Conducting reviews

- Recognizing and reinforcing

Leadership Team

The role of the unit leadership team is also summarized in Table 4-2. We define the unit as the entity responsible for identifying the improvement opportunities and chartering the Six Sigma projects. This could be a division, a facility, or a function. The unit leadership team (often called the Six Sigma Council) leads the overall effort within the unit. In the case of a manufacturing facility, the leadership team is typically the Plant Manager and selected members of his or her staff. In the case of the finance function the leadership team might be the CFO and selected members of his or her staff. A key difference between the roles of the two leadership teams is that the unit-level team has responsibility for the projects.

Champion

Each project has a Champion who serves as its business and political leader. Some organizations have used the term Champion to refer to the overall leader of the Six Sigma effort. The Project Champion is typically a member of the unit leadership team, has responsibility for the successful completion of projects, and is held accountable for the results of the projects. Key tasks for the Champion role are: facilitating the selection of the project; drafting the initial project charter; selecting the Black Belt and other resources; removing barriers to the successful completion of the project; and holding short weekly reviews with the Black Belt regarding the progress of the project.

The Champion has direct contact with and provides guidance and direction for the Black Belt. In some cases the Black Belt may be a direct re-

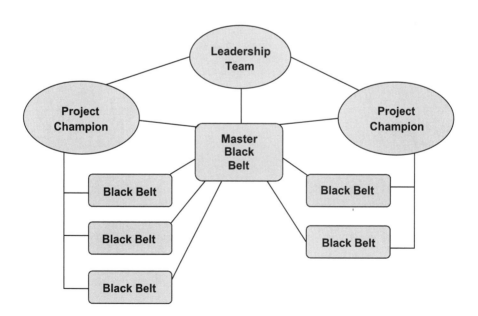

FIGURE 4-2   Organization of Multiple Project Champions and Black Belts

port of the Project Champion. In other situations the Black Belt may also report to a MBB. As shown in Figure 4-2, a unit typically has more than one Project Champion, with each directing one to three Black Belts. The Project Champion role is usually part time but can be a full-time responsibility in some organizations. In most cases the part-time role works best because it involves more managers in the Six Sigma improvement process.

Black Belt

The Black Belt leads the team that works on the project. A Black Belt should be—

- A technical leader in the area of the project
    - Helpful for the first project
    - Less important for subsequent projects
- Respected by the organization
- Computer literate
- An analytical thinker—not afraid of numbers
- Skilled in basic statistics
- A team leader—soft skills
- Skilled in project management
- A positive thinker—can-do attitude

These characteristics are clearly those of a leader and the people who possess them are the kinds you will want to lead your organizations in the future. In his latest book, *Jack, Straight from the Gut* (Welch [2001]), Jack Welch predicts that the person to follow Jeffrey Immelt as CEO of GE will be a former Black Belt.

Black Belts get things done. They are hands-on workers, work full time on their projects, and do much of the detailed work. They should be selected on the basis of what they can do, not on the basis of what they know (Hoerl [2001]). Black Belts also act as mentors for Green Belts, as do MBBs.

Green Belt

Green Belts may lead their own project under the direction of a Champion or MBB, or they may work on a portion of a Black Belt project under the direction of the Black Belt. Green Belts work part-time, devoting typically 25 percent of their time to the project. Green Belt projects are typically less strategic and more locally focused than are Black Belt projects. A Green Belt project is typically worth $50,000 to $75,000 per year to the bottom line and should be completed in less than four to six months. Since Green Belts work on improvement projects in addition to their existing job responsibilities, several companies (such as GE) have as an objective that eventually all professionals will be at least Green Belts. Some Green Belts will become Black Belts, so it is advisable for some of the Green Belts to have many of the Black Belt characteristics.

Master Black Belt

The MBB is the technical leader who enables the organization to integrate Six Sigma within its operations. The MBB should have strong leadership and technical skills and be politically savvy with a good understanding of the business, since he or she will work closely with Champions and the leadership team.

The MBB has typically completed several Black Belt projects and two to five weeks of training beyond the four weeks of Black Belt training. He or she helps the Champions select projects and reviews their progress. The MBB provides training and mentoring for Black Belts, and in some instances training for Green Belts. Like the Black Belts, the MBBs should be full-time.

MBBs play other roles as well. They should help lead mission-critical projects as needed. This work not only contributes to the success of the organization, but also enables the MBB to further develop process improvement skills. MBBs should also be responsible for ensuring that baseline and entitlement data are available and up-to-date for all key processes—important to effective project selection. MBBs are in an excellent position to identify and distribute best practices for process improvement and management and to distribute them around the organization. Many organizations develop a MBB network that meets periodically to share these best practices around the company.

In essence, MBBs are intended to combine technical skills beyond those of the Black Belt with managerial and leadership skills similar to those of a Champion. Most companies hire Six Sigma providers to deliver the initial Six Sigma training. It is the role of the MBB to gradually take over the responsibility for this training. Experience has shown that Six Sigma is internalized most quickly in those companies that develop their cadre of MBBs most rapidly.

Functional Support Groups

The functional support groups, such as HR, Finance, IT, Legal, Engineering, Quality Assurance, and so on assist the Six Sigma effort in four key ways. They:

- Provide data as needed by the Black Belt
- Provide expertise
- Provide members for the Black Belt project team
- Help identify improvement opportunities

The functional groups are typically involved in more aspects of the organization's work than are other groups and, as a result, they see where improvements are needed in cross-functional processes. For example, the finance organization interacts with Procurement, Manufacturing, Marketing, Logistics, Sales, and R&D, and therefore can more easily pinpoint cross-functional issues that need to be addressed.

Many companies overlook the role of the functional support groups and as a result slow the progress of the Six Sigma initiative. Sometimes Black Belts can't get the expertise and team members when they need them; worse yet, poor planning results in no resources to implement improvements. Careful planning and attention to the availability of functional resources as early as possible are time and effort well spent

Forming Teams

A key question is "How do I form the team that will work with the Black Belt or Green Belt?" The short answer is appoint no more than six people who are familiar with the process and will be involved with implementing the Six Sigma solution.

The team should not have more than 4-6 persons. Larger teams are generally ineffective because they have trouble finding a meeting time when all can attend. Large teams also often have trouble reaching consensus, and responsibility may be diluted. If it seems that the task is too great to be done by four to six people, the project is probably too large, and should be split into two or more smaller projects. These smaller projects can still be coordinated at periodic coordination meetings between the Project Champions.

The team needs to include people who are familiar with the process, can contribute to identifying the solution, and will be involved in its implementation. Experts and consultants, even internal or external customers and suppliers, can also be ad hoc members of the team, participating when needed. The core members of the team should be available 25% of the time to work on the project. The team receives any needed training delivered just in time by the Black Belt or MBB as appropriate.

The best approach to forming the team is for the Black Belt to create it in consultation with the Project Champion and the managers to whom the prospective team members report. The process might look like the following:

1. Black Belt and Champion discuss potential team members.
2. Black Belt or Champion gets the approval of the team members' management for them to be on the team.
3. Champion addresses any barriers identified, getting higher management involved as needed.
4. Black Belt and the team work on the project.

As in any partnership, the Black Belt and Champion work out who will do what in the team-forming process. A MBB may become involved if needed. It is important that both the Black Belt and Champion build support for the project with all the involved stakeholders. People are more likely to support a project when the purpose and value is understood, their role in the project is clear, and they see how they will benefit from the successful completion of the project. The Project Champion has the responsibility to see that any problems or barriers identified are resolved.

Where Do I Find the Resources?

This is the question most commonly asked when managers first hear about Six Sigma and every Six Sigma leader should have a ready answer. Help can come from reevaluating employees' responsibilities and from hiring from outside.

Some companies, to increase their capabilities and to move up the learning curve more quickly, may hire a MBB or a Vice President of Six Sigma to lead the implementation effort. Some will hire experienced Black Belts from other companies to lead projects, or new employees to backfill for Black Belts and MBBs.

Far and away the most popular resource strategy for companies deploying Six Sigma is to reevaluate existing work programs, and to reprioritize how they utilize their resources. As a result, Six Sigma is deployed using existing resources. This strategy is used most often, but is not initially the favorite of managers who must rethink priorities and deal with personnel changes. Fortunately, this stress decreases as managers learn to deploy Six Sigma and see it improve the performance of their organization.

Over time managers find many different ways to backfill for the employees that have become Black Belts or MBBs. Some projects will already be in the Black Belt's assigned area of responsibility, so even without Six Sigma they would likely have worked on this problem. If necessary, the Black Belt's previous responsibilities can be assigned to other employees and contractors; some work can be postponed; some work is non-value-added and can be eliminated. Resource sharing, while hard for some to do, is an effective way to create resources.

In short, look for two things—underutilized capacity and unrecognized capability. Some employees are not working to their full potential. Some employees can handle bigger workloads. Some are doing tactical work that could be better done by others, freeing these employees to do more strategic work, including Six Sigma. Many times engineers are seen creating budgets, writing talks for others, or doing paperwork rather than improving processes. We met one overworked and highly stressed vice president of sales who was reviewing *every* sales contract obtained by the company. Clearly a lot of time could be freed by delegating the review of smaller contracts to subordinates.

What Training Do I Need?

Six Sigma requires people to think and work in different ways. This requires that they be trained in the new way of thinking and working. There is a lot of training to be done as spelled out in the implementation plan. The key groups to be trained are executives, business teams, site leadership teams, functional leadership teams, Champions, MBBs, Black Belts, and Green Belts.

The Executive, Business Team, Site Leadership Team, and Functional Leadership Team workshops are typically one or two days and focus on what Six Sigma is, how it will be deployed, and roles of the groups involved. These are active workshops in which work is done on the deployment and implementation plans; not passive overviews. A draft deployment plan with carefully selected areas for initial projects is a key output of these workshops (Figure 4-3).

The Champion workshop is typically three to five days. Its focus is on developing a deeper understanding of Six Sigma, deployment in the organization, and roles of the Project Champion and the Black Belt. Project Champions are trained to guide the work of the Black Belts. The Champion also spends time learning the DMAIC process and understanding the Six Sigma tools the Black Belt will be using.

Black Belt training typically lasts four weeks, with each week focused on a phase of the DMAIC process. The usual sequence is Week 1 (define and measure), Week 2 (analyze), Week 3 (improve), and Week 4 (control). The recommended outlines for finance and manufacturing-oriented courses proposed by Hoerl (2001) are shown in the following two lists. Note that these outlines include both Design for Six Sigma (DFSS) methodology and tools. Some companies teach DFSS separately, while others prefer to integrate it with DMAIC training. Both approaches work.

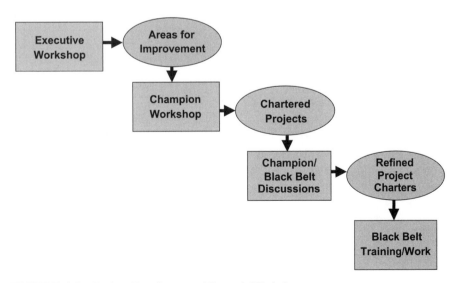

FIGURE 4-3   Project Development Through Workshops

Sample Black Belt Course for Finance

(This course is in three weeks, with Week 3 being a Black Belt addition to an existing Green Belt course)

Week 1

- The DMAIC and DFSS (Design for Six Sigma) improvement strategies
- Project selection and scoping (Define)
- QFD
- Sampling principles (quality and quantity)
- Measurement system analysis (also called "gage R&R")
- Process capability
- Basic graphs
- Hypothesis testing
- Regression

Week 2

- DOE (focus on 2-level factorials)
- Design for Six Sigma tools
- Requirements flowdown
- Capability flowup (prediction)
- Piloting
- Simulation
- FMEA
- Developing control plans
- Control charts

Week 3

- Power (impact of sample size)
- Impact of process instability on capability analysis
- Confidence Intervals (vs. hypothesis tests)
- Implications of the Central Limit Theorem
- Transformations
- How to detect "Lying With Statistics"
- General Linear Models
- Fractional Factorial DOEs

Sample Black Belt Course for Manufacturing

(The superscripts refer to the week in which the material would appear)

Context[1]

- Why Six Sigma
- DMAIC & DFSS processes (sequential case studies)
- Project management fundamentals
- Team effectiveness fundamentals

Define[1]

- Project selection
- Scoping projects
- Developing a project plan
- Multi-generational projects
- Process identification (SIPOC)

Measure[1]

- QFD
  - Identifying customer needs
  - Developing measurable critical-to-quality metrics (CTQ's)
- Sampling (data quantity and data quality)
- Measurement System Analysis (not just gauge R&R)
- SPC Part I
  - The concept of statistical control (process stability)
  - The implications of instability on capability measures
- Capability analysis

Analyze[2]

- Basic graphical improvement tools ("Magnificent 7")
- Management and planning tools (affinity, ID, etc.)
- Confidence intervals (emphasized)
- Hypothesis testing (de-emphasized)
- ANOVA (de-emphasized)
- Regression
- Multi-Vari Studies
- Developing conceptual designs in DFSS

Improve[3-4]

- DOE (focus on two level factorials, screening designs, and RSM)
- Piloting (of DMAIC improvements)
- FMEA
- Mistake-proofing
- DFSS design tools
  - CTQ flowdown
  - Capability flowup
  - Simulation

Control[4]

- Developing control plans
- SPC Part II
  - Using control charts
- Piloting new designs in DFSS

Green Belt training typically lasts two weeks with Week 1 focused on the define, measure, and analyze phases of DMAIC and the second week focused on the analyze and control phases. A recommended outline of topics for manufacturing Green Belt training is shown here—

Context[1]

- Why Six Sigma
- DMAIC (sequantial case studies)
- Project management fundamentals
- Team effectiveness fundamentals

Define[1]

- Project selection
- Scoping projects
- Developing a project plan
- Process identification (SIPOC)

Measure[1]
- QFD
  - Identifying customer needs
  - Developing measureable critical-to-quality (CTQs)
- Sampling (data quantity and data quality)
- Measurement System Analysis (not just gage R&R)
- SPC Part I
  - The concept of statistical control (process stability)
  - The implications of instability on capability measures
- Capability analysis

Analyze[1, 2]
- FMEA
- Basic graphical improvement tools ("Magnificent 7")
- Confidence intervals (emphasized)
- Hypothesis testing (de-emphasized)
- ANOVA (de-emphasized)
- Regression
- Multi-Vari Studies

Improve[2]
- DOE (focus on two level factorials)
- Piloting (of DMAIC improvements)
- Mistake-proofing

Control[2]
- Developing control plans
- SPC Part II
  - Using control charts

Black Belt and Green Belt training topics and areas of emphasis must be based on the specific needs and targeted applications of the organization. The sample curricula presented here form a base of reference or starting point, not the final answer for all organizations. Alternative curricula, as well as guidelines for conducting effective training, can be found in Hoerl (2001) and its associated discussion.

Key to the success of Black Belt and Green Belt training is the practice of working on real projects during the training. It is our firm belief that a real, significant project should be the admission ticket for the training: "No Project, No Training." As noted earlier, if the projects are completed, the resulting benefits should more than pay for the training.

Organizing and conducting Six Sigma training needs careful planning, coordination, and execution. It is so important for the training leaders to have experience in the deployment of similar efforts that most companies hire outside Six Sigma consultants to provide this service initially. Experienced providers have the knowledge, experience, capability, and capacity to do what is needed to create a successful deployment. Once the initiative has been successfully launched, and internal MBBs obtain sufficient experience, they should begin to assume leadership of this effort.

Selecting a Six Sigma Provider

Now that you have learned what is required to properly launch Six Sigma, you are in a position to decide whether to hire a Six Sigma provider (consulting firm) to help with the training and initial deployment of Six Sigma. Almost all companies get external help of some kind, which makes good business sense. Hiring a Six Sigma provider enables a company to learn from those who have gone before and move up the learning curve more quickly. The consultant costs should be much more than covered by the returns of the higher number of projects that can be completed using the expertise of a seasoned consultant. Black Belt projects can also produce bottom line results before the training is completed, as quick fixes are often found in the measure and analyze phases of the DMAIC process. It is not unusual for 30-50% of the projects to produce bottom line savings before the training is complete, and for these benefits to more than cover the training costs.

This point is so important it is worth repeating: employing an outside Six Sigma provider is cost effective and can help an organization move up the learning curve more quickly.

Using an outside provider is also a high-yield strategy because executives and managers will listen to those from the outside more readily than to the company's employees. It is difficult to be a prophet in your own land, even when the knowledge to do the work exists within the organization. Specific advice on how to choose a Six Sigma provider is presented with the questions and answers after Chapter 8.

Summary

The launch phase of Six Sigma is roughly the period between making the decision to deploy Six Sigma, and completing the initial wave of Black Belt training. This typically lasts 6-9 months. The purpose of this phase is to ensure that you "hit the ground running" in Six Sigma deployment. The key deliverables are:

- An overall deployment plan (strategy)
- The initial wave of projects
- Trained Black Belts, and other key roles, in place

As noted in Chapter 3, committed leadership is the key success factor in this phase. It will take committed leadership to make time to actively participate in leadership workshops, persevere through completion of the deployment and implementation plans, allocate the human resources and funding required for the effort, and address any resistance from within the organization. Leaders will need to provide clear vision and direction. Other important success factors are:

- Selection of good initial projects
- Selection of people for key roles
- Full-time allocation of Black Belts and MBBs
- Effective, tailored training for key roles
- Support from functional groups as needed

References

Conway, W. E. (1992). *The Quality Secret: The Right Way to Manage.* Conway Quality, Inc. Nashua, NH.

Conway, W. E. (1994). *Winning the War on Waste.* Conway Quality, Inc. Nashua, NH.

Gates, William H., III (1999). *Business @ The Speed of Thought.* Warner Books, New York, NY.

Harry, Mikel, and Richard Schroeder. (2000). *Six Sigma: The Breakthrough Management Strategy Revolutionizing The World's Top Corporations.* Currency Doubleday, New York, NY.

Hoerl, R. W. (2001). "Six Sigma Black Belts: What Do They Need to Know?" (with discussion), *J. Quality Technology,* Vol. 33, No. 4, 391-435.

Juran, J. M. (1989). *Leadership for Quality—An Executive Handbook.* Free Press, New York, NY, page 35.

Snee, R.D. "Dealing with the Achilles' Heel of Six Sigma Initiatives—Project Selection is Key to Success," *Quality Progress,* March 2001, 66-72.

Snee, R.D. and A. N. Parikh. "Implementing Six Sigma in Small and Medium Sized Companies," presented at the ASQ Six Sigma Conference 2001, San Diego, CA.

Snee, R.D. and W.F. Rodebaugh (2002). "Project Selection Process," *Quality Progress,* September 2002, 78–90.

Welch, J. (2001). *Jack, Straight from the Gut.* Warner Business Books, New York, NY.

5

MANAGING THE EFFORT

"Six Sigma works if you follow the process. If Six Sigma
is not working you're not following the process."

—AlliedSignal Manager

Your Six Sigma initiative is now under way. The Executive and
Champion workshops have been held. A deployment plan has been drafted, and an implementation plan is in place. The initial projects and Black
Belts have been selected, and the first wave of training has been held. It is
likely that the initial wave of enthusiasm has carried the Six Sigma effort
this far. You are now reaching a critical transition point.

Once the first set of projects has been completed, and the initiative begins to expand rapidly, you will need to make the transition from a short-term
launch to a well-managed long-term effort. The effort will simply become too
large to manage informally. You will need formal infrastructure to properly
manage Six Sigma deployment from this point onward. Otherwise, the initiative will become just another short-lived fad. You will also need top talent in
key leadership roles to implement the infrastructure and manage the effort.

We refer to this next step in our deployment process as managing
the effort. This phase goes roughly from the completion of the initial

wave of Black Belt training until we have trained everyone we originally intended to train, and completed projects in all the areas mentioned in the deployment plan. It typically lasts a minimum of 18 months, although organizations must continue to manage Six Sigma deployment in subsequent phases.

It is now time to put in place those systems and processes that will enable you to effectively manage the effort. You will have worked on many of these systems in the Executive and Champion workshops, and they are part of the deployment plan. At this point, you not only create systems to manage Six Sigma but also begin to think about how to make these systems part of your culture—how we do things around here. This will help you sustain the benefits and make Six Sigma the way we work (see Chapter 7).

The list on the next page, adapted from Snee et al (1998), notes the key types of leadership support needed for successful Black Belt projects. Clearly, Black Belts will not be successful on their own, and there is too much here to manage informally. Fortunately, your deployment plan can help you with each of these infrastructure elements. This chapter will focus on the elements of the deployment plan that are most needed at this point. Specifically, we will discuss:

- Management project reviews
- Project reporting and tracking system
- Communications plan
- Reward and recognition plan
- Project identification/prioritization system
- Project closure criteria
- Inclusion of Six Sigma into budgeting processes
- Deployment processes for Champions, Black Belts, MBBs, etc.

Implementation of these systems and processes is the key deliverable for this phase. Each of these infrastructure elements is an aspect of good management. When done well and integrated with your current management system, Six Sigma becomes part of your culture. The goal is to make Six Sigma part of how you do your work and not an add-on; i.e., not something extra that you have to do (see Chapter 7). Before we discuss each of the listed elements and provide examples and guidance for its implementation, we comment on the role of managerial systems and processes to set the stage.

**Leadership Support Needed for Successful
Black Belt Projects**

- Chartered project
  - Identified, approved and supported by management
  - Important to the organization—aligned with priorities
  - High impact—e.g. >$250K annual savings
  - Scope that can be completed in <4-6 months
  - Clear quantitative measure of success
- Time for Black Belt to work on the project
  - Recommend 100% dedicated, absolute minimum of 50-75%
  - Time for Black Belt to do the training & project work
  - Reassignment of current workload
- Directions to form project team: typically 4-6 team members
  - Access to people working on the process and others to be team members
  - Access to other specialists and subject matter experts
  - Guidance to keep the team small to speed up progress
- Training for team members as needed
- Priority use of organizational services such as lab services, access to the manufacturing line, etc.
- Regular reviews of project by management
  - Weekly by Champion
  - Monthly by leadership team
- Help with data systems to collect needed process data on a priority basis
  - Create temporary and manual systems as needed
- Communications—Inform all persons affected by project of:
  - Project purpose and value
  - Need to support work of Black Belts
- Assistance from Finance in estimating and documenting the bottom line savings ($)
- Recognize, reward and celebrate the success of the Black Belt and team appropriately

Managerial Systems and Processes

Since most of this chapter discusses implementation of managerial systems and processes, and since these terms are often used loosely in business circles, clarification is in order. All work is done through a series of processes. By process we simply mean a sequence of activities that transform inputs (raw materials, information, etc.) into outputs (a finished product, an invoice, etc.). There will always be a process, even if it cannot be seen, and even if it is not standardized. In manufacturing it is easy to see the process—just follow the pipes! Seeing the process is much more difficult in soft areas such as Finance or Legal. Understanding processes is critically important to making any improvement, however, since it is through improvement of the process that we improve outputs. As noted in Chapter 1, process thinking is a fundamental aspect of Six Sigma.

By managerial processes, we mean those that help us manage the organization, as opposed to making, distributing, or selling something. These typically include budgeting, reward and recognition, business planning, and reporting processes. Design and management of these processes generally define the core responsibilities of middle managers. Ideally, these processes help align all employees with strategic direction, such as by communicating or rewarding Six Sigma successes. Poor managerial processes usually produce a dysfunctional organization, while effective managerial processes usually produce an effective and efficient organization.

Figure 5-1 shows a diagram (IBM-Europe [1990]) that illustrates what IBM considers to be its core business processes. The diagram separates the core processes into three major categories: product development and production processes; general business processes, such as sales and marketing; and enterprise processes, the support processes that the customer does not usually see, but that are required to keep the company running. Most of the managerial processes we discuss in this chapter would fall into the category of enterprise processes, although the two other categories also have managerial processes.

Often you will need to integrate several processes together to form a system. By system we mean the collection of all relevant processes needed to complete some specific work. For example, your body has a cardio-vascular system that performs the work of circulating blood. The beating of your heart is one process that is part of the cardio-vascular system, but it could not circulate blood effectively without the action of other muscles, or the use of veins and arteries. All muscles, veins and arteries, and other parts of the cardio-vascular system must work in harmony for our blood to properly circulate. To return to the business world, most organizations

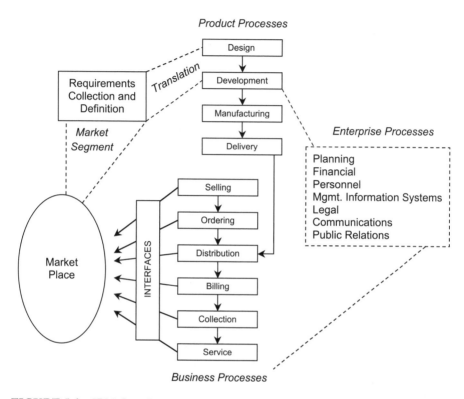

FIGURE 5-1   IBM Core Processes

have an overall reward and recognition system. Annual performance appraisal is typically one process in this system, but there are other processes as well that form an overall system.

An understanding of systems is important because you need to make sure that all processes are properly integrated for overall system optimization. It is common in the business word for people to optimize one process at the expense of others, resulting in poor overall system performance. For example, in a company's sales system four regional managers may compete with each other to land a national account, the net result being a less profitable contract for the company. Each regional manager attempted to optimize his or her regional sales process, but did so to the detriment of the overall corporate sales system. This is called sub-optimization, and has been one of the central themes of management author Peter Senge's work (Senge 1990).

Improving systems can have a profound impact on entire organizations, and will institutionalize change, since systems and their processes define how you do your work. It goes without saying that top talent in leadership roles is required to properly design, implement, and manage these systems.

In the discussion of managerial systems and processes organizations need to change or implement to properly manage Six Sigma deployment, there will undoubtedly be instances where we use the word "system" when the reader feels "process" may be more accurate, and vice versa. This distinction is often gray, rather than black and white. The key point is that we need formal infrastructure, be it a process, a system, or some other mechanism, to effectively manage the effort. The specific term we use is not critical.

The key infrastructure elements are discussed in roughly the order in which they are typically considered in deployment.

Management Project Reviews

Management review is a critical success factor for Six Sigma. Regular management review keeps the effort focused and on track. We know of no successful Six Sigma implementation in which management reviews were not a key part of the deployment process. We focus here on management project reviews, and address management reviews of the overall implementation in Chapter 6. Project reviews should be done weekly and monthly, while reviews of the overall initiative are preferably done quarterly, or at a minimum, annually. We begin with management project reviews, since you should already be reviewing status of the initial wave of projects by this time.

Six Sigma projects are most successful when Champions review them weekly, and the business unit and function leaders review them monthly. Such a drumbeat prevents projects from dragging on, and provides leadership with early warning of any problems. A useful agenda for the Champion review is:

- Activity this week
- Accomplishments this week
- Recommended management actions
- Help needed
- Plan for next week

This review is informal and is not time-consuming—taking approximately 30 minutes. The idea is to have a quick check to keep the project on track by finding out what has been accomplished, what is planned, and what barriers need to be addressed. Typically Champions guide only one or two Black Belts, so the time requirements are not great. These reviews help the Champion fulfill his/her role of guiding the project

and addressing barriers. Master Black Belts (MBBs) also attend these reviews as needed, and the MBB and Black Belt also meet separately to resolve any technical issues that might have arisen.

All current projects are typically reviewed each month as well. This
monthly review with the business unit or function leader is shorter than the
weekly review, being no more than 10-15 minutes per project. The purpose
is to keep the project on schedule with respect to time and results, and to
identify any problems or roadblocks. This review helps the business unit
and functional leaders stay involved in Six Sigma, and directly inform them
of any issues they need to address. A useful agenda for these reviews is:

- Project purpose
- Process and financial metrics—progress versus goals
- Accomplishments since the last review
- Plans for future work
- Key lessons learned and findings

Notice that this agenda is similar to that for the weekly review with
the Champion. In the monthly review much more emphasis is placed on performance versus schedule, progress towards process and financial goals, and
key lessons learned and findings. As Six Sigma grows, the number of projects
may become large, requiring a lot of time for the reviews. The review time
can be reduced by rating projects as Green (on schedule), Yellow (in danger
of falling behind schedule if something isn't done) and Red (behind schedule
and in need of help), and reviewing only those rated as Red and Yellow.

One way to increase the speed, clarity, and understanding of the review process is to use a common reporting format, such as the one shown
in Figure 5-2. This format is similar to templates used by GE, AlliedSignal,
DuPont, and other companies. An overall project summary is shown on
one page using the four headings of project description, metrics, accomplishments, and needs. Additional backup slides to support the material in
the summary can be added as needed. A good way to show progress toward entitlement is to use the graph shown in Figure 5-3 (Rodebaugh
[2001]). There will be a separate graph for each process measure impacted
by the project.

We all need feedback. Feedback is required to know how your're
doing and to improve. Former New York City Mayor Ed Koch used to ask
at every opportunity "How am I doing?" The Beatles also needed feedback. The rock group's last outdoor concert was held in Candlestick Park
(San Francisco) in 1966. The crowd noise was extremely loud so they knew
their music was appreciated, but because of the noise they couldn't hear

Project Description

- Reduce Days Sales Outstanding (DSO) for Concrete Products U.S. from 55 to 45 days
- Team Members:
  - –SAP Business Analyst
  - –District Sales Manager
  - –Project Champion
  - –Senior Credit Specialists
  - –Mgr. of Treasury Services
  - –Customer Service & Logistics Mgr.
- Projected Savings: $500,000   Projected Completion 4-15-00

Accomplishments Since Last Review

- Requested Credit Dept. to verify customer address, identify customers with different bill to and payer address, and note date of invoice requested.
- Southeast region is the pilot for Point of Delivery project. This can reduce billing cycle from 5 days to 1.
- Developed a report that measures days to bill
- Developed process and procedures for calling late paying customers 35 days after delivery

Metrics

	BSL	Goal	ENT
DSO	55	45	35
Days to Bill	5	1	1

- Reasons for late payments
- Reasons for credits
- Reasons for billing errors

Issues/Needs

- Identify why some customers do not have an invoice (2-1-00)
- Call late paying customers on day 35 (2-1-00)
- Implement credit checks for bulk shipments (88% of business) prior to shipment
- Implement credit hold & credit block procedures
- Reduce billing cycle time (3-1-00)
- Reduce billing errors- pricing & sales tax (2-15-00)

Key Takeaway
Call customer early to modify their accounts payable policy and resolve any problems

FIGURE 5-2   Example Project Status Reporting Form

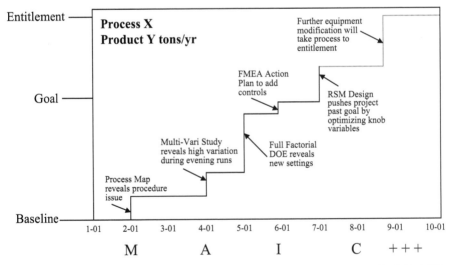

Adapted from Rodebaugh (2001)

FIGURE 5-3   Progress Toward Process Entitlement for Sample Project

themselves sing; they had no direct feedback of their voices. Without this feedback the Beatles couldn't monitor their own performance, and improve it where necessary. This led them to discontinue outdoor concerts.

Feedback provided during reviews is an important aid to improvement. Black Belts want and need feedback, and management reviews are one important form of providing it.

In all project reviews it is important to ask questions to identify the *methods, logic,* and *data* used to support decisions. It is also important to pay attention to both *social* and *technical* issues. Sometimes the social concerns such as interpersonal relationships and leadership skills are more important than the technical issues.

It is important to do a lot of listening. Open-ended questions, rather than those that can be answered yes or no, generally lead to more informative answers. Two helpful questions are: "Could you explain that in more detail?" and "Could you help me understand how you arrived at that conclusion?"

When you want to learn how the project—or any activity for that matter—is progressing, ask two questions; "What's working?" or "What are we doing well?" and "What do we need to do better?" The answers will take you a long way toward understanding what is going on in the project or activity. A more detailed list of good questions to ask is given in Chapter 8.

The Black Belts, the Champions, or a combination of Black Belts and Champions can present the project reports at the monthly reviews. Having the Champions give the reports involves them more deeply in the Six Sigma initiative, as well as increasing understanding and ownership. When appropriate, Champions can report on several projects, reducing the amount of time required for the reviews. Project reviews are critical to success. Infrequent review of projects is a good predictor of a Six Sigma initiative in trouble, as we saw in the case studies of Royal Chemicals and Diversified Paper in Chapter 2.

We noted in Chapter 4 that 30-50% of the projects would produce improvements that have bottom-line results even before the project is completed. Champions and other leaders should be on the lookout for such situations and make sure that the project, the Black Belt, and the Six Sigma initiative get credit for the results as soon as possible. The weekly and monthly reviews are a good place to identify these opportunities and will speed up the impact of the Six Sigma initiative.

Project Reporting and Tracking System

As noted, it is important to have a regular drumbeat of reporting on the progress and results of projects. Developing a formal reporting and tracking system should therefore be an early priority during this phase of Six Sigma deployment. The reporting system will provide electronic or paper documents to back up and facilitate the project reviews. The reporting structure for Six Sigma projects depends on the needs of the organization. A target frequency is:

- Weekly highlights from the Black Belt to the Champion. A summary of the weekly review is usually sufficient for this purpose.

- Monthly reports for the business or function leader, typically using information provided by the Champions.

- Quarterly reports for corporate leadership, typically using information provided by the business and function leaders.

The purpose of the reporting system is to keep the various levels of management informed of progress and results of the initiative. These reports also become the raw material for internal and external communications (see communications plan section).

The reports should, of course, be designed to meet the needs of the organization. A good way to report on a project is to create a short summary of the project, analogous to the review template. Such a summary typically contains three parts: problem/issue description, work done, and results/impact/implications. Depending on the required length, it is usually appropriate to include a two or three sentence description for each of the three areas, plus relevant metrics and graphs. It is critical that your summary include the results obtained in terms of improvement of process performance and bottom line results. Six Sigma is about getting results.

Typically, the Black Belt enters the project-level information into a computer system that is able to roll up the results across projects, functions, and business units, and drill down to greater detail on individual projects. Using workflow software, users can track status of a project portfolio at a high level, and also find links to additional, more detailed information, such as PowerPoint™ presentations or statistical analyses.

A key element of this reporting system is the financial tracking system. Leadership needs to know how the total bottom line savings is progressing. By tracking the projects, leadership not only knows how the Six

Sigma initiative is performing, but also communicates the importance of the initiative to the organization. Recall the old saying: "What we measure and pay attention to gets done."

Project tracking is typically led by Finance because of the need to validate the financial data. Some key measures (English [2001]) typically tracked are:

- Hard and soft dollar savings

- Number of projects completed

- Savings per project

- Projects per Black Belt and Green Belt

- Time to project completion

- Number of Black Belts and Green Belts

Leaders will want reports of these measures for the whole organization, as well as the ability to drill down by business unit, function, plant or site, region of the world, country, and so on. It is easy keeping track of a few projects; an Excel™ spreadsheet will usually do the trick. As the projects grow in number and as Six Sigma moves throughout the organization, a more sophisticated system will be needed. This system may be a database such as Lotus Notes™, Microsoft Access™, or Oracle™, or software specifically designed for tracking Six Sigma projects. We are also aware of instances in which an existing project tracking system (e.g., for R&D projects) has been enhanced to track Six Sigma projects, thereby integrating Six Sigma with existing management systems.

A question people commonly ask when tracking projects is "How do I calculate the financial impact of a project?" While the answer is dependent on the financial rules of each organization, we can provide some general guidance.

Financial impact is typically divided into hard and soft dollars (Snee and Rodenbaugh [2002]). Hard dollars are those dollars that clearly flow to the bottom line and will show up on the balance sheet. Examples include dollars from cost reductions, increased capacity that is immediately sold (because the product is in a sold out condition), and decreased holding costs from increased inventory turns. As a general rule, companies only report the hard dollars as Six Sigma savings because these are the funds that indisputably affect the profitability of the organization. For example, W. R. Grace reported a $26 million bottom-line impact in 2000, and an additional $7 million in cost avoidance (soft dollars).

Soft dollars are improvements in operations that do not affect the bottom line directly, but typically do so indirectly. Some examples are improving meeting efficiency so that less time is wasted in meetings, preventing problems that typically occur in new product introduction, and simplifying accounting processes so fewer resources are needed to close the books.

In each case, we could calculate a theoretical savings (in soft dollars) due to reduction of either the effort required or typical waste and rework levels. However, we cannot clearly demonstrate how these soft savings will show up on the balance sheet.

To clarify the difference between hard and soft dollars, consider a process that is improved, requiring three fewer people to operate it. If these three people are reassigned to other work we have a cost avoidance (soft dollars). They are now freed to do more value-adding work to the benefit of the organization elsewhere. However, they are still employed and are still a cost to the organization, so we cannot claim hard dollar savings. If, on the other hand, three positions are removed from the employee rolls after reassignment, we have a cost reduction (hard dollars), because we will clearly see this savings on our payroll expenses.

It is not unusual for a project to have both hard and soft dollar savings. It is also not unusual for the financial impact of a project to come from several different places. Black Belts and the financial organization should search for all possible sources of project impacts, and capture the true savings to make sure that no tangible savings are missed. Typically, the finance organization makes the final decisions about what qualifies as hard savings.

Communication Plan

We noted in Chapter 4 that clear communication of the vision and strategy for Six Sigma was a critical responsibility of leadership. Communication will have a huge impact on the organization's perception of Six Sigma, and subsequently on everyone's receptiveness to it. We also noted that many organizations wait until they have achieved some tangible success before making major pronouncements about the initiative, hence we did not address the communications plan until this chapter. The information provided here is relevant whenever leadership wishes to begin formal communications about the effort.

The project reporting for management described in the previous section is one form of communication. In this section we discuss communications more generally. Answering the six questions Who? What? When? Where? Why? and How? will take us a long way toward designing an effective communications plan for Six Sigma. The answers to these questions are:

Question	**Answer**
Who?	Different target audiences
What?	Six Sigma need, vision, strategy, and results
When?	Continual, ongoing
Where?	Use a variety of media
Why?	Set the tone, keep the organization informed
How?	Clear, concise, continual using a variety of media

An informed organization will make a more rapid, effective implementation of Six Sigma. Many studies of change initiatives have demonstrated that people are more likely to embrace change when they understand the rationale, vision, and strategy of the change (Weisbord [1989]).

Fundamental to communicating well is recognizing that there is a lot of variation in both the information to be communicated, and the target audiences. For example, the information that we need to communicate to the investment community is likely much different from the information we need to communicate to rank and file employees. The communication plan should take this type of variation into account. Communication is a process just like any other process used to run the business. There are a variety of target audiences, each with different needs, wants, and desires. People are individuals who take in, process, and understand information in different ways. Their differences dictate that we utilize different media to communicate the message, even to the same target audience.

Note that leaders communicate by their actions—what they do, as well as by what they say. Each contact, in person or otherwise, is an opportunity to communicate. Communication is a key responsibility of leaders and they need to communicate their message over and over again, and in different ways, in order for it to be understood and internalized by the organization. People may have to hear something new at least five times before internalizing it. A message delivered only one time will likely go unnoticed.

The design of the communications plan depends on the organization. We summarize some communication principles here—

- We communicate by what we do and by what we say
- Use a variety of communication vehicles: face-to-face, video, newsletters, memos, emails, skits, pocket cards
  - Leaders must be seen and heard as well as read

- Communication is:
  - An on-going process, not an event
  - A two-way process: talk top-down, listen bottom-up
  - A key aspect of leadership and a job responsibility
  - Also horizontal: employee-to-employee
- Each contact is an opportunity to communicate
- Leaders clarify complex issues

And the following are communication methods—

- Systems that share information throughout the organization and include customer views
- Discussion of strategic direction and initiatives
- Periodic reports on progress of projects and initiatives
- Periodic reviews at all levels
- Connecting all initiatives to the strategic plan
- Using the strategic plan to guide work processes
- Behaviors that match the values of the organization
- Horizontal: employee-to-employee
- Visual management and measurement
- Process management
  - Communicates how we serve our customers

The next two lists illustrate specific examples of awareness training from one company (first list), and the outline of an overall communications plan in another company (second list). The first company decided to do a two-hour awareness training to introduce the organization to Six Sigma.

Two-hour awareness training for the organization

- A standard script and visual aids were created for use by all managers
- Agenda—Presentation followed by Question and Answer session
- Feedback and Follow-up
- Barriers and issues identified in Question and Answer session were collected, reviewed by senior management team, and needed actions taken

Overall Communications Plan

- Plan covers the first 6-9 months
- Themes to be communicated
  - Six Sigma tie to business strategy
  - Building of what was done before
  - Goals
  - Role of individuals
- Media to be used
  - Corporate and Plant newspapers, Lotus Notes™, bulletin board postings, staff meetings, corporate television, Six Sigma web site

Topics for First 9 Weeks

- Six Sigma strategy and goals
- Meet the Six Sigma Champions
- How other companies are using Six Sigma
- Customer Feedback Surveys
- Six Sigma improvement process
- How projects are being selected
- How Six Sigma is different
- Executive, Champion, and Black Belt training
- How Six Sigma will affect the organization

Periodic Communications as Needed

- Answers to frequently asked questions
- Comments from the President
- Results of Six Sigma projects
- Success Stories and celebrations
- Six Sigma financial updates

Note that the awareness session followed the principles that communication is a process and that it is two-way: delivering and receiving. An awareness session usually answers the questions:

- What is Six Sigma?

- Why are we pursuing Six Sigma?

- How will we deploy Six Sigma?

The answers are intended to communicate the organization's rationale for deploying Six Sigma, its vision, and its overall strategy. This is a critically important message and should be an integral part of any communication plan. Our experience is that it usually takes 2 hours to 4 hours for a group of any size to develop a useful awareness of Six Sigma.

The last list summarizes the overall communications plan for another company. This plan has a time frame of the first 6-9 months of deployment. Note that the plan does not contain any awareness training. Those participating in the Executive and Champion workshops were told to do awareness training for their organizations using the materials they had received in the workshops. This unique approach illustrates how organizations differ in their deployment of Six Sigma.

Some organizations prepare presentations for the managers to use to communicate Six Sigma. Other companies ask the managers to prepare their own awareness materials. There are pros and cons for both approaches. A common presentation helps ensure a consistent message. However, managers who prepare their own awareness training will develop a deeper understanding of Six Sigma in the process. Since first impressions often last, we recommend using common materials to hit the rationale, vision, and strategy, combined with tailored materials for each organization developed by their own management.

Reward and Recognition Plan

As noted in Chapter 4, we believe that the most effective motivation is intrinsic motivation; i.e., people doing something because they believe in it or want to do it. For example, throughout history mercenary armies have never performed well against armies that believed in what they were fighting for. On the other hand, if there are no tangible rewards for accomplishments in Six Sigma, this omission will essentially be a de-motivator. People may say: "I would love to be involved in Six Sigma, but I'm concerned about what it might do to my career."

We must balance intrinsic motivation with extrinsic motivation. Extrinsic motivation means providing a carrot or stick to motivate someone to do something they would not do otherwise, such as rewarding children for cleaning their rooms. Providing extrinsic motivation will help ensure that there are no barriers to our top talent getting involved in Six Sigma.

We are all motivated to work on those things that will be beneficial to our career. This fact leads us to consider what reward and recognition system we will use to support Six Sigma. In fact, some companies have the reward and recognition plan for Six Sigma designed prior to deployment. Jack Welch comments that at GE: "As with every initiative, we backed Six Sigma up with our rewards system" (Welch [2001]). This included 40% of the annual managerial bonus based on Six Sigma results, stock option grants for Black Belts and MBBs, and Green Belt certification being required for promotion.

Every successful implementation of Six Sigma we are familiar with has developed a special reward and recognition system to support Six Sigma.

Conversely, during previous improvement initiatives (such as TQM) leadership may have stated that they wanted one behavior (e.g., quality improvement), but rewarded something totally different (e.g., making the financial numbers). Such disconnects between leadership's words and actions are immediately obvious to employees, and can lead to cynicism. The reward and recognition system is a statement by leadership about what it values and is a much more important document than a printed values statement. Leaders must think carefully about the message they want to convey.

Like communications, the form of the reward and recognition plan is greatly dependent on the culture and existing plan of the company involved. Some companies choose to use their existing system, as they feel it has the capability to adequately reward the contributions of those involved in Six Sigma. This may be the case in some instances, but in general a special reward and recognition system should be developed. The following list summarizes the Black Belt recognition program for one company we have worked with. This plan recognizes that Black Belts are critical to our success, and special rewards are needed to ensure that top performers are anxious to take this role. Unfortunately, this plan makes no mention of rewarding others involved in Six Sigma work.

- Base Pay
  - Potential increase at time of selection
  - Retain current salary grade
  - Normal group performance review and merit pay

- Incentive Compensation
  - Special plan for Black Belts
  - Target award at 15% of base pay
  - Performance rating on 0 - 150% of scale
  - Measured against key project objectives
  - Participation ends at end of Black Belt assignment

The Six Sigma reward and recognition plan for another company is summarized in the next list. Note the completeness of this plan, including recognition of Green Belts and team members (including MBBs and Champions), and an annual celebration event complete with leadership participation.

- BB Selection—Receive Six Sigma Pin
- BB Certification—$5,000 Certification Bonus plus plaque
- BB Project Completion
  - $500 to $5,000 in cash or stock options for first project
  - Plaque with project name engraved for first and subsequent projects
- BB Six Sigma Activity Awards
  - Recognizes efforts and achievements during projects with individual and team awards—Cash, tickets, dinners, shirts, etc.
- Green Belt Recognition
  - Similar to Black Belt recognition
  - No certification bonus
- Project Team Member Recognition
  - Similar to BB and GB recognition
  - No certification awards
- Annual Six Sigma Celebration Event
  - Presentation of key projects
  - Dinner reception with senior leadership

Note also that all rewards do not have to be monetary. For many people peer and management recognition, such as an opportunity to present their project, is a greater reward than money.

In evaluating these reward and recognition plans, and those of other organizations, we conclude that the most appropriate plan is company dependent. What works for one company, or even one employee, will not necessarily work for another. Reward and recognition plans are also not static. The points listed on pages 119 and 120 will likely change over time as experience with Six Sigma grows, and the reward and recognition needs become clear. The one constant is to make sure you are rewarding the behavior you want to encourage.

Six Sigma goals and objectives should be part of performance plans for all those involved in the Six Sigma initiative. If the company intends for Six Sigma to involve the entire organization, then these goals and objectives must be included in the performance plans for the entire organization. This is consistent with our earlier recognition that we are all motivated to work on those things that will be beneficial to our career. Six Sigma responsibilities should be part of people's individual goals and objectives, and their performance should be evaluated relative to these goals and objectives. Once again, what we measure and pay attention to gets done.

Project Identification/Prioritization System

We discussed initial project selection in Chapter 4. When the Black Belts have completed their first project, they are ready to take on another project. You don't want to lose any momentum. After this new project has gotten under way, full-time Black Belts will be ready to take on a second project simultaneously. This ramp-up will continue until fully operational Black Belts are handling three or four projects at a time.

Clearly, with a lot of Black Belts working in an organization you need to plan carefully to ensure that you have important, high-impact projects identified and ready to go when the Black Belts are ready. A frequent mistake companies make is waiting for the Black Belt to finish a project before looking for another one. Such a strategy wastes the time of the Black Belts, a valuable resource. A Black Belt without a project is a sin in the Six Sigma world. Lack of planning also often results in mediocre projects being worked on, because sufficient thought had not been put into the selection process. Good project selection is a key to success.

Now that you have numerous projects and Black Belts you cannot rely on ad-hoc project selection, but must implement a formal selection and prioritization system. A schematic of an ongoing project selection process and its associated project hopper is shown in Figure 5-4 (Rodebaugh [2001]). Project selection should be an ongoing process that ensures we always have a collection of projects ready for Black Belts to tackle. One strategy for keeping the project hopper "evergreen" is to require that a new project be added to the hopper each time a project is removed and assigned to a Black Belt or Green Belt.

The project hopper can be thought of as an organizational to-do list and should be managed in much the same way. Projects are continually being put into the hopper, the list is continually being prioritized, and prioritized projects are assigned to Black Belts or Green Belts as these resources become available. By continually searching for projects, and reprioritizing the list of projects in the project hopper, you ensure that problems most important to the organization are being addressed by using Six Sigma.

Each business or functional unit should have a project hopper. It is also appropriate to have a corporate project hopper to handle those projects that do not naturally fit into the hoppers of the business and functional units. For example, a project to improve integration of business units or functions does not fit squarely within any one business or function. The hopper should always be full, containing at least a six-month supply of projects (a year's supply is even better), and at least one project that would naturally fit into the work of each individual Black Belt. As noted earlier, Black Belts should never be without a full load of projects. It is important to review the hopper contents as part of the quarterly Six Sigma initiative review (discussed further in Chapter 6).

The discussion of initial project selection in Chapter 4 provides most of the guidelines for project selection. These apply to the ongoing project selection and prioritization system as well. We recommend focusing projects strategically on business priorities, and also wherever the organization is experiencing significant pain, such as responding to critical customer issues. Information that is helpful in selecting specific projects is contained in the baseline and entitlement database. These data tell you how the processes are performing today and how they could be performing in the future, as well as identifying the sources of important improvement opportunities.

Process baseline and entitlement data should be maintained and updated for all key process performance metrics associated with all key manufacturing and non-manufacturing processes used to run the organiza-

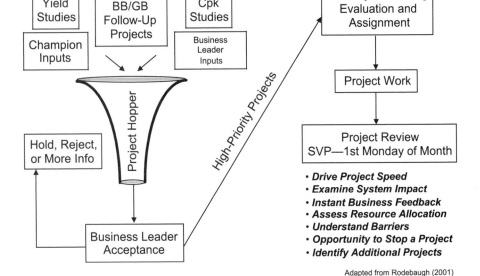

FIGURE 5-4   Project Selection and Management Process System

tion. The job of creating and maintaining this database is typically assigned to a MBB or experienced Black Belt. This database should be updated every 6 months or so and be an item for at least every other quarterly Six Sigma initiative review (see Chapter 6).

While development and maintenance of such databases is simply good management practice, our experience is that typically they either don't exist at all, or are solely focused on accounting information, and therefore are inadequate for improvement purposes. Lack of good data is probably the greatest issue faced by Black Belt teams. This is one reason why evaluation of the measurement system is a key element of the measure phase of DMAIC projects.

Once you have spent time and effort developing an adequate measurement system for improvement purposes, you should make sure it is properly maintained so that you don't have to recreate the system for future projects.

Project Closure—Moving On to the Next Project

Project closure is an important event. It is the signal that the project is done, that the Black Belt can move on to the next project, and that you can ring the cash register with money flowing to the bottom line. Project closure criteria form an important part of the project identification/prioritization system, because they help Black Belts and others move on to their next projects promptly. They should neither linger on projects too long nor leave prematurely before critical controls are in place.

Some perfectionists will not want to move on until they have reached entitlement, even though they have met their original objectives, and there are now bigger issues elsewhere. Other Black Belts or Green Belts may be anxious to tackle the next problem, and want to leave before critical controls are in place. The key players in this event are the Black Belt or Green Belt, Champion, finance representative, and the person who owns the process. The process owner is needed because the process improvements developed by the Black Belt or Green Belt will become standard operating procedure for the process in the future.

Key to project closure is the verification of the process improvements and associated financial impact (determined by Finance), the completion of the process control plan, completion of the training associated with the new way of operating, and completion of the project report that summarizes the work done and the key findings. When this work is done the Black Belt or Green Belt will often make a presentation to management, and the rest of the organization is informed through the project reporting system or other methods of communication used by the organization (e.g., newsletters, web sites, story boards, etc.).

You can manage project closure by having a standard set of steps to close out a project, a project closure form that is an integral part of the project tracking system, and a method for electronically archiving the project in the reporting system so the results will be available to the whole organization. This last item is important because Black Belts working in nonstandard areas, such as risk management, find documentation of previous projects in this same area extremely helpful. The specific closure steps and form should be tailored to each organization, but we recommend that the following steps be required:

- Successful completion of each phase of the DMAIC (or DFSS) process
- Finance sign-off on the savings claimed
- Control plan in place and being used by process owner
- Any needed training implemented
- Final Champion and management reviews

Inclusion of Six Sigma in Budgeting Processes

Most organizations that implement Six Sigma do not have the implementation costs or benefits in their budget at the time they decide to launch. This happens simply because most didn't realize in the previous year, when the current year's budget was developed, that they would be implementing Six Sigma now. Therefore, Six Sigma is generally launched with special funding allocated by senior leadership. This is certainly acceptable to get started, but as organizations begin to formally manage the effort it is critically important that Six Sigma be included in their key budgeting processes.

This inclusion is important for several reasons. First, leadership needs to make sure that Six Sigma receives the same degree of financial scrutiny as any other budgetary area. Since virtually all public corporations, and most private and even non-profit organizations, have existing budgeting and financial control systems, they can simply include Six Sigma in these, rather than having to create new infrastructure.

Second, inclusion into the budget will help Six Sigma move from being viewed as a separate, and potentially short-term initiative, to being a normal part of how you work.

Third, this budget will document and formalize leadership expectations of all layers of management. These expectations will be clear when each business unit budget shows a line item for financial benefits from Six Sigma, in addition to a line item for expenditures for Six Sigma. Leadership is providing financial resources to implement Six Sigma, but it expects a payoff. Ideally, business unit managers will be intrinsically motivated to enthusiastically deploy Six Sigma because they believe in what it can do. However, just in case some managers are not, knowing that they are accountable to obtain financial benefits through Six Sigma will provide significant extrinsic motivation to succeed.

Deployment Processes for Leaders

After you have selected your first group of Champions, Black Belts, and other roles in the launching the initiative phase, they will begin working on their initial projects. We explained in Chapter 4 how to go about initial project and people selection. During the managing the effort phase, however, the number of projects will be growing too quickly to pick Black Belts and others on an ad-hoc basis. You will need to develop a formal process for selecting Black Belts and other roles, and assigning them to projects. This process will become even more important later, as Black Belts begin rotating out of their assignments and have to be replaced. It may be appropriate for some Black Belts to remain in the role for many years. But the world is dynamic, and Black Belts will leave the initiative for a variety of reasons, just like people leave other assignments over time. A few will leave because they are not suited for the work; others because of a transfer or promotion. A few will become MBBs. Some will move on to other companies and other careers.

A formal process is needed, typically lead by HR, that continually looks at the improvement needs of the organization (for example, strategy and project hopper contents), and the career development needs of the top performers in the organization, and selects those who should take Champion, Black Belt, MBB, or other Six Sigma roles.

It will also look to move top Green Belts into Black Belt roles, Black Belts into MBB roles, and so on. After about two years into the initiative, Black Belts and others will begin to rotate out of Six Sigma roles, and will be looking for big jobs. It is important that a placement process is ready to properly place them into important roles.

As noted in our discussion of reward and recognition, people need tangible evidence that making the commitment to Six Sigma will help their career. Seeing others get big and important jobs after their Six Sigma assignment is one way to make this happen. Conversely, if you do not place these resources in important positions, you will be wasting the significant leadership development they have received.

HR may primarily manage the people selection process, or it may be managed by a business Quality Council with support from HR. Most organizations soon see the need for an active, formal, Six Sigma organization to effectively manage many of these systems and processes (see Chapter 6). The people selection process should follow the criteria given in Chapter 4 for selection of Black Belts and others. The process of assigning these resources to projects should be based on the project identification and prioritization system. In other words, you should first select the projects, and then select the appropriate Black Belts to work on them. Such an approach simplifies the process of assigning Black Belts once they have been selected.

The placement process often presents a greater challenge, since big jobs are by definition few in number, and there may not be a suitable job waiting for each Black Belt or MBB that rotates out of Six Sigma. Therefore, many companies will make the timing flexible, allowing Black Belts and others to begin looking for their next job after about 18 months, while still in their Six Sigma position. This enables them to wait until they find a good fit and still complete their current project.

Initially, HR may need to help those leaving Six Sigma roles obtain the job they desire. After a while, managers will be actively seeking Black Belts and MBBs with no prompting from HR because they will see how these assignments have grown and matured the people in them. Recall from Chapter 3 that a key benefit of Six Sigma is that it becomes an excellent leadership development system for our top talent.

Integrating Six Sigma with Current Management Systems

Organizations should look for every opportunity to integrate Six Sigma management systems with their current management systems. Integration will help make Six Sigma part of their culture, reduce bureaucracy and the amount of effort needed to manage the initiative, and increase its impact. This approach to integration will be discussed in detail in Chapter 7, which shows how to make the transition from Six Sigma being an initiative to it being the way you work. However, you should begin integrating Six Sigma now, at the point where you implement Six Sigma management systems. The more integration you do now, the less you will have to do later.

For example, Six Sigma reviews can become part of normal staff and management meetings as long as they are given adequate time on the agenda. As noted, Six Sigma should be part of your budgeting processes, not a stand-alone item. In some companies, Six Sigma identifies a gap in the communications process that has to be filled by creating new media. We noted previously that the reward and recognition system usually has to be revised to support the needs of Six Sigma, but there will eventually be only one reward and recognition system. Most organizations will need to create a project tracking system. In some instances existing project management systems can be enhanced to enable Six Sigma project tracking.

In most cases, project closure procedures and supporting forms have to be created and integrated with the project tracking system. The project selection process and its associated project hopper also have to be created in most organizations. Whenever possible the project selection process should be integrated with the capital project system, and other similar systems. Early focus on integration of Six Sigma managing processes with current systems greatly speeds up acceptance of the methodology and its bottom-line impact, not to mention simplifying the final transition to the way you work.

Summary

We define the managing the effort phase to be the period between completion of the initial wave of Black Belt training, and the point when we have trained everyone originally intended, and implemented all projects identified in your original deployment plan. This phase typically lasts about 18 months, although management of the effort lasts indefinitely. The critical transition that occurs here is from a new launch to a formal long-term initiative. The effort will become too large to manage informally, requiring the implementation of formal management systems and processes. These systems and processes are all infrastructure elements of the deployment plan discussed in Chapter 4. The key deliverable is implementation of these infrastructure elements, which typically include:

- Management project reviews
- Project reporting and tracking system
- Communications plan
- Reward and recognition plan
- Project identification/prioritization system
- Project closure criteria
- Inclusion of Six Sigma into budgeting processes
- Deployment processes for Champions, Black Belts, MBBs, etc.

Obtaining top talent for key Six Sigma roles and implementation of this key infrastructure are key success factors in this phase. Top talent is needed to properly design, implement, and manage these systems and processes. Designing management systems is not easy work, and a poor system can negatively impact the entire organization. Other important success factors in this phase are:

- Making improvement opportunities possible with a good process baseline and entitlement database.

- Using Six Sigma assignments as a leadership development system.

- Integrating Six Sigma management processes with normal operating procedures. This reduces the effort required to manage the initiative, reduces bureaucracy, and sets the stage for making Six Sigma the way we work.

References

English, W. (2001). "Implementing Six Sigma—The Iomega Story." Presented at the Conference on Six Sigma in the Pharmaceutical Industry, Philadelphia, PA, November 27–28, 2001.

IBM Europe. (1990). "Business Process Quality Mangement." *Quality Today*, June 1990, 10–11.

Rodebaugh, W. R. (2001). "Six Sigma in Measurement Systems— Evaluating the Hidden Factory." Presented at the Penn State Great Valley Symposium on Statistical Methods for Quality Practitioners. October, 2001.

Senge, P. (1990). *The Fifth Discipline: The Art and Practice of the Learning Organization.* Doubleday/Currency, New York, New York.

Snee, R. D., K.H. Kelleher, and S. Reynard. (1998). "Improving Team Effectiveness," *Quality Progress.* May 1998, 43–48.

Snee, R.D. and W.F. Rodebaugh (2002). "Project Selection Process," *Quality Progress*, September 2002, 78–80.

Weisbord, M. R. (1989). *Productive Workplaces.* Jossey-Bass, San Francisco.

Welch, J. F. (2001). *Jack, Straight from the Gut.* Warner Business Books, New York, N.Y., page 331.

6

SUSTAINING MOMENTUM AND GROWING

"To improve is to change. To be perfect is to change often."

—Winston Churchill

You have successfully launched your Six Sigma initiative (Chapter 4), and have been working on putting in place those systems that are needed to effectively manage the deployment (Chapter 5). Many Six Sigma initiatives begin to hit a lull at this point as other priorities gradually erode the momentum. Now is the time to implement systems and processes that will instead help you sustain the energy. Sometimes the best defense is a good offense, and growth of the program can be a good offensive tactic that helps maintain momentum. This chapter focuses on the defensive effort needed to sustain impetus, and the offensive effort needed to expand the Six Sigma initiative. This sustaining phase is defined as the time between the completion of the training and projects identified in the original deployment plan, and the transformation of Six Sigma from an initiative to the normal way you work. This phase may last several years.

The momentum of Six Sigma is maintained by holding the gains of completed projects, and by sustaining the gains of the overall Six Sigma system. Some of the methods discussed in this chapter are shown schematically in Figure 6-1. As you will see, and as should come as no surprise, the key is consistent implementation of periodic reviews, including audits. It is also important to implement a complete training system (as opposed to individual training courses), create a formal Six Sigma organizational structure, and develop Leadership Green Belts. Note from Figure 6-1 that all the other elements are done within the context and direction of the Six Sigma organizational structure. This makes up your defensive effort to maintain what you already have.

At this stage, you will also want to play offense and extend the deployment into new areas. You can accomplish this primarily by expanding Six Sigma to the whole organization, introducing customers and suppliers to Six Sigma, and using Six Sigma to increase revenue as well as reduce costs. Much of the literature on Six Sigma to date has emphasized cost reductions, but, as you will see, it also can have a huge impact on top-line growth, that is, revenue generation. We will first review the key elements of our defensive strategy, and then discuss the offensive elements.

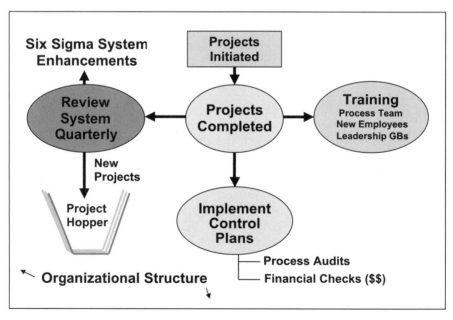

FIGURE 6-1   Sustaining the Gains

Playing Defense—Sustaining Momentum

After a couple of years, Six Sigma may become old news, and more recent issues or problems may divert managerial attention. This phenomenon has been faced by all organizations deploying Six Sigma, so it is leadership's response to it that determines whether or not the deployment will be successful in the long term. In Chapter 3 we noted that implementing the remaining infrastructure elements was the key to successfully making this transition. Recall that these infrastructure elements were identified as part of the overall deployment plan developed in the launching the initiative phase (Chapter 4). Some of these infrastructure elements were implemented during the managing the effort phase (Chapter 5), such as the systems for selecting projects and Black Belts. You are now going to close the loop and implement the remaining infrastructure elements identified in your deployment plan. These elements will enable you to sustain momentum without the same level of personal attention from senior leadership that you have had up until now.

HOLDING PROJECT GAINS

The improvements obtained from Six Sigma projects are held by implementing the project control plans, ensuring that all employees associated with the process are trained in the new way of operating the process and performing periodic process and financial audits. A control plan (AIAG [1994]) contains the information needed to monitor and control a process and to maintain improvements, and is finalized during the control phase of a DMAIC project. It contains specific activities required to monitor and control the process, including answers to the questions who, what, when and how? It also contains the reaction plan that defines what should be done by whom, and who should be informed when something goes wrong.

The control plan is effective when it contains all the information needed to ensure that the process is in a state of control, is in a form easily used by the operators (process workers), and is, in fact, used to operate the process. An evergreen document, it is continually updated to reflect the current methods and measurements used to monitor and control the process. Clarity, completeness, conciseness, and simplicity are key characteristics of effective control plans.

An example of a control plan adapted from the Automotive Industry Action Group (AIAG) is shown in Figure 6-2. Control plans are process-specific, having many different forms and including a variety of types of information such as process steps, FMEA findings, measurement system indices (such as Gage R&R values) and process capability indices. The right control plan for your process is the one that contains the information needed to monitor and control your process and to maintain the gains of improvements projects.

Part of the control plan and project closure report is a schedule for the process and financial audits. The goal of the process audit is to see whether the process is being operated as directed by the control plan and standard operating procedures, and whether the process performance levels are being maintained. An effective way to integrate process audits into the normal work procedures is to make them part of the ISO 9000 audit. Both control plans and ISO 9000 audits have provisions for changing the standard operating procedures as more effective means to operate the process are found.

The financial audits determine whether the projected monetary gains are being realized. These audits, typically done by the financial organization, generally follow the financial performance of a project for 12 months after project closure. They help validate the results, build credibility for Six Sigma, and identify opportunities for improvement. Recall that documentation of financial benefits is a key success factor for Six Sigma. It is equally important to maintain the financial gains.

There also needs to be a concerted effort to ensure that all persons connected with the process, whether old hands or recently assigned, are trained in the new way of working. The adequacy of the training can also be checked as part of the ISO 9000 audit. The overall training system will be discussed later in this chapter. Some organizations train all process operators as Six Sigma Yellow Belts. Yellow Belt training is usually given by the Black Belt, typically lasts two days, and focuses on the measure and control phases of DMAIC. Although accountabilities vary considerably based on organizational philosophy and structure, in typical organizations the operators' (process workers') principal responsibilities are to take process data and to control the process.

QUARTERLY AND ANNUAL REVIEWS
Quarterly reviews conducted by the chief executive serve to monitor the health and effectiveness of the overall Six Sigma system. In large organizations these reviews should also be held at the business and function

Prototype	Pre-Launch	Production X									
Control Plan Number						Date (Orig.)				Date (Rev.)	
Part Number/Latest Change Level	Key Contact/Phone					Customer Engineering Approval/Date (If Req'd)					
Part Name/Description						Customer Quality Approval/Date (If Req'd)					
Supplier/Plant	Supplier Code					Supplier/Plant Approval/Date					
						Other Approval/Date (If Req'd)					
						Other Approval/Date (If Req'd)					

Part/Process Number	Process Name/Operation Description	Machine, Device Jig, Tools for MFG	No.	Characteristics		Special Char. Class	Product/Process Spec/Tolerance	Evaluation Measurement Technique	Sample		Control Method	Reaction Plan
				Product	Process				Size	Freq.		
3	Machine Surface "A"	Rotary Machine	51	Depth of Cut		*	2 ± 0.25"	Depth Gage	5	per hour per fixture	x-R chart	Quarantine adjust and reset
		Holding Fixture #10	52	Perpendicular Cut		*	90° ± 1°	Gage 050	1 pc	every 4 hrs	x-MR chart	Quarantine adjust and reset
		Holding Fixture #10	53		Hold casting in fixture for proper orientation		Fixture free from debris	Visual inspection	1 pc	after each cycle	Air blow-off	Readjust air blow-off

Adapted from Automotive Industry Action Group (1994)   Advanced Product Quality Planning and Control Plan

FIGURE 6-2 Control Plan Example

level. The goal is to check on the functioning of the overall Six Sigma infrastructure, including all relevant systems and processes. Table 6-1 is based on the elements of the deployment plan (see Chapter 4), but augmented with some specifics that have been developed since, such as review of selected projects and overall financial results. Table 6-2 shows a typical outline for such a quarterly meeting. The key Six Sigma processes to be reviewed are progress toward financial goals, training progress (particularly in the first two years), and the project selection process including the project hopper. It is not imperative that all processes be checked in each quarterly review, but certainly all processes should be checked at least once per year.

A good strategy is to formally review the critical processes in each of the first three quarterly reviews. The fourth quarter or annual review should probe in more depth, reviewing all the processes and developing an annual plan and goals for the coming year. Obviously, the annual plan and goals should link tightly to the overall strategic plan and goals from the deployment plan.

The annual review is a good time to check the project hopper for sufficient projects to reach the financial goals set for the coming year, and

TABLE 6-1   Elements of Six Sigma System Review

- Goals and strategy
- Budgeting—costs and benefits
- Project selection including financial impact ($$)
- Project hopper review
- Personnel selection
- Training
- Project reviews
- Project reporting
- Project tracking
- Project closure and handoff
- Audits—process and financial
- MBB, BB, GB, and Champion performance management
- MBB, BB, and GB career development including certification
- Communications
- Recognition, reward, and compensation
- Six Sigma system review and enhancement

TABLE 6-2   Typical Outline for Six Sigma System Quarterly Review

---

- Review Format
  - Presentation of program status
  - Questions for clarification
  - Discussion
  - Action items
  - Review evaluation—went well, do differently at next review
- Materials for Quarterly Review
  - Summary status for all projects
  - Trends in key process performance metrics
  - Financial impact assessment
  - Status of communications
  - Assessment of other Six Sigma system elements as needed
  - Actions needed
  - Key learnings

Note: Materials to be discussed at the review should be sent to review team 2-3 days prior to review.

---

whether the project portfolio (mix of projects) is sufficient to satisfy the goals of the organization. Do you have the right mix of projects as categorized by business unit, functional unit, cost reduction vs. cost avoidance, strategic vs. tactical, revenue enhancement vs. cost reduction, quality improvement, etc.?

Consider taking an organizational survey of the Six Sigma deployment every 18–24 months to check on deployment progress, and to identify opportunities for improvement (Snee [1995]). This survey should measure the feelings and attitudes of all employees. Honest, unfiltered feedback from employees is difficult information for senior leadership to obtain, but very important. The results of the survey are useful input for the annual planning sessions. Organizations change slowly and the 18–24 month frequency is usually sufficient to detect improvement needs and any trends that have occurred.

THE TRAINING SYSTEM

To sustain Six Sigma long term, organizations will need an overall training system. Portions of this system will already exist by this phase, and Executive, Business Leader, Champion, Black Belt, Master Black Belt

(MBB), and Green Belt training will be under way. It is now time to think holistically about the organization's overall training needs relative to Six Sigma for years to come.

Key elements of a long-term training system are:

- Six Sigma Awareness training for new people
- Ongoing Champion, MBB, BB, and GB training
- Champion, MBB, BB, and GB refresher training
- Advanced Black Belt training
- Initial MBB training
- Six Sigma training in different languages
- Six Sigma curricula for operations, administration/transactional, and new product development processes
- Leadership Green Belt training

Advanced Black Belt training is typically needed because some skills specific to certain technical areas are not part of the general Black Belt training. Some examples include mixture experimentation for the chemical, coatings, and foods industries; multidimensional tolerancing for the assembly industries; and advanced process control and process variance component studies for the process industries. There are additional or advanced skills that the Black Belts need that couldn't be part of their original training because of time limitations. Some examples include advanced regression analysis and modeling techniques, complex multi-vari studies, and advanced design of experiments. Supplemental Black Belt materials and topics from Hoerl (2001) are given in Table 6-3.

Organizations are dynamic and people move in and out for various reasons. The training system must include processes for training new executives, Champions, Black Belts, MBBs, and Green Belts. Some training will be job dependent; for example, engineers and financial personnel will need different kinds of training. In general, we recommend tailored training to the degree feasible. Existing executives, Champions, Black Belts, MBBs, and Green Belts can also benefit from brief refresher courses, particularly when they stay in these roles for an extended period of time. New topics or techniques will likely be added to courses over time, and refreshers provide a convenient means for those previously trained to stay up to date. To sustain Six Sigma momentum, training needs to be a sustained system, not simply a one-time event.

TABLE 6-3   Supplemental Materials for Black Belts

- Failure Modes and Effects Analysis—Automotive Industry Action Group (1995b)
- Design of Experiments—Box, Hunter, and Hunter (1978); Montgomery (2000)
- General Statistics—Walpole, Myers, and Myers (1997)
- Measurement Systems Analysis—Wheeler and Lyday (1990); Automotive Industry Action Group (1990)
- Mixture Designs—Cornell (1990)
- Quality Function Deployment (QFD)—Cohen (1995)
- Regression—Draper and Smith (1998); Montgomery, Peck, and Vining (2001)
- Reliability—Meeker and Escobar (1998)
- Response Surface Methodology—Myers and Montgomery (1995)
- Statistical Process Control—Wheeler and Chambers (1992); Automotive Industry Action Group (1995a); Montgomery (2001)
- Statistical Thinking—Hoerl and Snee (2002)
- Time Series—Box, Jenkins, and Reinsel (1994)

Adapted from Hoerl (2001)

Multinational companies will need to develop training materials and instructors to deliver Six Sigma training in multiple languages. In our experience you can often deliver Executive, Champion, MBB, and Black Belt training in English in most industrialized countries, but Green Belt training needs to be in the native language. Learning Six Sigma is challenging enough without having to struggle with the nuances of a foreign language. Accurate translation of technical material is very difficult, and for digital training systems there are often unique challenges translating into double-byte languages such as Chinese or Japanese (for which characters are stored as two bytes instead of one).

A training system is much more extensive than a list of courses. A good system will include processes for developing and presenting new courses, keeping track of who has attended courses and/or passed exams, identifying people in need of specific training, translating materials, qualifying instructors, and providing managerial reports.

The organization must think carefully about how the training system will be managed over time. In most situations, a Six Sigma provider manages the training system initially, but what happens when the contract expires? Taking over the responsibility for managing the training system from the Six Sigma provider helps make Six Sigma part of the culture—how things are done around here. Many organizations put MBBs in charge of managing the training system, perhaps through a Training Council, since training is a key role of MBBs.

Leadership Green Belt Training

It takes time before your entire management team has the required Six Sigma skills and experience. GE recognized this and decided to train all its professionals as Green Belts, as well as making Green Belt status a condition of promotion for professionals. Jack Welch said, "with Six Sigma permeating much of what you do, it will be unthinkable to hire, promote or tolerate those who cannot, or will not, commit to this way of work" (*USA Today*, 2/27/98).

When management supports it in this manner, Six Sigma is an effective leadership developmental tool. Leaders learn how to use Six Sigma to improve an organization and its processes in all businesses, all functions, and all cultures. They see how Six Sigma develops personnel, providing breadth of experience by allowing people to work on a variety of processes, empowering people to improve processes, teaching teamwork, and developing leaders. Leadership Green Belt training also results in all leaders hearing a common message that helps create alignment around the objectives and goals of Six Sigma. Leaders with such perspective will ensure that the gains of Six Sigma are maintained.

Iomega reported, "Six Sigma is the best people development tool we have ever deployed" (English [2001]). Through its Six Sigma projects Iomega, which provides storage products for digital items, developed a common language and common approach for process design, improvement, and management. DuPont, Honeywell, and 3M are also providing Six Sigma training for their leadership.

We focus on Green Belt training as a leadership tool to ensure that all leaders have experienced Six Sigma at the gut level. Green Belt training is needed at the beginning of implementation, because none of the senior leaders will have held MBB or Black Belt positions. The need for Leadership Green Belt training will decrease over time as more leaders have Black Belt and MBB experience.

The goal of the Green Belt Leadership training is for the leaders to develop a deeper understanding of Six Sigma, and to learn how to use it to improve the organization. Six Sigma training works best when it is project-based, but it can be difficult to find appropriate projects for the leaders to work on. Training without a project is of less value; it can leave the impression that the leaders are just getting their tickets punched and are not serious about learning the methodology. A similar result can occur if the projects are not viewed as important, or the leaders don't do a good job and poor results are obtained. So we have come full circle, finding that project selection is a potential Achilles heel of Leadership Green Belt training, just as it is for other types of Six Sigma projects. Here are a few suggestions for finding appropriate projects.

Focus on the work the leader *actually does*. This will ensure that the project is meaningful, not duties added to an already overflowing plate. Recall from the discussion of non-manufacturing applications that all work can be viewed as a process, but with general business processes it is much harder to actually see the process. Experienced MBBs should be able to help the Leadership Green Belts see the underlying processes in managerial activities such as budgeting, evaluating performance, and allocating resources. Many senior executives feel that they spend too much time in unproductive meetings. All would appreciate improvements to the meeting process. Implementing and managing the systems and processes that are part of the Six Sigma infrastructure (the focus of Chapters 5 and 6) would make excellent leadership DFSS projects. A senior HR leader could implement a new reward and recognition system; an IT leader could design a new tracking and reporting system; finance leaders could work on designing the financial auditing system for projects. Large projects such as these might need to be split up into several smaller projects, and additional team members will likely be needed to address details (such as writing computer code). Nevertheless, relevant, important project areas like these tend to be much more fruitful than projects that are perceived as "moving the water cooler." Other examples of topics for Leadership Green Belt projects are given in Table 6-4.

Our recommendation is that every Green Belt, including senior leadership, do at least one formal project. We do not believe you can get a "gut-level" appreciation for Six Sigma without actually doing it yourself. Through careful project selection, and mentoring from experienced MBBs, Leadership Green Belts can successfully complete meaningful projects. While extra mentoring from the MBB can be extremely helpful, the MBB must carefully avoid even the perception that he or she is doing the project for the Leadership Green Belt.

TABLE 6-4   Examples of Leadership Green Belt Projects

- Reduce the amount of expedited freight usage in the Eastern Region (Business Executive Vice President)
- Improve the customer complaint handling process to reduce response time (Quality Manager)
- Increase the impact of the employee training process (Human Resources Manager)
- Improve the management reporting process to increase the timeliness of reports and to eliminate little used reports (Assistant Plant Manager)
- Reduce the cost and and increase the job offer acceptance rate of the college recruiting process (Corporate College Recruiting Director)
- Speed up the transfer of manufacturing processes from pilot plant to manufacturing in order to reduce amount of backorders (Director of Manufacturing)
- Streamline the operations forecasting process to improve timeliness and accuracy (Planning and Scheduling Manager)
- Reduce the corporate budgeting process cycle time from 12 months to 9 months (Corporate Financial Officer)
- Reduce the cycle time of the new acquisitions process (President)
- Improve shipping contracting process to improve on-time delivery performance (Logistics Vice President)

Six Sigma Organizational Structure

By now you have realized that some Six Sigma infrastructure is needed to sustain momentum. If properly designed and implemented, this infrastructure will be value-added, with minimal bureaucracy. Note that we recommend a lean infrastructure, one that is primarily automated and requires *minimal* human staffing. For example, the project tracking and reporting system should be digital, so that additional personnel are not required to process paper reports. Despite its leanness, the infrastructure will require some human guidance to manage and improve it over time. Therefore you will need a formal Six Sigma organizational structure to clarify roles and responsibilities for managing the infrastructure. This organizational structure will likely have begun in the managing the effort phase, but needs to be completed and invigorated now because of the extension of supporting systems and processes in this phase.

Organizational structure is particularly important now that the direct involvement of the Six Sigma provider is winding down. In many Six Sigma deployments the provider handles much of the initial organizational effort. Transition to an internal organizational structure is an important step in becoming self-sufficient. It is particularly important that the training system is well managed, and does not miss a beat as the provider's efforts wind down.

If the transition is not properly handled, a leadership vacuum will be created when the provider fades out of the picture. The best way to avoid this is to have a formal, functioning organizational structure, such as an active Six Sigma Council led by the overall Six Sigma Leader, to manage the effort going forward. This implies more than just naming Champions, MBBs, Black Belts, and so on. You need a functioning team that works like a "well-oiled machine" to properly lead and coordinate all aspects of the Six Sigma deployment.

By "active" we mean that all members must participate regularly. It does little good to list the company's top leaders as council members if they do not participate. As noted earlier, we may also set up Six Sigma Councils within individual business units or functions. The leaders of the business unit and functional councils are usually members of the overall council, resulting in interlocking membership, which aids in communication and coordination across the organization.

For example, when Roger Hoerl was Quality Leader (Six Sigma Leader) of the GE Corporate Audit Staff (CAS), he also was a participant in the GE Quality Leaders' Council (overall Six Sigma Council). In addition, he led the CAS Quality Council that also consisted of:

- The CAS Vice President (head of CAS)
- Head of all financial service business audits (GE Capital)
- Head of all industrial business audits
- CAS HR manager
- CAS IT leader
- An MBB

This organizational structure worked well for a couple of reasons: (1) it ensured that the CAS Six Sigma effort was aligned with the overall direction of GE's Six Sigma deployment, due to the interlocking membership; (2) the participation of the key decision makers in the CAS council ensured alignment within CAS.

For example, when the council made policy decisions about certification criteria, training requirements, and so on, all the key leaders conveyed the same message. If the leaders had not participated in these decisions, there would have been an opportunity for second-guessing, misalignment, or organizational conflict at the top. All members, including the vice president, made their active participation in this council a priority. The HR and

IT representatives contributed significantly to training, reward and recognition, career development issues (HR), and tracking systems for projects, training, and certification (IT). Six Sigma Councils typically include the Six Sigma Leader, representative (not all) Champions, representative MBBs, leaders of Finance, HR, IT, and any other relevant functions or participants.

Six Sigma Leaders Must Work Together as a Team

It is important not only that an organizational structure be in place to lead and manage the Six Sigma effort, but that the key Six Sigma players work together as a team. A team functions well when each player does his or her job well and knows what the roles and functions of all the other players on the team are. For example, it is important that the Black Belts understand the roles of the Champion and other Six Sigma team members so they will know where to go for help.

Similarly, it is critical that the functional group leaders know the role of the Black Belts so they can provide them with data, expertise, and resources. This attitude helps everyone learn his or her role and function effectively. The Six Sigma Sweep sports analogy can help us deepen understanding of this requirement.

"The Six Sigma Sweep"

Columnist George Will tells us "sports serve society by providing vivid examples of excellence." This can be true with Six Sigma. Sports provides vivid examples and analogies that help us understand why Six Sigma is so effective—the fact that it provides a strategy, methodology, and an infrastructure that enables all the leaders to work together as a team improving the performance of the organization.

When you think of excellence and success in the sports world, Vince Lombardi quickly comes to mind. He was the coach of the Green Bay Packer football team that won five National Football League titles and the first two Super Bowls in the 1960s. Many subsequent successful football coaches were students of Lombardi's. How did he do it? His success came from careful thought, detailed planning, lots of practice and hard work, and a clear focus on the goal. These success factors also apply to Six Sigma.

What was his methodology? The famous Packer Sweep was Lombardi's signature play, and a key component of his success. This was a running play where the running back carried the ball to the outside behind two lineman (pulling guards). Lombardi practiced this play more than any other, refining it until his players knew that they could run it anytime against any opponent. Anyone who saw Green Bay play football during the Lombardi years will recall the sweep in which the guards Jerry Kramer (64) and Fuzzy Thurston (63) pulled out of the line and led the running back Jim Taylor (31) around the end while each of the other players completed their assignments.

"The Six Sigma Sweep" *(continued)*

Interestingly, Lombardi did not invent this play—he borrowed it from the then-Los Angeles Rams—but he certainly perfected it. He also developed many variations. On every play each player knew his job, and that if each did his assignment the play would be successful. The play was so important to Lombardi's offense that Coach John Madden recalls him devoting an entire one-day seminar to the subject (Madden [1985]). Lombardi discussed the play, its philosophy, its fundamentals, its objectives, what each player's role was, and why the play couldn't be stopped if each player executed well. Each variation of the sweep was discussed in the same detail.

There are many similarities between the Packer Sweep and Six Sigma. First, Six Sigma was not totally original. It built on the work of others and continues to be enhanced. Six Sigma works because it emphasizes focus, planning, constant practice (every project is a practice session), and dedicated leadership. There are well-defined roles and if each person does his or her job, as defined by the process, the projects will be successful and Six Sigma will achieve its goals.

Six Sigma can be the signature business strategy and management process that separates an organization from its competition—providing focus, reducing costs, growing revenues, empowering and developing people, enhancing teamwork, and providing a common corporate language and methodology. In the process, Six Sigma improves an organization's performance, sweeping money to the bottom line, just as Lombardi's Green Bay Sweep gained yards, put points on the scoreboard, won games, won conference titles, and won Super Bowls. We refer to this use of Six Sigma as a signature business strategy as the Six Sigma Sweep.

This analogy actually goes much deeper. There are 11 roles on the Six Sigma Sweep team just as there are 11 positions on a football team. These roles are detailed in Table 6-A (also see Chapter 4) and are shown schematically with linkages in Figure 6-A. While there are many analogies, we will resist the temptation to match the roles on the Six Sigma team with those on a football team. The important point is that these roles have to work together as a team just as the players on a football team have to work together to be successful.

If the people in these roles perform their job as defined and understand the roles of the others on the team, just as Lombardi required of his players, the Six Sigma Sweep will work. Organizational performance will improve, money will be swept to the bottom line, and the organization will be well down the road to success. In fact, when an organization moves out in front of its competition using Six Sigma, and continues to use Six Sigma effectively, the organization will most likely always be ahead of its competition. It is unlikely that the competition will ever catch up.

We again recall the AlliedSignal manager's admonishment, "Six Sigma works if you follow the process. If it is not working you are not following the process."

(Madden, J. (1985). *Hey, Wait a Minute! I Wrote a Book.* Random House, New York, NY.)

continued on next page...

"The Six Sigma Sweep" *(continued)*

TABLE 6-A   Six Sigma Sweep Team Roles

- Chief Executive Officer—Provides strategy, goals, promotion, resources, review, recognition, and feedback
- Six Sigma Leaders—Build infrastructure, provide training, coordinate initiative, track progress, identify best practices
- Leadership Teams—Provide strategy, goals and resources, identify and approve projects, report progress, provide review, recognition and feedback
- Champions—Project business and political leaders, remove barriers, review BB progress, promote initiative
- Black Belts—Learn methods and tools, complete strategic projects, train and promote Six Sigma
- Green Belts—Learn methods and tools, complete tactical projects, promote Six Sigma
- Master Black Belts—Technical Leaders, train, complete "mission critical" projects, and coach
- Functional Groups—Provide data, expertise, and personnel for BB and GB teams
- Finance—Determines and tracks financial impact of projects and Six Sigma initiative
- Human Resources—Creates and administers communications process, career development, and recognition and reward systems
- Information Technology—Provides process data collection and management systems

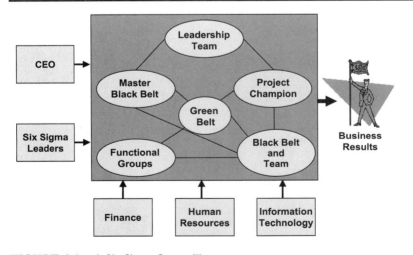

FIGURE 6-A   A Six Sigma Sweep Team

Playing Offense—Growing the Effort

While your efforts to hold project gains and the benefits of the overall Six Sigma system help sustain momentum, this is basically a defensive strategy. You don't want to lose the benefits you have worked so hard to obtain. As in all of life, however, the best defense is a good offense.

While you work on holding gains, you also want to take proactive steps to grow and expand the deployment into new areas. This is your offensive strategy. Continuing to drive Six Sigma into new areas will keep the initiative fresh, and prevent it from losing steam.

Some key areas that may prove particularly fruitful are extending Six Sigma to the entire organization, taking it to suppliers and customers, and using it to drive top line growth to complement the bottom line benefits already achieved.

EXPANDING SIX SIGMA THROUGHOUT THE ORGANIZATION

Most Six Sigma initiatives begin in manufacturing or operations because manufacturing typically has better measurement systems than other functions. These measurement systems enable you to get going on improvement projects faster, and the money to be made is more obvious and easier to quantify than in other parts of the organization. Nothing shows that Sigma works better than speed and results.

These two ingredients—speed and results—help you demonstrate the success of Six Sigma and allow the organization to see that "Six Sigma will work here!" In the process you gain experience in Six Sigma, build confidence that you can deploy it successfully, and produce bottom line results. Six Sigma is shown to more than pay for itself.

But there is much more to be gained. Many believe that more than half of an organization's improvement opportunity lies outside manufacturing or operations. This additional improvement is a huge opportunity the organization must capture. Organizations typically move Six Sigma in one of two directions after manufacturing/operations—to administrative and transactional processes, or to new product development (R&D). Some organizations may want to improve both areas at the same time. Most, however, move first to the administrative and transactional processes, such as accounts receivable, transportation and shipping, human resources, finance, and other areas listed in Table 6-5. The list on pages 26 and 27 shows additional examples of financial applications.

TABLE 6-5   Some Opportunities in Administrative and Transactional Processes

• Supply Chain	• Human Resources
• Logistics, distribution, warehousing	• Recruiting
• Inventory reduction	• Performance evaluation
• On-time delivery	• Retention of "hi-pots"
• eCommerce	(high potential employees)
• Web site development (eSell)	• Legal
• Fulfillment (eSell)	• Compliance
• Procurement (eBuy)	• Patent filing
• Digitization (eMake)	• Business Development
• Finance	• Mergers and acquisitions
• Accounts payable	• Due diligence
• Accounts receivable	• Marketing
• Manual account reconciliations	• Advertising & promotions
• Environmental	• Marketing research process
• Waste disposal	• Customer Service
• Emission control	• Response time
	• Issue resolution

Transactional and administrative areas have unique characteristics that are unlike those of manufacturing processes.

■ The culture is usually less scientific and people don't think in terms of processes, measurements, and data.

■ The work typically requires considerable human intervention, such as customer interaction, underwriting or approval decisions, and manual report generation. Human intervention is, of course, an additional source of variation and errors.

■ Transactional and administrative processes are often invisible, complex, and not well-defined or well-documented. Such characteristics make opportunities for improvement difficult to identify, and projects difficult to define.

■ Measurements are often nonexistent or ill-defined, resulting in the need to create measurement systems first, and then begin to collect the data.

- The process output is often intangible, and can be unique. For example, the actual output of a due diligence study is knowledge, possibly documented in the form of a report, and each due diligence study will be unique.

- Similar activities are often done in varying ways. Three people in three different company locations are unlikely to do the same job in the same manner.

The most important of these unique attributes is the frequent lack of process measurements. In our experience, four key measures of the performance of non-manufacturing processes come up repeatedly: accuracy, cycle time, cost, and customer satisfaction.

Accuracy is measured by correct financial figures, completeness of information, or freedom from data errors.

Cycle time is how long it takes to do something, such as pay an invoice.

By *cost* we mean the internal cost of process steps, as opposed to the price charged for services. In many cases, cost is largely determined by the accuracy and/or cycle time of the process; the longer it takes, and the more mistakes that have to be fixed, the higher the cost.

Customer satisfaction is the fourth common measurement. For a situation in which the key process outputs are intangible, such as customer service processes, customer satisfaction (often measured through surveys) will likely be the primary measure of success.

Fortunately, there are more similarities than differences between manufacturing and non-manufacturing processes. One of the key similarities is that both types of processes have "hidden factories," places where the defective product is sent to be reworked or scrapped (revised, corrected, or discarded in non-manufacturing terms). In reality, every process has a hidden factory (Figures 6-3 and 6-4). Find the hidden factory (performing manual account reconciliation, revising budgets until management will "accept" them, and making repeat sales calls to customers because there wasn't all the requested information on the first visit) and you have found one good place to look for opportunities to improve the process.

Use of Six Sigma in new product development (R&D) is commonly referred to as Design for Six Sigma (DFSS). This is another area in which you must expand the Six Sigma effort, since the entitlement of a process is often determined in the design phase. The goal is to improve the product development process so that the company can get new and better products to market quicker and at less cost to both the consumer and the company.

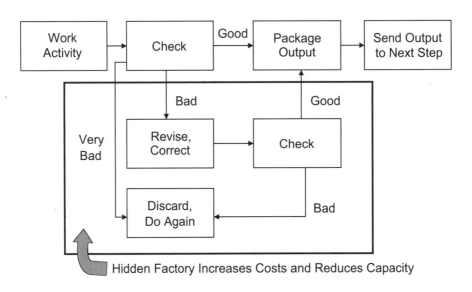

FIGURE 6-3   Every Process Has a Hidden Factory: A Non-Manufacturing View

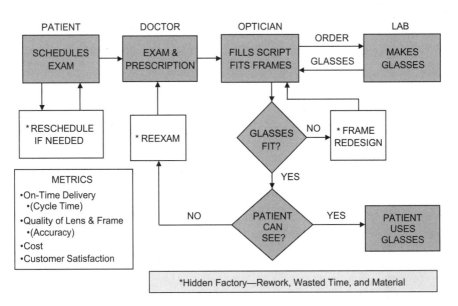

FIGURE 6-4   Every Process Has a Hidden Factory: Eyeglasses Fitting Process

The strategy is to build the Six Sigma methods and tools into the company's new-product development process (usually a stage-gate process).

Close interaction with marketing also greatly improves the development process, and therefore the new products and services that are ultimately produced. The payoff on DFSS projects usually has a longer time frame because of the time required to get a new product to market. The training is still project focused (no project, no training), and is done at both the Black Belt/MBB and Green Belt levels. More will be said about DFSS when top-line growth is discussed later in this chapter.

USING SIX SIGMA TO IMPROVE SUPPLIER PERFORMANCE

You will quickly learn that the average level and variability of quality and the cost of the materials from suppliers have a big effect on the quality and cost of products and services. It is not unusual for 40–60% of the final cost of a company's product to derive from the costs of materials purchased from suppliers. Since you cannot overlook such a high cost, or the effects of variation in materials on the performance of processes, you may wonder how to get suppliers to use Six Sigma to improve their performance.

You will have more credibility going to suppliers with a recommendation to use Six Sigma once you have used it in your organization and demonstrated that it works. For this reason supplier Six Sigma programs typically don't start until after the first or second year of a Six Sigma deployment.

The first step in getting suppliers to use Six Sigma is to determine how the quality and cost of supplier materials are affecting the performance of your organization. One way to accomplish this is to track supplier materials as they flow through your processes and determine the scrap, waste, downtime, and yield loss they cause. (You will also see that a large portion of the loss is due to your company's processes, thereby identifying additional opportunities for internal improvement.)

We *do not* recommend focusing improvement efforts on beating up suppliers, without a clear understanding of how their materials affect your process. This misguided step is popular because it requires no change or hard work on the part of your organization. A more effective method is to first focus Six Sigma on what you can control and, as you learn about root causes coming from materials, integrate suppliers into your improvement efforts.

This approach works in both manufacturing and non-manufacturing environments. For example, a newspaper company initiated a Six Sigma project to reduce errors in the paper. Such errors were generally found prior to publication, but finding and fixing them is an expensive form of rework. Data from the project ultimately revealed that the root causes of many errors were in the information obtained from external sources, such as wrong facts, wrong names, and wrong figures (see Hoerl and Snee [2002], Chapter 10). Armed with this information, the newspaper communicated to reporters and copy editors which information sources (suppliers) could be trusted and should be used. Other sources needed to initiate improvement efforts in order to be trusted and used.

Once you know the magnitude of the problems coming from suppliers, you can set an improvement goal for them to attain. A common goal is 5% reduction per year in price, adjusted for inflation. The intent is that the price reduction would be based on supplier improvement projects that reduced the supplier's costs. In this way, both the supplier and customer benefit financially. The price reduction goal may be mandatory, or suppliers that meet this price reduction goal may receive preferential treatment.

To the extent that these goals are based on actual data, and can be achieved via a win-win approach, communicating such expectations is not simply beating up suppliers. It may also be appropriate, when it makes business sense, to have unique improvement goals for different organizations or processes within a given supplier.

Next, you have to determine which suppliers you are going to approach with encouragement to use the Six Sigma approach. One way is to do a Pareto analysis of the key sources of costs, such as supplier-caused scrap, rework, and other losses. Focus on those materials and suppliers that are associated with the highest costs; the biggest problems usually represent the biggest opportunity. You may also wish to approach key suppliers with which you desire a long-term strategic relationship.

Companies have introduced suppliers to Six Sigma in a variety of ways. One way is to identify a few high-impact projects, and form customer-supplier teams to complete the projects using Six Sigma. If the supplier doesn't have Black Belts available to work on the project, then the customer supplies the Six Sigma expertise and any needed training. Tremendous progress is made when both the customer and the supplier have one or more Black Belts on the project team.

Another approach is for the company to make available supplier training programs that are partially funded by the customer and that make available both Champion and Black Belt training, at a minimum. An effective way to create such a program is to start with a few good projects and then use their success to expand the program. It is essential that the supplier's management be involved in the program. An executive workshop is a good way to help build this involvement, as it helps communicate what Six Sigma is and the benefits the supplier organization can expect to receive.

Clearly, careful planning is needed to have a successful Six Sigma supplier program. Any financial arrangements must be defined and agreed to up front so that the expectations of both parties are met. The goals and objectives have to be carefully thought out and clearly communicated.

Six Sigma must be positioned as a "how" rather than a "what." In other words, your purpose is not to have the supplier use Six Sigma. Your purpose is for suppliers to make tangible improvements that positively affect you and your organization, and Six Sigma is just a means to help you accomplish this objective. Six Sigma can be an effective methodology for achieving customer and supplier goals, once those goals have been clearly defined and communicated.

IMPROVING TOP-LINE GROWTH

A common question from those implementing Six Sigma is: "I can see how to use Six Sigma to reduce costs, but how can I use Six Sigma to increase revenues?" It often goes unnoticed that Six Sigma can grow the top line as well as improve the bottom line. In general, revenues are increased by:

- Getting new customers (find more)
- Getting current customers to buy more (get more)
- Regaining old customers who have left to do business with your competitors (keep more)

Fortunately, Six Sigma can be applied in many ways that directly tie to one or more of these revenue-increasing areas.

For example, consider the following specific approaches, with the principle revenue-increasing areas noted:

- Use DFSS to create new and better products (find, get, and keep more)
- Increase capacity (productivity) when the product line is sold out (find and get more)
- Improve product quality and price (find, get, and keep more)
- Improve the service processes that touch the customer such as delivery, billing, and customer service (get and keep more)
- Show customers how to benefit from Six Sigma (get more)
  - "At the customer, for the customer" Six Sigma projects
- Successfully complete strategic sales and marketing Six Sigma projects (find, get, and keep more)

Developing new and better products or services are obviously key means to growing the top line. DFSS is the Six Sigma approach to accomplishing this objective. We've seen that DFSS is typically started about one year after the initiation of the DMAIC methodology for improving existing processes, and you have gained confidence that Six Sigma will work in the company. Conceptually, you can consider product design a process and apply Six Sigma in a straightforward manner to improve it. In most cases, however, organizations wish to apply Six Sigma to the design of a specific new product or service. While it applies equally well here, Six Sigma requires a different roadmap more tailored to design. If a team applies the DMAIC roadmap to designing a new product, it will likely stumble in the measure phase, since there is no existing process on which to take measurements.

GE developed the DMADV roadmap, adopted by many others since then, to apply to design projects. The define stage is analogous to define in DMAIC, although typically more complicated, since you are designing a new product or service, not improving an existing process. In the DMADV measure phase, you determine the CTQ characteristics, and ensure that you have measurement capability, but you do not measure an existing process, unless the new design is an enhancement of a current design.

The analyze phase focuses on conceptual design, in which you use creative "out of the box" thinking to determine the most promising high-level design to satisfy your CTQs. For product designs, you may develop prototypes. The details of this design are completed in the design phase, where you make calculations to predict final design capability. If these calculations are not promising, the team must repeat the analyze phase and design phase to improve the design capability. In the verify phase you pilot the new design under realistic conditions to obtain real data verifying design capability.

For example, if you were designing a manufactured product, you would utilize a pilot run in a real manufacturing facility, using regular workers and raw materials for the verify phase. This contrasts with a prototype made under ideal conditions that might be used to prove the design concept in the analyze phase. If you are designing a web-based insurance application and underwriting system, you would utilize people with computer skills similar to your targeted market to access the system, and do so during normal business hours using standard platforms. In many cases you may go through a mini-DMAIC cycle to improve design flaws observed in the pilot. If there are major discrepancies in capability, you may have to loop back through the analyze phase and design phase again.

This approach to DFSS maintains the key technical elements of DMAIC:

- Disciplined approach
- Use of metrics throughout the process
- Use of analytical tools
- Emphasis on variation
- Data-based decision making

There are other ways to use Six Sigma to improve the top line besides DFSS. One way is to find situations in which a product is in a sold out condition today, or is forecast to be sold out in the near future. Here you can use Six Sigma in a traditional manner (DMAIC) to increase capacity (productivity). While Six Sigma is often thought of as primarily a quality improvement methodology, it applies equally well to improving productivity. When you increase capacity closer and closer to the theoretical maximum capacity (capacity entitlement), you have the opportunity to sell more to new or existing customers, resulting in top-line growth. When you have reached theoretical maximum capacity, you will likely need DFSS projects or capital expenditures to further increase output.

Often customers will buy more if the quality of your product is improved, or you are able to reduce price. In these situations you can use Six Sigma to improve your quality and decrease your internal costs. Part of the cost savings can be passed on to the customer if you desire, thereby increasing volume without having to sacrifice margin. You may also be able to obtain new customers because of the improved quality and decreased price. Better yet, you may regain some customers that you lost because of poor quality or high price in the past.

In many instances the key problem is a service issue, such as customer response time or CRT—the time between placing an order and receiving the product or service. Resolving service issues can require you to analyze the whole process: order, manufacture, delivery, bill, and return. The root cause of the problem may be in some or all of these steps.

A point often missed is that manufacturing is only one step in the process of serving the customer. We know of one instance in which the customer response time for a piece of heavy equipment was 12 months. A look at the subprocess cycle times revealed that the physical manufacture took only three months, so reducing manufacturing time to just a few days still left 75% of the cycle time untouched. Clearly you will sometimes have to move outside manufacturing to obtain significant reductions in total cycle time.

Variation in customer response time is as important as, if not more important than, the average level of CRT. For example, if a customer receives two orders, one 30 days early and one 30 days late, the average CRT is perfect, but neither order was on time!

In some instances early orders are worse than late ones, because the customer is not prepared to handle the early delivery and may tell the shipper to return the order to the vendor. GE, noting this, focused on reducing variation as a way of creating greater customer satisfaction (see the "Message to the Shareholders" in the 1998 GE Annual Report).

The opportunity to increase revenues by improving quality and/or service requires input from the customer. (Price reduction is universally appreciated!) You need to know those key problems that, if fixed, would result in the customer buying more. Asking the customer, "What changes can I make in my products or services that would allow you to buy more from me?" is not without risk. It can lead the customer to expect that any improvements requested will be made. Of course, you can also ask noncustomers or previous customers the same question to try to win their business as well.

Another way to use Six Sigma to grow the top line is to introduce your customers to Six Sigma, and show them how Six Sigma can help them improve. The theory is that customers with a better bottom line will be happier customers with a closer working relationship with you, and will repay you by buying more products and services from you.

Helping your customers solve their problems as a method for developing better business relationships is not new, and has been used for many years by many different companies. What is new is the use of Six Sigma in working with customers in this way.

GE is now using Six Sigma as the model for this type of relationship, and is having its Black Belts work with customers on solving customer problems. GE calls the program "Six Sigma at the Customer for the Customer."

Welch (2001) reports that in 2000 GE helped 50 GE Aircraft Engine customers complete 1,500 projects that saved $230 million. Also in 2000, a total of 1,000 projects were completed for GE Medical Systems customers returning $100 million to the customers' bottom lines. Many of these projects were done primarily by GE Black Belts as at the customer, for the customer projects.

Six Sigma can be applied to strategic sales and marketing processes. DMAIC projects in these areas will primarily improve top-line growth, but they may have secondary benefits for cost savings as well. Such projects are generally initiated as part of the effort to spread Six Sigma across the organization, as discussed earlier. Potential applications include:

- Improving the impact of advertising (more bang for the buck)
- Improving marketing research studies, which drive DFSS projects
- Increasing sales force effectiveness

With the exception of improving capacity, all the approaches discussed require close working relationships with customers. This aspect of using Six Sigma is somewhat different from the uses of Six Sigma in cost reduction projects. Of course all Six Sigma projects have a link to customers in one way or another; some links are just stronger than others.

Summary

Sustaining momentum and growing occurs between the completion of all the training and projects identified in the original deployment plan and the completion of deployment across the organization, when you are ready to make the transition from Six Sigma as an initiative to Six Sigma as the normal way you work.

This phase may last several years. It consists of both a defensive strategy (sustaining momentum) and an offensive strategy (growing the effort). Keys to the defensive strategy are taking proactive steps to hold the gains from completed projects, and also hold the gains from the overall Six Sigma initiative.

Implementing the remaining infrastructure elements is the critical success factor in this defensive strategy. These elements include:

- Process and financial audits verifying the benefits
- Six Sigma system reviews
- A comprehensive training system (vs. a mass training event)
- A formal Six Sigma organizational structure

The offensive strategy consists of expanding the effort across the organization, involving strategic suppliers and customers, and using Six Sigma to grow the top line. Utilizing a DFSS approach to new product and service design is a critical success factor, as it influences each of these elements of the offensive strategy. Using the philosophy that the best defense is a good offense, you want to make sure you are aggressively deploying Six Sigma in new areas to ensure that you maintain momentum, and reach the entire organization and all its activities. Once Six Sigma has become the modus operandi across the organization, you will be well positioned to make the transition to the way you work, to ensure Six Sigma benefits are permanent.

References

Automotive Industry Action Group. (1990). *Measurement Systems Analysis Reference Manual.* Available from AIAG, Suite 200, 26200 Lahser Road, Southfield, MI 48034 (313-358-3570).

Automotive Industry Action Group. (1994). *Advanced Product Quality Planning and Control Plan.* Available from AIAG, Suite 200, 26200 Lahser Road, Southfield, MI 48034 (313-358-3570).

Automotive Industry Action Group. (1995a). *Statistical Process Control Reference Manual,* 2nd ed. Available from AIAG, Suite 200, 26200 Lahser Road, Southfield, MI 48034 (313-358-3570).

Automotive Industry Action Group. (1995b). *Potential Failure Mode and Effects Analysis Reference Manual,* 2nd ed. Available from AIAG, Suite 200, 26200 Lahser Road, Southfield, MI 48034 (313-358-3570).

Box, G. E. P., W. G. Hunter, and J. S. Hunter. (1978). *Statistics for Experimenters.* John Wiley and Sons, Inc., New York, NY.

Box, G. E. P., G. M. Jenkins, and G. Reinsel. (1994). *Time Series Analysis: Forecasting and Control,* rev. ed. Holden Day, San Francisco.

Cohen, L. (1995). *Quality Function Deployment: How to Make QFD Work for You.* Addison-Wesley, Reading, MA.

Cornell, J. A. (1990). *Experiments With Mixtures: Designs, Models, and the Analysis of Mixture Data,* 2nd ed. John Wiley and Sons, New York.

Draper, N. R., and H. Smith. (1998). *Applied Regression Analysis,* 3rd ed. John Wiley and Sons, New York.

English, Bill. (2001). "Implementing Six Sigma—The Iomega Story." Presented at the Conference on Six Sigma in the Pharmaceutical Industry, Philadelphia, PA, November 27-28, 2001.

Hoerl, R. W. (2001). "Six Sigma Black Belts—What Do They Need to Know? (With Discussion)." *J. Quality Technology*, Vol. 33, No. 4, 391-435.

Hoerl, R. W., and R. D. Snee. (2002). *Statistical Thinking: Improving Business Performance*. Duxbury Press/Thomson Learning, San Jose, CA.

General Electric Company. (1998). Annual Report, General Electric Company, Fairfield, CT.

Meeker, W. Q., and L. A. Escobar. (1998). *Statistical Methods for Reliability Data*. John Wiley and Sons, New York, NY.

Montgomery, D. C. (2001). *Statistical Quality Control*, 3rd ed. John Wiley and Sons, New York, NY.

Montgomery, D. C. (2000). *The Design and Analysis of Experiments*, rev. ed. John Wiley and Sons, New York, NY.

Montgomery, D. C., E. A. Peck, and G. Vining. (2001). *Introduction to Linear Regression Analysis*. John Wiley and Sons, New York, NY.

Myers, R. H., and D. C. Montgomery. (1995). *Response Surface Methodology*, Wiley-Interscience, New York, NY.

Snee, R. D. (1995). "Listening to the Voice of the Employee." *Quality Progress*, January 1995, 91-95.

Walpole, R. E., and R. H Myers. (1993). *Probability and Statistics for Engineers and Scientists*, 5th ed., Prentice Hall, Englewood Cliffs, NJ.

Welch, J. (2001). *Jack, Straight From the Gut*. Warner Business Books, New York, NY.

Wheeler, D. J., and D. Chambers. (1992). *Understanding Statistical Process Control*, 2nd ed. SPC Press, Knoxville, TN.

Wheeler, D. J., and R. W. Lyday. (1989). *Evaluating the Measurement Process*, 2nd ed. SPC Press, Knoxville, TN.

7

THE WAY WE WORK

"With Six Sigma permeating much of what we do, it
will be unthinkable to hire, promote, or tolerate those
who cannot, or will not, commit to this way of working."

—Jack Welch, former CEO, General Electric

In Chapters 5 and 6 we discussed managing the Six Sigma initiative, sustaining the gains, and expanding the initiative to all parts of the enterprise, including suppliers and customers, in order to make the organization perform better. A central theme was the need to integrate Six Sigma activities with existing management processes and procedures.

In this chapter we take Six Sigma one step further and discuss how to integrate it into daily work. The changes an organization makes in its work as a result of Six Sigma comprise its control plan for the overall initiative and ensures that it maintains the gains it has achieved. The desired end game is that Six Sigma becomes such an integral part of the way the organization manages that there is no longer a need for a formal Six Sigma initiative.

The recognition that Six Sigma has been institutionalized into your culture is not based on a Gantt chart or predetermined deadline. Rather, you will know that Six Sigma is an integral part of the way you do your work when you see the key elements of Six Sigma being used on a daily basis. Some examples include:

- Continuously working to find better ways of doing things
- Recognizing the importance of the bottom line and finding ways to improve it
- Thinking of everything you do as a process
- Recognizing the ubiquitous nature of variation and its effects on your work
- Working to reduce variation
- Using data to guide your decisions
- Using Six Sigma tools to make your processes more effective and productive

These key elements will be clearer as we discuss ways of making Six Sigma part of daily work processes.

In our experience, the most effective ways to make Six Sigma a part of daily work include integrating Six Sigma concepts, methods, and tools with process management systems (for both your operational and managerial processes), creating and managing an overall improvement system that guides and integrates all types of organizational improvement, and integrating Six Sigma with other strategic initiatives such as ISO 9000, the Malcolm Baldrige Award criteria, and Lean manufacturing. We address each of these methods in turn, and conclude by discussing the long–term impact that Six Sigma should have on your organization.

Integrating Six Sigma With Process Management Systems

By process management systems we mean the set of procedures, methods, requirements, operating manuals, and so on that you use to manage a given work process. The work process itself may be an operational one, such as an assembly line, or a managerial one, such as the budgeting process. Every process has a process management system, although in many cases it is ad-hoc, undocumented, inconsistent, and totally ineffective. Effective work processes almost always have a good process management system, which helps explain why the process is effective. The ISO 9000 standards are one means of documenting a process management system.

Clearly, if you are able to integrate Six Sigma concepts and methods into formal, documented process management systems, Six Sigma will be ingrained into the way you work. It will no longer be a separate initiative. If you already have documented process management systems, you simply need to appropriately integrate the Six Sigma approach into them. If your process management system is not documented or consistently followed, then you will first have to develop a process management system based on Six Sigma, and then formally implement and document it.

The process management system should be a living document, which accurately depicts what people actually do, and is periodically reviewed and updated as better methods of process management are found. Someone should be accountable for the system, and senior management should review the use and results of the system on a regular basis. Obviously, there are strong similarities between Six Sigma and the use of good process management systems.

Process Control and Improvement

Process management is often broken into two main components: process control and process improvement. Process control makes adjustments to the process, often in real time, in order to maintain the performance level. It also fixes problems that have caused deterioration in performance, and returns the process to standard conditions. Process improvement makes fundamental changes to the process itself, or the way it is operated, in order to achieve higher levels of performance. For example, most DMAIC Six Sigma projects focus on process improvement rather than process control.

Most companies are trying to achieve new levels of performance with Six Sigma, rather than getting back to normal after a problem. This is not to diminish the importance of process control. Process improvement works best on a solid platform of good process control, which is required to sustain the gains of the improvement projects.

There are many ways to integrate Six Sigma into process management systems and processes. A few guiding principles are helpful:

- Focus on key processes

- Routinely monitor key processes using data generated by the process

■ Have people at various levels in the organization routinely analyze process data using relevant tools and take appropriate actions

■ Utilize two types of actions: controlling (adjusting) the process to maintain performance; and making improvements to the process to achieve even higher performance

Figure 7-1 (Snee [1999a]) depicts a high-level schematic of a typical process management system based on these principles. The organization collects data from the process on a routine basis. Various levels of management review these data on a regular basis to decide what process actions should be taken. Typical review groups for high-throughput environments (manufacturing, billing, logistics, etc.) are as follows:

Review Team	**Review Timing**
Process Operators	Continuously and Daily
Process Managers and Staff	Weekly
Site Manager and Staff	Monthly
Business Manager and Staff	Quarterly

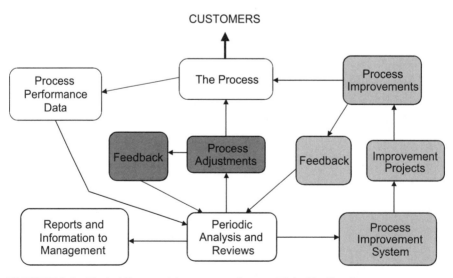

FIGURE 7-1 Typical Process Management System. Light Shading Represents Improvement, Dark Shading Represents Control

Process operators, such as assembly line workers, accountants, and salespeople review the process performance data continuously to look for out-of-control situations, and review daily summaries to detect other sources of problems. Analysis tools often present the data in a statistical control chart format, or other graphical presentations.

The process control plan, developed in the control phase of the Six Sigma improvement project, documents for the operators what to look for, what actions to take, and whom to inform when additional assistance is needed. The control plan typically details the process adjustments needed to bring the outputs back to the desired target and range. The Six Sigma tools used by the operators for troubleshooting typically include process maps, control charts, histograms, and Pareto charts. The role of Six Sigma tools is discussed in more detail in Chapter 8.

Examples of such process adjustments are changing the pressure setting on a piece of stamping equipment to eliminate bad stamps, calling in additional accountants to close the books on time, or having a salesperson work overtime to meet a sales quota. However, such efforts are primarily aimed at sustaining current performance levels, rather than improving to new levels. Improvement to new performance levels often requires the involvement of additional people with specialized skills, such as engineers in manufacturing, or experienced underwriters in insurance. True improvement is usually made by project teams that include process operators, technical specialists, and perhaps someone trained in improvement methodologies if needed.

Note that in Figure 7-1 the reviews of the data also feed the process improvement system. This process improvement system has similarities to the project selection system in Six Sigma: the organization identifies good improvement opportunities, identifies specific projects, makes improvements, and provides feedback on how the overall system is working so that it can be improved. Utilizing Six Sigma projects to make these improvements as part of the process management system will ensure that you continue to receive benefits from Six Sigma long into the future. The process management infrastructure, which has hopefully existed all along, gradually replaces the Six Sigma infrastructure. Fortunately, once it is properly set up, the process management infrastructure should be smaller since you are no longer ramping up a new initiative.

Process Management Systems for Operational Processes

By operational processes we mean those processes that are directly related to providing products and services to customers, as opposed to the processes that manage, organize, or strategically direct the organization. Examples in a manufacturing environment include buying materials, manufacturing a product, distributing finished goods, marketing, and selling.

Obviously, there are many other operational processes in manufacturing, and somewhat different ones in businesses such as banking, insurance, retail sales, and so on. Serving customers who come into a branch bank, processing insurance applications, and ringing up charges for purchases at a store are also examples of operational processes.

Consider the following hypothetical manufacturing scenario. Operators on the production floor are reviewing data continuously, and making process adjustments based on it. As new operators come in to begin their shift, they review summary data and graphs of how the process has been running, and may decide to address a problem that appears to have occurred. Each week, typically at 8 a.m. Monday, the process manager and staff will review the data for last week's performance, including: process adjustments made; the effects of those process adjustments; current level of process performance; additional process adjustments needed; and potential process improvement needs. The focus of this meeting is on making process adjustments to keep the process on target with acceptable levels of variation, and staying on the look out for problems that need to be addressed by improvement projects.

Once a month the site manager and staff meet to review the performance of the processes under their guidance and assess the need for process improvements. The agenda for this meeting includes review of process performance, feedback on process improvements put in place since the last meeting, and assessment of the need for additional Black Belt and Green Belt improvement projects, including potential redesign (DFSS).

This is the group that manages the improvement of the process, particularly the Green Belt projects and the identification of the Black Belt projects that will be championed at the business unit level. The distinction between Green Belt and Black Belt projects recognizes that local managers can generally assign whatever Green Belt projects they desire, but depending on the organizational structure, they may require business unit approval or resources for Black Belt projects.

Once a quarter the manager of the overall business unit and staff review the key processes in the unit. The focus is on performance versus process and financial goals, impact of Black Belt and Green Belt improvement projects, and assessment of the need for additional Black Belt projects, with special emphasis on potential process redesign (DFSS). These reviews can be part of the Six Sigma quarterly review that focuses on the performance of the overall Six Sigma system for the business unit, as discussed in Chapter 6.

A process management system, such as that outlined, integrates process control and process improvement into the daily activities that organizations perform to serve their customers and stakeholders. Six Sigma concepts, methods, and tools are an integral part of the system. Even though formal Six Sigma projects are generally done as part of the process improvement aspect of the system, Six Sigma concepts and tools should be integral to the process control efforts of the operators. As we have noted, the key to success of such a system is regular management reviews. In this approach the reviews are built into the system.

Let's look at two real examples of Six Sigma operational process management systems.

A major U.S. corporation used a process management system similar to that described earlier to manage and improve its billing process. It was taking 17 days to get the bills out compared to the process goal of eight. Customers were very unhappy. Employees were unhappy and stressed because of Herculean efforts required by some to get the bills out. At this point, the corporation instigated a system of process management and data collection to monitor the overall cycle time and critical subprocess cycle times. Each day at 10 a.m. the team of process workers (operators) met and analyzed the process cycle times to address problems. The process manager and his staff met at 11 a.m. and analyzed the same data to address managerial issues. This frequent review by the process manager and his staff was needed because of the critical importance of this process.

At the end of the monthly billing cycle management reviewed the process performance and effects of process improvements, identifying additional improvement projects as needed. In six months, as a result of this system of data collection, management review and systematic improvement, the monthly cycle time was reduced to the target of eight days, customer and employee satisfaction increased, and there was a bottom line saving of $4 million. Interestingly, the 10 a.m. review by process workers had been in place for some time but there had been minimal improvement in process performance. The daily reviews by the process managers, as well as reviews at the end of the billing cycle, led to the needed improvements. In general, both process control and process improvement are needed to see lasting results. See Chapter 1 of Hoerl and Snee (2002) for additional details on this case.

In another situation we were involved in, a major service corporation was plagued by low service ratings that had received much unwanted attention by the media. The corporation had gone through a major reorganization and downsizing and had taken its eye off the goal—providing service to its customers. The president of the company had grown up in the business and knew the operational processes well. He put an extensive process monitoring system in place, and led weekly reviews of process performance at 7 a.m. on Fridays by conference call. The corporation identified problems and took actions in each meeting. The president held managers accountable, often in public, for the improvement needed on their watch.

This was not an easy process; being reviewed in front of your peers is not fun. But it worked, and after a year the service levels rose significantly. Data-based process control and improvement can be integrated into daily work and can produce significant bottom line impact.

Process Management Systems for Managerial Processes

Six Sigma can also be integrated with managerial processes, such as goal setting, budgeting, planning, employee selection, training and development, reporting, project management, performance management, communication, and recognition and rewards. Managerial systems and processes were defined and discussed in more detail at the beginning of Chapter 5. The approach for managerial processes is essentially the same as for operational processes, that is, integration of Six Sigma concepts, methods, and tools with the process management systems for these managerial processes. The key steps are:

1. Identify a key managerial process
2. Select a set of performance measurements
3. Collect data on the process and review them at appropriate levels of management
4. Take action to make process adjustments
5. Make fundamental improvements to the process by defining and completing Black Belt and Green Belt projects

In the ongoing effort to collect the process data, analyze the data, and take action based on the Black Belt and Green Belt projects, Six Sigma concepts, methods, and tools become part of your daily work.

There are some unique challenges in deploying process management systems for managerial processes, so the integration of Six Sigma is not easy, but is certainly doable. Perhaps the most challenging aspect is selecting the right process metrics. As we noted in Chapter 4, the key metrics for non-manufacturing processes are typically accuracy (correctness, completeness, errors, defects, and so on), cycle time, cost, and customer satisfaction. However, many managerial processes do not have existing measurement systems that provide useful data for improvement. For example, few companies measure and analyze metrics on the effectiveness of their budgeting processes. An example of a set of metrics used to measure the performance of a Six Sigma training process is shown in Table 7-1 (Snee [2001]). As in any important work activity, leadership, including regular reviews by various levels of management, is the key success factor.

Another challenge in many managerial processes is that the data are often sparse. One company wished to improve its annual college campus recruiting process. However, once a Green Belt got into the project she realized that the most important data for improvement purposes were only generated once a year, after each wave of campus recruiting!

A less obvious challenge is that there will sometimes be resistance to the introduction of process management systems for managerial processes, because some people will view them as threatening. As noted in Chapter 5, when we introduce formal metrics and reviews to manage these processes, the process owners, such as HR, Finance, IT, and so on, may feel that Big Brother is watching them, or that they are going to be micromanaged. As long as the emphasis is on improving the process, however, and not on assigning blame, this concern will be quickly seen to be groundless.

Stoner and Werner (1994) present an example of using Six Sigma in the management and improvement of a managerial process. The process of interest is Motorola's internal financial audit process. The first step, and a major breakthrough in thinking, was to view each internal audit not as an event, but as a process with five key steps:

1. Schedule the audit
2. Plan the audit
3. Perform the audit
4. Report the results
5. Perform the post audit check

The performance measurements used were internal errors, cycle time required to complete the audit, customer feedback on the audit, and

TABLE 7-1   Six Sigma Training Metrics

- Participants Like the Training Experience
  - Survey of participant evaluations of content, exercises, delivery, materials, instructors, facilities, food, etc.
  - Participant evaluation of each day—What went well? What needs to be done differently?
- Participants Learn the Methodology
  - Score on weekly quiz on tools used
  - Written exam at the end of the training as part of the certification requirements
- Participants Use the Methodology
  - Number of tools used per project
  - Percent of tools used appropriately
  - Project completion cycle time
  - Projects completed per training session (%)
  - Number of persons certified as BB
  - Other tools used for success
  - Time devoted by BB to project work
  - Number of meetings per month between Champions and BBs
- Participants Get Results
  - Project results, for individual projects and for business and functional groups
  - Improvement in key process metrics
  - Improvement in bottom line results ($$)

---

cost in terms of person-hours to do the audit. Additional audit process measures included the time and cost for the audit of the corporate books by an external auditor. Accuracy of the external audit was the responsibility of the external auditor, and to maintain independence, Motorola could not be involved in evaluating accuracy.

Impressive results were obtained through this approach. Between 1988 and 1991 Motorola reduced internal errors from 10,000 ppm to 20 ppm (parts, or errors, per million opportunities). The company reduced report cycle time from 51 days to five days. The quality of the customer feedback report was 21 times better in two years. Audit person-hours dropped from 24,000 hours in 1983 to 12,000 hours in 1991, while annual sales increased from $4.8 billion to $11.3 billion during the same time period.

Clearly higher quality work was being done in less time and at less cost. But there is more. The external audit cycle time dropped by 50 percent due to better internal audit information, producing $1.8 million cost avoidance per year. Unfortunately, many companies cannot achieve this same level of improvement because they still view internal audit as an event rather than a process that can be managed and improved.

Accounting scandals at major corporations such as Enron and WorldCom have only reinforced the need to apply improvement methodologies like Six Sigma to auditing.

Six Sigma tools can also be used to improve the quality of managerial decisions. One clearly beneficial action is to include relevant data to support decisions and guide the decision making process. In the absence of data, everyone is an expert and whoever yells the loudest wins.

Another improvement is to create a flow chart of the project plan to implement the decision and analyze it to ensure that the plan will work. The flowchart also helps to communicate the plan to the organization ("a picture is worth 1000 words"). A simple Gantt chart is one example of such a managerial flow chart, and is often used when the steps are to be implemented concurrently rather than consecutively.

Another effective use of Six Sigma tools is doing a failure modes and effects analysis (FMEA) of key decisions to identify ways in which the decision or its implementation might fail. Once the potential failure modes are identified, contingency plans can be put into place to prevent or mitigate them. It is also appropriate to create and monitor one or more key metrics to assess the effectiveness of the decision (to guide improvement, not to second-guess the decision). These measurements should be part of a control plan to ensure that management decisions are implemented properly.

The cause and effect matrix used by the Black Belts and Green Belts is a form of prioritization matrix (Brassard [1989]). We have seen the cause and effect matrix used to rank job candidates (rows of the matrix) according to job criteria (columns of the matrix). Another use is the ranking of the effects of various corporate initiatives (matrix rows) on the core strategies of the organization (matrix columns).

The way to increase the use of these tools in the daily work of the organization is to formalize it as part of the hiring process and the strategic and annual planning processes. People will use the Six Sigma tools in their work when they are encouraged to do so through the use of best practices, and when they see that the tools work.

Six Sigma organizations can apply the concepts underlying experimental design (Box, Hunter, and Hunter [1978]) to the managerial decision-making process by considering each decision as an experiment. Managers begin with a conjecture or theory as to why something needs to be changed. Next, they identify the change, plan the change, and implement it. Thus they have planned and implemented the experiment. The management decision is an experiment because managers don't know for sure that it will work. They next collect and analyze data on the results of the management change to assess its effectiveness. Based on the results, management may alter their approach and even decide to make another change. Thus they have a new theory or conjecture and run another experiment producing another cycle of experimentation (management decision and change). This thought process increases use of the scientific method and data to guide and support the management decision-making process.

In summary, deploying process management systems for managerial processes presents unique challenges. However, as shown by Motorola and other companies, the same levels of improvement is possible with these processes as with operational processes. Once organizations have implemented good process management systems, complete with metrics and measurement systems, integrating Six Sigma methods and tools is straightforward and further ingrains Six Sigma into the organization's culture, that is, into the way it works.

Creating an Overall Organizational Improvement System

As you progress in your Six Sigma deployment you will see that other improvement activities compete for resources and management attention, such as capital improvements. Your long-term goal should be to combine all your improvement initiatives into an overall improvement system, make Six Sigma an integral part of this system, and create the supporting management systems required to sustain it. This is the process improvement system indicated in Figure 7-1 on page 164; it will make improvement a routine managerial process just like any other, such as the annual budgeting process, the internal audit process, and the recruiting process.

Some guiding principles for an overall improvement system incorporating Six Sigma are:

- Improvement and growth occur project-by-project

- A project is a problem scheduled for solution

- Projects come from many different sources and should be managed by a common system

- Projects should be linked to the strategic needs and priorities of the organization

- Continual review, assessment, and evaluation of the combined list of projects will keep it up to date

- Effective project management skills are needed for success

- A joint focus on both control and improvement is essential; process performance deteriorates after improvement if there is insufficient focus on control

The organization's improvement portfolio will generally include a mixture of projects in three main categories:

- Projects with known solutions, such as capital projects (repairing the roof, paving the parking lot, building a new facility)

- Six Sigma projects where the problem has no known solution

- Other improvement initiatives, such as ISO 9000, digitization, or a new performance management system

An organization's annual improvement plan should be a blend of these three types of initiatives, and include projects related to such diverse areas as productivity improvement, cash generation, revenue growth, and organization learning and improvement. Note that Six Sigma does not address all the improvement needs of the organization, although it is a critical component of the improvement system.

Table 7-2 shows an example of an overall improvement plan. There are 12 projects shown in this example—seven Six Sigma, three capital, and two others. Table 7-2 is shown for illustrative purposes; actual plans typically contain many more than 12 projects. Putting all improvement projects in a single list aids the budgeting process, and focuses the organization on what needs to be done, given the available resources. The list will also raise necessary questions regarding capital projects and whether there are sufficient data to justify each.

In some cases planners charter a Six Sigma project to assess whether the solution proposed by the capital project is in fact the best solution, or whether the same level of improvement can be obtained without significant capital. For example, in the case of capacity improvement projects, planners want to make sure the process is at entitlement before they spend capital to upgrade it. Six Sigma projects can also result in capital expenditures. Our experience is that such capital projects are approved more quickly because of the data provided by the Six Sigma improvement process.

TABLE 7-2   Sample Projects for Annual Improvement Plan

Project	Category
• Increase Capacity of Process Z	Six Sigma
• Relocate Milling Process	Capital
• Secure Environmental Permits	Other
• Upgrade DCS Software	Other
• Automate Packaging Line	Capital
• Increase Yield of Process XX	Six Sigma
• Reduce Downtime of Mixer M	Six Sigma
• Reduce Manufacturing Cost of Product P	Six Sigma
• Improve Steam Trap Performance	Six Sigma
• Install New Pump on Line K	Capital
• Reduce Plant B Reactor Cycle Time	Six Sigma
• Reduce the Impurity of Product 741	Six Sigma

Integration of Six Sigma With Other Strategic Initiatives

Over the past 10-15 years many companies have implemented an ISO 9000 quality management system, used the Baldrige Criteria for Performance Excellence (Baldrige National Quality Program [2002]) to assess and improve the performance of their organization, or adopted lean manufacturing concepts. The popularity of these and other strategic initiatives raises the question: "How does Six Sigma fit with ISO 9000 (or Baldrige, Lean, etc.)?" The short answer is that there is a very good fit between Six Sigma and modern quality management systems, as shown in Figure 7-2 (Snee [1999b]). We will discuss Lean manufacturing later in this chapter.

Each quality initiative in Figure 7-2 adds something different to an organization's management system. The key to their smooth integration is the recognition that all three (ISO, Baldrige, Six Sigma) are process-focused, data-based, and management led. We have found anecdotal evidence that organizations working aggressively on the Baldrige criteria, becoming ISO certified, or practicing lean manufacturing principles, are able to implement Six Sigma faster and more effectively than organizations

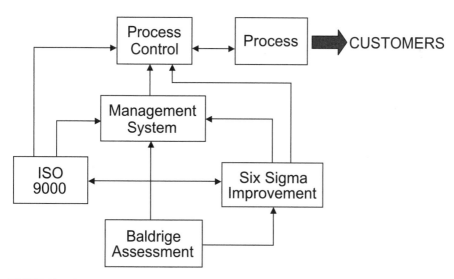

FIGURE 7-2   Integration of Quality Systems

new to formal process management and improvement systems. We next discuss the linkages between Six Sigma and these other strategic initiatives.

Six Sigma and ISO 9000

ISO 9000 is widely used by many different companies (ISO 9000 Standards, 2000). Many customers, particularly in the European Community, require ISO certification as a condition of doing business. Six Sigma supports ISO 9000 and helps an organization satisfy the ISO 9000 requirements. Further, ISO 9000 is an excellent vehicle for documenting and maintaining the process management systems involving Six Sigma. In other words, ISO 9000 can help make Six Sigma the way you work. Keep in mind from the outset that ISO 9000 and Six Sigma serve two different purposes. ISO 9000 is a quality management system, while Six Sigma is a strategy and methodology for business performance improvement. Both purposes are important and required.

ISO 9000 requires that you have a continuous improvement process in place (see Figure 7-3), but doesn't tell you what the process should look like. Six Sigma can provide the needed improvement process. ISO 9000-2000 requires that you measure (M), analyze (A), and improve (I). MAI are 3 phases of the Six Sigma DMAIC process improvement methodology. ISO 9000 helps create the process mindset that is required for Six Sigma to be successful. Both ISO 9000 and Six Sigma contribute to improving business performance. When expanded to working with suppliers, Six Sigma also supports each of the ISO 9000-2000 quality management principles:

- Customer focus
- Leadership
- Involvement of people
- Process approach
- System approach to management
- Continual improvement
- Factual approach to decision making
- Mutually beneficial supplier relationships

Implementing Six Sigma partially fulfills many of the elements required by ISO 9000-2000 in the following key areas: quality management system; management responsibility; resource management; product realization; and measurement, analysis, and improvement.

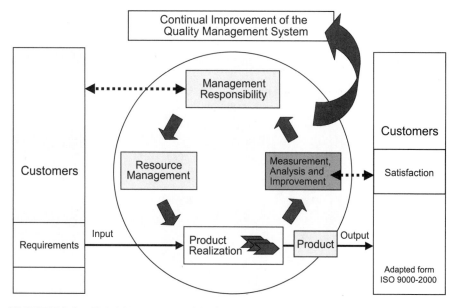

FIGURE 7-3   ISO 9000-2000 Model of a Process-Based Quality Management System

These five areas are the heart of the ISO 9000-2000 standard. Table 7-3 provides details on some of the specific ways Six Sigma supports the ISO 9000-2000 Standard. ISO can also provide valuable support to the Six Sigma initiative. ISO audits can be expanded to include monitoring the performance of processes improved via Six Sigma, and monitoring the use of the Six Sigma process control plans. In short, use Six Sigma to change the way you work, and use ISO audits to check on whether the changes are still in use and effective.

TABLE 7-3   Ways That Six Sigma Supports ISO 9000-2000

Quality Management System
- Six Sigma:
  - Identifies processes and their interrelationships
  - Develops control plans to monitor and control processes
  - Provides resources (people, hardware and software) to measure, improve and sustain processes
  - Provides a method for continual improvement
  - Documents how processes should be operated in process control plans
  - Maintains records of process improvement projects in project data bases and project tracking systems

continued on next page

TABLE 7-3   Ways That Six Sigma Supports ISO 9000-2000   *(continued)*

Management Responsibility
- Management commitment demonstrated by:
  - Annual Six Sigma plans
  - Weekly, monthly and quarterly Six Sigma reviews
  - Providing Champion, Black Belt, and Green Belt resources
  - Providing training resources
  - Communication of purpose and progress using a variety of media

Resource Management
- Six Sigma resource management includes:
  - Training of Executives, Champions, Black Belts, Green Belts, and others as needed
  - Certification of Master Black Belts (MBBs), Black Belts, and Green Belts
  - Maintaining focus by identifying and monitoring of critical few process inputs
  - Work environment improvement by identifying critical noise variables via multi-vari studies

Product Realization
- Planning—annual Six Sigma improvement plan
- Review of customer requirements through cause and effect and process capability studies
- Product and process design and development using Design for Six Sigma (DFSS) techniques
- Improvement of purchased materials through supply chain Six Sigma studies and encouraging suppliers to use Six Sigma
- Creation and use of process control plans which include process maps, targets, specs, measurement methods, measurement system performance data, sampling methods, reaction plans, etc.

Measurement, Analysis and Improvement
- Six Sigma process improvement strategy, and its roadmap and tools provide the methods and tools to measure, analyze and improve processes
  - Improvement phases—define, measure, analyze, improve, and control
  - Key tools–maps, metrics, cause and effect analysis, measurement system analysis, capability studies, failure modes and effects analysis, multi-vari studies, design of experiments, statistical process control, and control plans

Six Sigma and the Malcolm Baldrige Criteria

The Baldrige criteria for performance excellence form a widely used tool for improving corporate performance, as well as identifying outstanding companies through the Baldrige National Quality Program (2002) and its annual awards. The Baldrige criteria have also been used in whole or in part to establish various state awards for performance excellence. Table 7-4 summarizes how Six Sigma supports the core concepts and values of Baldrige. A quick review of this list leads us to conclude that Six Sigma supports each of the core values and concepts very nicely.

Baldrige Criteria have seven categories of performance excellence:

1. Leadership
2. Strategic planning
3. Customer focus
4. Information and analysis
5. HR focus
6. Process management
7. Business results

You can easily see that Six Sigma supports all the categories of the Baldrige criteria. In addition, the use of Six Sigma can significantly enhance the performance of the organization so that it will better satisfy the Baldrige criteria.

Many companies use the Baldrige Criteria as a means to identify their best opportunities for improvement. Leadership typically charters an assessment team to perform an organizational assessment; identify, categorize, and prioritize the opportunities; and assign them to improvement teams for solution. These improvement teams generally have annual goals, and report on progress monthly to leadership.

Sometimes leadership provides organizational incentive compensation to support the improvement process. Some common problems that these improvement teams encounter include projects with too broad a scope, no measurements, poor project management processes, and infrequent management reviews. The need to address these problems provides an opportunity to further enhance the synergy between Baldrige and Six Sigma.

TABLE 7-4 Ways That Six Sigma Supports the Baldridge Core Values

Visionary Leadership
- Six Sigma strategy and goals are set by top management. Projects are linked directly to strategic direction

Customer-Driven Excellence
- Projects are selected to increase customer satisfaction and to enhance the bottom line

Organizational and Personal Learning
- Extensive training is part of the process. Key learnings are shared across the organization

Valuing Employees and Partners
- Black Belts typically come from the top talent in the organization and get extensive training. Many employees are Green Belts and team members. Many companies see Six Sigma as their key employee development process

Agility
- Six Sigma focuses on rapid improvement with projects scheduled to be completed in 4–6 months. Projects are focused where the greatest need is

Focus on the Future
- Six Sigma is focused on improvement; making the organization better for future customers, employees, and the community

Managing for Innovation
- Design for Six Sigma (DFSS) is focused on improving new product development and the R&D process

Management by Fact
- Six Sigma is data-based. A project is not worked on unless it has data to measure its important variables. All decisions are guided by data

Public Responsibility and Citizenship
- Six Sigma addresses these issues through the projects it pursues. Health, safety, and environmental issues are candidates for projects just as are other business performance issues

Focus on Results and Creating Value
- Six Sigma is about getting business results and growth

Systems Perspective
- Six Sigma is focused on process improvement and the recognition that all processes are part of an overall system

Six Sigma is a natural methodology for addressing the issues noted earlier, and can produce huge benefits to Baldrige-based improvement initiatives. As shown in Figure 7-4, Six Sigma methods including project selection, DMAIC process improvement projects, and project reviews and reporting, can be very effective in turning the opportunities identified by the Baldrige assessment into projects that produce high impact, lasting organizational improvements (Snee [1999b]). Baldrige assessments are typically done every 18–24 months, as organizations tend to change slowly. When an organization uses such assessments, their outputs should be given high priority for Six Sigma improvement projects.

A word of caution: the most difficult aspect of using Six Sigma to capture the opportunities identified in a Baldrige assessment will be properly defining the projects. The opportunities identified by the Baldrige criteria are frequently areas of opportunity that have a broad scope, making project definition challenging. Performing an affinity analysis (Hoerl and Snee [2002]) to first group the areas of opportunity into logical categories, and then putting the resulting categories through a project screening process to identify good candidate Six Sigma projects, helps considerably.

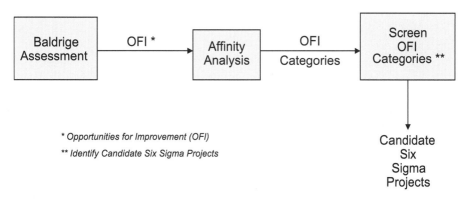

FIGURE 7-4   Integration of Baldrige Assessment and Six Sigma Improvement

Six Sigma and Lean Manufacturing

Lean manufacturing principles (Womack and Jones 1996) have their roots in the Toyota Production System (Monden 1983). As we will see in the following paragraphs, the fit with Six Sigma is again very good. Both approaches have unique strengths, and they integrate well because they are both focused on improving results through improving processes. Forward thinking organizations are taking Lean manufacturing principles from manufacturing to other processes, resulting in Lean operations.

Lean can be defined in many different ways. A key focus in any definition is the elimination of waste of all types: excess floor space, excess inventories, scrap, rework, excess raw materials, wasted capital, wasted labor, and wasted time. Womack and Jones (1996) comment that Lean thinking can "help managers clearly specify *value*, to line up all the value-creating activities for a specific product along a *value stream*, and to make value *flow* smoothly at the *pull* of the customer in pursuit of *perfection*."

This view leads Womack and Jones (1996) to identify five key principles:

- Specify *value* by specific product
- Identify the *value stream* for each product
- Make value *flow* without interruptions
- Let the customer *pull* value from the producer
- Pursue *perfection*

Note that value, value stream, flow, and perfection are part of the focus of Six Sigma, quickly revealing the synergy between Six Sigma and Lean.

Lean is well-suited for achieving the following objectives:

- Factory and line layout
- Work station design
- Waste reduction
- Cycle time reduction
- Work in progress (WIP) and inventory reduction
- One piece flow

Some of the tools used by Lean manufacturing to accomplish these objectives include:

- Process mapping
- 5S method (sort, store, shine, standardize, sustain)
- Standard work
- Line balancing
- Spaghetti maps
- Videotaping
- U-shaped work cells
- Single-minute exchange of dies (SMED)
- Poka-yoke (mistake-proofing)
- Kanban (just in time)

Womack and Jones (1996) provide a description of these tools. Many of the Lean manufacturing objectives (waste, cycle time, WIP, and inventory reduction) are also the subject of Six Sigma projects, particularly when the solution to the problem is unknown. Further, some of the Lean tools are used in Six Sigma projects when they are needed, such as process mapping, spaghetti maps, and mistake-proofing.

Another key tool of Lean is the Kaizen event in which over a short time period (typically three days) a process is torn apart and reassembled. Kaizen events are useful when the goal is to reduce waste, streamline the process, eliminate wasted floor space, and standardize the workflow, and you know how to solve the problem using common sense approaches.

In a similar situation you may want to reduce process variation and process waste, and increase process capability, but don't know how to do it. When the solution to the problem is unknown, we recommend use of Six Sigma and the scientific method. Such a project will take four to six months versus the three days of the Kaizen event, but of course the effort over the longer period will be nowhere near as intense. While we are certainly proponents of Lean, we believe that Six Sigma provides a richer infrastructure and toolset for problems with unknown solutions.

The critical question, however, is not whether to use Lean or Six Sigma exclusively, but rather how to take advantage of the strengths of both approaches depending on the nature of the problem. Experience has shown that there are some useful strategies for doing just this. For example, when the objective is process design, factory layout, waste reduction, and the other objectives that come under the Lean umbrella, *and* the way to accomplish these objectives is known, Lean tools and approaches are recommended.

Conversely, for design or improvement problems with unknown solutions, Six Sigma is recommended. In addition, it is often found in doing Lean projects that problems arise that have no known solution. These issues can naturally be addressed through one or more Six Sigma projects. Since the overall improvement system discussed earlier will include both solution known and solution unknown projects, there is room for both Six Sigma and Lean in the system.

Another strategy that is widely used is to include the Lean philosophy, objectives, and tools in the training of Six Sigma MBBs and Black Belts. The tools taught typically include the common-sense methods listed earlier, including cycle time reduction, Kaizen events, Kanban, poka-yoke, and 5S. Table 7-5 shows one way to integrate the Lean tools with the DMAIC improvement process identified by Ficalora (2001).

The Black Belts thus have the Lean methodologies and tools at their disposal to be used as needed on their projects. In those organizations using Six Sigma and Lean approaches it is important that the Six Sigma

TABLE 7-5   Integration of Lean Tools with DMAIC

- Define
  - Define value and waste
- Measure
  - Measure value and waste
  - Videotape processes
  - Observe product and employee movements
- Analyze
  - Analyze videotapes, value and waste measurements, process space utilization
- Improve
  - Identify and implement ways to reduce waste of all types
- Control
  - Standard work procedures, poka-yoke, 5S, SMED

Adapted from Ficalora (2001)

MBBs be skilled in Lean methods and tools so that they can assist the Black Belts or Green Belts when needed, and deliver the appropriate training.

There are two significant limitations of the Lean approach. First, Lean tools are not statistical in nature, and as a result they are not effective in dealing with variation. Variation is present in all processes and must be addressed if the process is to be improved, or operated in an effective manner over time. As an example, Ficalora (2002) notes that some Lean proponents argue that all excess inventory, excess floor space, and capital equipment are waste. That would be true if there were no variation in demand, no variation in supply, and no variation in production yields. In reality, however, variation is always present in each of these; hence the inventory, capital, and floor space that are currently excess may be needed to buffer variation in the future. Finding the right balance of such resources is a classic problem in the field of operations research.

A company that was using Six Sigma to reduce inventory found that variability was the root cause of the excess inventory, and then applied the Six Sigma tools to reduce the variability (Ficalora [2002]). For example, when there was excessive raw materials inventory, the company explored the variation in forecasting, delivery quantities, supplier yields, and so on. Black Belt teams were successful in each case, and the raw material, work in progress, and finished goods inventories were all significantly reduced once the variability that caused excess inventory was reduced. The approach taken by this company views excess inventory of any kind as a process output (Y), and then looks for the process variables (Xs) producing the excess inventory. Once these causal variables are identified, analyzed, and controlled, the excess inventory will naturally decrease.

The second limitation is that the Lean methodology is most useful in manufacturing environments, although it has applications elsewhere. Our experience has been that Six Sigma is much more effective for creating a common language and methodology usable across the whole organization, not only for improving processes but for empowering employees, developing employees, and creating leaders of tomorrow. We believe the effectiveness of the Lean methods is greatly enhanced when used in the Six Sigma framework. We acknowledge that many Lean proponents feel the opposite—that Six Sigma methods are enhanced when used in a Lean context. Each organization should decide at the beginning of its Six Sigma deployment, whether, how, and where it will use Lean, and how the two approaches will be integrated.

The Long-Term Impact of Six Sigma

The long-term impact of Six Sigma is summarized in Figure 7-5. Most organizations initiate Six Sigma in operations. This start is usually followed in 12–18 months by expansions into administrative and transactional processes, and R&D processes (beginning in the managing the effort phase, and expanding in the sustaining momentum and growing phase).

Top management has fueled the deployment through its leadership, evidenced by such things as clear goals, resources, breakthrough expectations, and a deployment plan. Of particular importance is the clear communication of breakthrough expectations—what we need to do to be successful, how we are going to do it, and what will happen when we are successful. Without these expectations the organization is confused about what is expected and what will happen.

The work done in the first 12–18 months produces many useful results, including some very worthwhile by-products. Most important are

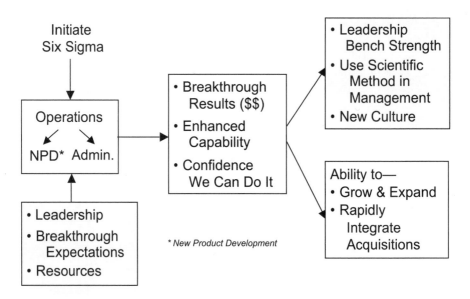

FIGURE 7-5   The Long-Term Impact of Six Sigma

business results in the form of improvement to the bottom line, and increased customer satisfaction. This helps Six Sigma build credibility, pay for itself, and provide fuel for continued growth. The capability of the organization is thereby greatly increased, including enhanced teamwork and cross-functional cooperation. Most importantly, the organization begins to believe that Six Sigma will work here, and each person can benefit from Six Sigma personally.

Two to three years into the initiative, typically during the sustaining momentum and growing phase, the longer-term benefits begin to appear. The leadership team bench strength begins to increase as the Six Sigma experience provides the organization with a larger number of highly skilled leaders. Organizations typically see greater use of scientific thinking in how they manage, including focusing on processes, using data to guide decisions, and understanding the effects of variation on the decision making process.

The discussion of the impact of variation on customer satisfaction in the 1998 GE Annual Report is one illustration of this type of thinking. As a result, people are working in a new way and a new culture begins to emerge. This solid foundation enhances the organization's ability to expand and grow. The cadre of MBBs, Black Belts, and other experienced Six Sigma leaders, and the focus on improving processes, creates a better climate for rapid assimilation of new acquisitions. This climate also makes it possible to move acquired processes to new locations and get them productive in record time.

The list on the following page summarizes some of the mindset changes seen in the organization along the way. People believe that a focus on breakthrough process improvement is the way to improve business performance and growth. They see that this improvement comes when improvement is part of the budget and annual planning, with both the costs and the benefits of improvement built into the budget. They believe that Six Sigma is about improvement, and not training per se. Training is needed to build the improvement skills, but is not an end in itself. Process improvement rises to a new and higher level of importance, a part of how you run the business. The use of data and facts as a guide to decision making has become the norm. "Please show me the data that this recommendation is based on" is a common request when evaluating proposals and recommendations. A new way of working evolves and higher and higher levels of performance results are achieved.

Mindset Changes Produced by Deployment of Six Sigma

- Breakthrough process improvement is the route to increased business performance and growth.

- We focus on improvement, not training per se. Training is aimed at building the skills needed to get business results.

- We are bringing our improvement processes to a new, higher level of importance.

- Budgeting process—annual allocations include costs and benefits of Six Sigma projects.

- Goal setting process—improvement goals using Six Sigma and other means are well defined.

- Decision making–guided by data when possible.

- Management reviews are done as scheduled.

- Data systems include data for improvement as well as finance.

- Delivery of results is a key component of performance management, recognition and rewards, and career development.

- Hiring process searches for people who will be successful in new culture.

- Communications process reports the new way of working including purpose, expectations and accomplishments.

- You are making Six Sigma part of everything you do.

Summary

Deploying Six Sigma is a major organizational initiative requiring a lot of effort and resources. To maintain the gains long term, and continuously improve using Six Sigma, organizations need to integrate Six Sigma into the way they work. In other words, they need to institutionalize it. In this way, they are able to retain the benefits without retaining a separate infrastructure permanently. Of course, without integrating Six Sigma into the way you work, the benefits will disappear with the separate infrastructure, and Six Sigma will have been just another fad that had temporary benefits.

Successfully transitioning is therefore the key to making the financial and organizational benefits permanent.

The three main means of integrating Six Sigma into the way we work reviewed in this chapter were integrating Six Sigma concepts, methods, and tools with your process management systems; creating and managing an overall improvement system that guides and integrates all types of organizational improvement; and integrating Six Sigma with other strategic initiatives such as ISO 9000, the Malcolm Baldrige Award criteria, and Lean manufacturing. Process management systems are extremely important and valuable, with or without Six Sigma. They are particularly critical when transitioning from a Six Sigma initiative to the way you work because they replace much of the Six Sigma infrastructure while maintaining the gains of Six Sigma. One key element of the process management system is the improvement system, which integrates Six Sigma as well as other improvement approaches, such as capital projects. Integration of Six Sigma with organizational initiatives, such as ISO 9000, Baldrige assessment, and Lean manufacturing, ensures that Six Sigma remains critical to how you do your work.

References

Baldrige National Quality Program. (2002). *Criteria for Performance Excellence.* National Institute for Standards and Technology, Gaithersburg, MD.

Box, G. E. P., W. G. Hunter, and J. S. Hunter. (1978). *Statistics for Experimenters.* John Wiley and Sons, New York, NY.

Brassard, M. (1989). *The Memory Jogger Plus—Featuring the Seven Management Planning Tools.* GOAL/QPC, Methuen, MA.

Ficalora, J. (2001). "A Six Sigma Perspective on Lean Manufacturing." ASQ Metropolitan Section Annual Conference, Newark, NJ.

Ficalora, J. (2002). "Variation and Lean Manufacturing," Personal Communication.

Hoerl, R. W. and R. D. Snee. (2002). *Statistical Thinking: Improving Business Performance.* Duxbury Press/Thomson Learning, Pacific Grove, CA.

ISO 9000 Standards. (2000). *ISO 9000-2000 Quality Management Systems—Fundamentals and Vocabulary, ISO 9001-2000 Quality Manage-*

ment Systems—Requirements, ISO 9004-2000 Guidelines for Performance Improvements. American Society for Quality, Milwaukee, WI.

Monden, Y. (1983). *Toyota Production System*. Industrial and Management Engineering Press, Norcross, GA.

Snee, R. D. (1999a). "Statisticians Must Develop Data-Based Management and Improvement Systems as Well as Create Measurement Systems," *International Statistical Review*, Vol. 67, No. 2, 139-144.

Snee, R. D. (1999b). "The Impact of Six Sigma: Today and in the Future," Presented at the Quality and Productivity Research Conference Sponsored by the American Statistical Association and American Society for Quality, General Electric Corporate R & D Center, Schenectady, NY, May 19-21, 1999.

Snee, R. D. (2001). "Make the View Worth the Climb—Focus Training on Getting Better Business Results," *Quality Progress*. November 2001, 58-61.

Stoner, J. A. F. and F. M. Werner. (1994). *Managing Finance for Quality*. ASQ Quality Press, Milwaukee, WI.

Womack, J. P. and D. T. Jones. (1996). *Lean Thinking: Banish Waste and Create Wealth in Your Corporation*. Simon and Schuster, New York, NY.

8

FINAL THOUGHTS FOR LEADERS

"The ability to learn faster than your competitors may be the only sustainable competitive advantage."

—Arie DeGeus, Royal Dutch Shell

In this final chapter we discuss three issues that are of particular importance to leaders: understanding and use of the Six Sigma tools; ensuring project success; and ensuring success of the overall initiative.

Our discussion of how leaders should think about the Six Sigma improvement tools is not intended as a technical reference, since this is not the primary need of leaders. Rather, it is motivated by our belief that the Six Sigma literature has provided conflicting advice as to what level of knowledge, understanding, and competency leaders need to have in the Six Sigma tools. Our goal is to clarify leaders' responsibilities regarding deployment of the Six Sigma tools within their organizations.

Some publications seem to indicate that leaders need to become ministatisticians, while others give the impression that no familiarity with tools is needed at all, since the technical details of Six Sigma can be delegated to others (MBBs, Black Belts, etc.). As we shall see, the truth is somewhere in between. First we will provide a case study of a DMAIC Black

Belt project. It represents neither the most technical Black Belt project, nor the project with the greatest financial return. Rather, it is an excellent example of the major points we want to make about Six Sigma tools, and relates to an industry whose issues can be easily grasped (newspaper publishing).

After presenting the case study, we will discuss what leaders need to know about Six Sigma tools, and how these tools fit into the bigger picture, using the case for illustration. Next, we summarize our advice for ensuring the success of Six Sigma projects, including pitfalls to avoid. This is followed by guidance on pitfalls and success factors for the overall Six Sigma initiative. Finally, we summarize the key points of previous chapters, and provide references for further study. Following this final chapter we provide additional material on frequently asked questions about deployment, and our answers to them.

Understanding the Role of the Six Sigma Tools—A Case Study

The successful deployment of Six Sigma depends on leaders having an understanding of the Six Sigma tools—what they are, when they are to be used, when they work, and when they don't. Certainly the more leaders know about the tools the better, although familiarity is more important to acquire than a high degree of technical expertise. The tools we refer to are general improvement tools, some of which may involve the use of two or more statistical methods.

The case study we will discuss is an elaboration of the Newspaper Accuracy case from Hoerl and Snee (2002). While this case is about reducing errors in newspaper publishing, it is illustrative of reducing errors in processes in general.

One of the first questions leaders should ask is "Is this problem important?" The answer here was a clear yes. Nothing is more important to a newspaper than the accuracy of the names, facts, figures, and other information it publishes. In this case the newspaper reported the promotion of a new CEO in a major U.S. corporation and misspelled the new executive's name. The newspaper received a call from an unhappy reader—not the new CEO, not the company's public relations department, not the CEO's spouse, but the CEO's mother! This points out that the requirement of accurate information can come from many different sources, some of which may not be anticipated.

Before delving further into this case study, let us look at the DMA-IC process with emphasis on the tools used in each phase, the purpose of each tool, and what we can learn from the application of each tool. A brief description of the most common Six Sigma improvement tools is below. A depiction of the purpose, deliverables, and key tools of each step in the DMAIC process is shown in Figure 8-1.

Key Six Sigma Tools

- Process Map—A schematic of a process showing process inputs, steps and outputs.

- Cause and Effect Matrix—A prioritization matrix that enables you to select those process input variables (Xs) that have the greatest effect on the process output variables (Ys).

- Measurement System Analysis—Study of the measurement system typically using Gage R&R studies to quantify the measurement repeatability and reproducibility.

- Capability Study—Analysis of process variation versus process specifications to assess the ability of the process to meet the specifications

- Failure Mode and Effects Analysis—Analytical approach for identifying process problems by prioritizing failure modes, their causes, and process improvements

- Multi-vari Study—A study that samples the process as it operates and by statistical and graphical analysis identifies the important controlled and uncontrolled (noise) variables.

- Design of Experiments—A method of experimentation that identifies, with minimum testing, how key process input variables affect the output of the process

- Control Plan—document that summarizes the results of a Six Sigma project and aids the operator in controlling the process.

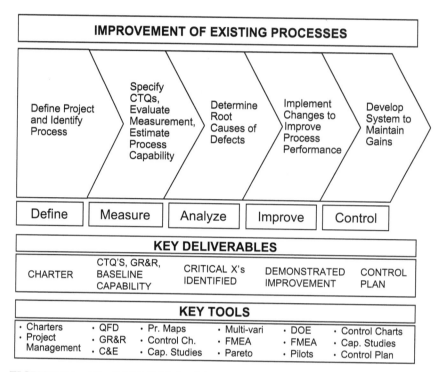

FIGURE 8-1 The DMAIC Methodology and Key Tools

Define Phase

In the define phase we select a project to work on, and define the specific problem to be solved and process to be improved. We use key process metrics to guide project selection and identify the goals, and we summarize the resulting project and its objectives in the project charter. The project charter is a key tool of the project definition phase.

A common cause of failure in improvement projects is lack of common understanding of what the projects will do and accomplish. This can lead to disappointment and finger pointing at project closure.

In the newspaper accuracy study leadership established error reduction as an important issue. In order for a Black Belt to work on this issue the newspaper needed a project charter which, as discussed in Chapter 4, defines the work to be done including the process involved, problem statement, the metrics (process baseline, project goal, process entitlement) associated with the problem, the project objective, the financial impact of the project, the team members, and project scope.

Common problems encountered in constructing an effective project charter are discussed in Chapter 4. Leadership must ensure that for each project a charter is created by the project Champion, is refined by the Champion and Black Belt, contains all the relevant metrics, defines the proper scope, specifies all the metrics, names the team members, and so on. In short, the charter must be complete with no shortcuts taken. It then serves as an internal contract among all project stakeholders. The project scope is very important because it defines the boundaries of the project. The scope of the newspaper accuracy project was the editorial process beginning with assignment of the story and ending with transmission of the story to production. Anything before or after these boundaries would be out of scope for this project.

Some baseline data showed that while the copy desk might catch and fix as many as 40 errors per day, the rate on a typical day was 20 errors. Each error caused significant problems in the production process, so improvement was needed. A goal was set for this project to reduce the errors by 50 percent to less than 10 per day.

The financial impact of an error was established as $62 if caught at the copy desk, $88 if caught at the composing room, $768 if a page had to be redone, and $5,000 if the presses had to be stopped and restarted. Of course, the cost of an error being published is unknown and unknowable.

The team developed an operational definition for an error before any data were collected, so that the data would be accurate, and everyone would be talking about the same thing when errors were discussed. This definition was (1) any deviation from truth, accuracy, or widely accepted standards of English usage, or (2) a departure from accepted procedures that causes delay or requires reworking a story or a graphic. The team also decided to divide the errors into nine categories: misspelled words, wrong number, wrong name, bad grammar, libel, word missing, duplicated word, fact wrong, and other. Obviously, all of these errors are not equally serious.

The 11-person team consisted of the Black Belt, the editor, two copy editors, two graphics editors, one reporter, and four supervisors. This team was large (we recommend teams of four to six), but it was effective. Larger teams have difficulty finding mutually agreeable meeting times, reaching consensus, and making decisions. Fortunately, team size turned out not to be a problem in this case.

Measure Phase

The measure phase is intended to ensure that you are working on improving the right metrics, those that are truly in need of improvement and that you can measure well. In this phase you select the appropriate process outputs to be improved, based on the objectives of the project and customer needs. You determine what is acceptable performance and gather baseline data to evaluate current performance. This work includes the evaluation of the performance of the measurement system, as well as the performance of the process being studied. The tools used during the measure phase include the process map, cause and effect diagram or cause and effect matrix, measurement system analysis, capability analysis, and a control chart analysis of the baseline data on the process output. Quality function deployment (QFD) may also be used to refine and validate the output metrics (often referred to as CTQs).

Process mapping, cause and effect diagrams, capability studies, and control charts are popular improvement tools discussed by Hoerl and Snee (2002) and other authors. More detailed discussions of the analysis of measurement systems are found in AIAG (1990) and Wheeler and Lyday (1989). Breyfogle (1999) elaborates on the use of the cause and effect matrix.

The process map is prepared by the team, not the Black Belt alone, and provides a picture of the process, as well as identifying non-value-added work and the hidden factory where the reworking is done. Reworking refers to redoing substandard work done previously, such as finding and correcting errors in financial reports. Non-value-added work refers to that which adds no value to the product or service, but is currently required due to inefficiencies in the process. For example, warehousing finished goods adds no value from a customer point of view, but some level of warehousing is typically needed to maintain a supply chain.

The first process map is prepared at a macro level, and usually consists of five to ten steps. If the team needs further detail for some key steps, it can map them further, creating substeps for each macro step.

The team usually identifies important process input and output variables during the process mapping work. The newspaper writing and editing five-step process map is shown in Figure 8-2. Note the revision cycle that may be a source of both non-value-added work and rework. The size of the paper (number of pages), number of employees absent each day, and a major change in front page (cover) story (yes, no) were identified by the team as variables that could have an effect on errors.

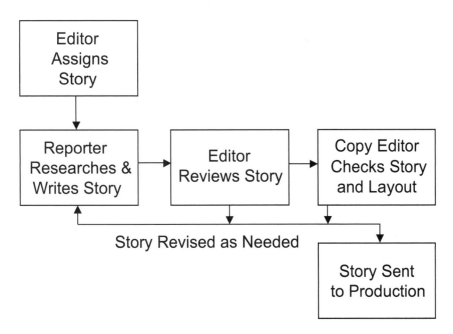

FIGURE 8-2 Newspaper Writing and Editing Process

The purpose of both the cause and effect diagram and cause and effect matrix is to enable the Black Belt and the team to study the relationships between the process input variables and the process output variables. In the case of the newspaper accuracy study, the key output variable was errors. The diagram serves as a visual display of the effect, or output variable, and its important causes or input/process variables. The cause and effect diagram for errors is shown in Figure 8-3. The cause and effect matrix rates the process input variables in terms of their relative impact on the process output variables. It is actually one of the houses (typically the third house) created in a full-blown QFD analysis (see Breyfogle [1999]).

For this project the cause and effect diagram was adequate and the cause and effect matrix was not needed. As a general rule, we do not have to use every tool on every project; rather we use whatever tools are needed to successfully complete each phase of the DMAIC methodology. Note also that both the cause and effect diagram and matrix are examples of knowledge-based tools; they are developed based on our existing knowledge of the process, rather than on objective data. Eventually, we need ob-

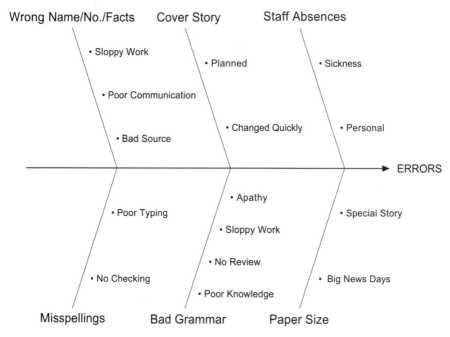

FIGURE 8-3   Cause and Effect Diagram Showing Causes of Newspaper Errors

jective data to ensure our current understanding is correct, and to enhance this understanding.

In this case the measurement system analysis consisted of developing the measurement system and errors collection scheme, and validating it. In other instances, particularly in manufacturing, gage repeatability and reproducibility studies (AIAG 1990) are used to evaluate the adequacy of the measurement system. Gage repeatability and reproducibility studies evaluate your ability to replicate results when you take multiple measurements (repeatability), and the ability of several people or pieces of measurement equipment to obtain similar measurements (reproducibility). Such analysis is a particularly important step because, in our experience, as many as 50% of the measurement systems in use are in significant need of improvement. Of course, there can be other measurement issues besides repeatability and reproducibility, such as accuracy (ability to achieve the correct average measurement).

In Six Sigma projects outside manufacturing, such as the newspaper study or projects in finance, most of the measurement system work focuses on the creation of the measurement system and the construction of the data collection process.

A process capability study is conducted to measure how well the process is capable of meeting the customer specifications. Typical outputs of these studies are short-term capability indices (short-term sigma level, Cp, Cpk) in the measure phase and long-term capability indices (long-term sigma level, Pp, Ppk) in the control phase. See AIAG (1995a) for definitions of these capability indices. Black Belts often conduct such studies using control charts (AIAG [1995a], Montgomery [2001])—graphical depictions of performance level and variation over time. A control chart analysis of 44 days of baseline data for the newspaper study showed that the errors were being produced by a stable process with an average value of approximately 20 errors per day, and daily variations from just below 10 to just below 40.

A control chart is a plot of data over time with statistically determined limits of normal variation. A run chart is analogous to a control chart, but does not have the statistically determined limits. Figure 8-4 shows a run chart of this data that illustrates the degree of stability, average level, and variation of the process.

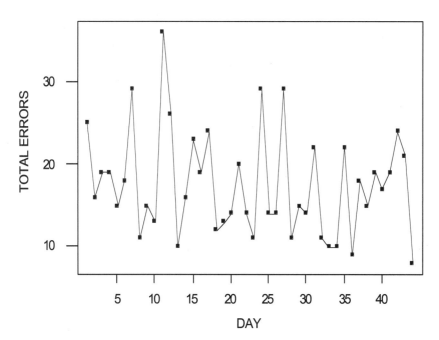

FIGURE 8-4 Run Chart of Newspaper Errors March–April

Analyze Phase

The analyze phase helps us avoid the ready, fire, aim approach by accurately diagnosing the root causes of problems. In this phase we evaluate the baseline data to further document current performance and to identify root causes of the observed variation and defects, collecting additional data as needed.

Two of the improvement tools most commonly used in the analysis phase are multi-vari studies and FMEA. Multi-vari studies are process studies in which we collect data on the key process and input variables as well as on the key outputs. We then analyze the data using graphical and statistical tools such as regression analysis and hypothesis testing, to identify the variables having the most significant impact on the output variables. FMEA is a disciplined methodology for identifying potential defects, and taking proactive steps to avoid them. More detailed explanations of these tools are given in the references on page 220.

When we evaluate data on errors we often use a Pareto analysis to determine which categories of errors are the biggest problems. The Pareto chart (Figure 8-5) is basically a bar graph whose bars are ordered by number or magnitude of occurrence. The theory is that a few categories will account for the majority of the errors, and it holds in the newspaper errors study. In Figure 8-5 we see that the majority of the errors during the March-April time period were due to misspelling, wrong names, numbers, and facts, and poor grammar.

The team initially focused attention on addressing these categories, and identified one root cause: reporters were not using the spell checker. The typical attitude was "I don't have time to spell check. Besides, the copy editors will catch the errors anyway." The reporters were also not routinely checking their facts and their sources, which was a job requirement. We address how to deal with these root causes in the improve phase.

A multi-vari study is conducted to identify variables that may be producing the errors. The variables studied in the newspaper case were those identified in the measure phase; namely, size of paper, number of employees absent, and major changes in the front-page story. While the size of the paper is controllable, the other two variables are not. The team also studied day of the week and month of the year differences. Work teams often perform differently on Mondays and Fridays than on the other days of the week. Analysis of the data indicated that the only variables with an effect on errors were size of the paper (more pages leads to more errors) and changes in the front cover story (new stories had to be created under very tight schedules increasing the error rate).

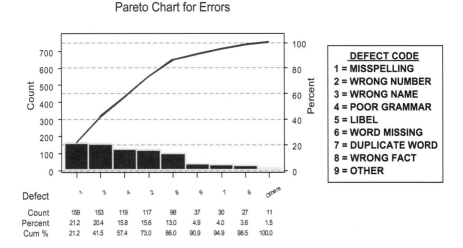

FIGURE 8-5   Pareto Chart of Newspaper Errors March–April

Improve Phase

In the improve phase teams figure out how to change the process to address the root causes identified in the analyze phase, and thereby improve the performance of the process. Each process change is tested with a confirmatory study to verify that the predicted improvements in fact happen. It may take several rounds of improvements to reach the desired level of performance. Note that this is the only phase in the DMAIC process that actually *makes* improvement. The other phases are intended to properly set up (DMA) and maintain (C) the improvements from this phase.

At this point in the newspaper case, management reaffirmed that reporters were responsible for checking the accuracy of their articles. Three job aids were also created: a "Spell Check How-To," a list of "10 Rules of Grammar," and the "Pyramid of Trust" which detailed the sources that could be trusted to produce accurate names, facts, and numbers.

These new working methods were communicated in an all-hands meeting in July. The importance of being careful when the front cover story changed with little notice and problems of large editions of the newspaper were also discussed. The interim goal of letting less than 10 errors reach the copy desk per day was also reviewed and reaffirmed.

One month went by, and it was now time to test whether the changes were having an effect. Data for the month of August were analyzed, and total errors had not changed! The leadership team assembled and reviewed the situation. Why were errors still high? Leadership learned that the new procedures were simply not being used. Many employees did not feel that leadership was serious about the changes, and therefore did not take them seriously. This emphasizes the point that deciding on improvements, and actually implementing them effectively, are two different things. The editor reiterated that the new procedures were to be used and that the leadership team was expected to lead this new way of working. Another all-hands meeting was held to address the issue.

One month later when the latest data were analyzed, total errors had dropped significantly (Figure 8-6). In another month the total errors had dropped by approximately 65%, compared to the goal of 50%. The new procedures were clearly working.

It is not uncommon to find that new procedures are not being used. It is leadership's responsibility to ensure that the new way of working is used. Otherwise, the benefits of the project will not be realized. Project reviews, confirmatory studies, and process audits are effective ways to identify whether the process changes are being used and are effective.

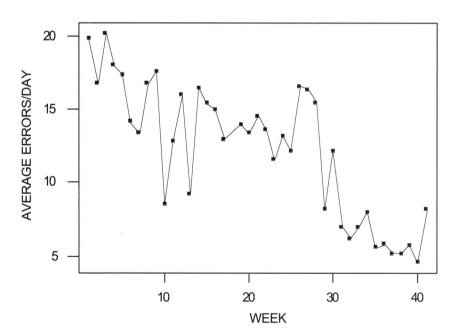

FIGURE 8-6   Run Chart of Weekly Average Newspaper Errors March to December

In some instances, particularly in manufacturing processes, additional work needs to be done in the improve phase to obtain the desired process performance. Typical studies include verifying cause-and-effect relationships identified in the measure and analyze phases, identifying optimum operating conditions, and defining process specification limits. The tools of statistical design of experiments (DOE) and response surface methodology can be very helpful in these instances (Box, Hunter, and Hunter 1978; Myers and Montgomery [1995]). Designed experiments have been successfully used in non-manufacturing studies and their use continues to grow in this important area of improvement (Koselka [1996]).

Control Phase

In the control phase we implement a system that will ensure that the improved performance of the process is sustained after the Six Sigma team has completed its work and moved on to another project. The key tools of this phase are the control plan (AIAG 1994) including control charts (part of statistical process control—Montgomery [2001] and AIAG [1995a]) and long-term capability studies.

Returning to our newspaper case, we see that while the errors were significantly reduced, errors were not yet at zero, and more work was needed to achieve further improvement. In the meantime, a control plan was put in place to hold the gains of the work done to date, and to keep the errors at the level obtained. This is the purpose of the control phase in Six Sigma, to hold the gains. The control plan specified that the following measures would be monitored using control charts:

- Total errors
- Errors by category
- Percent of articles checked by the author
- Percent of articles spell-checked

The latter two measurements were particularly useful in detecting when the reporters were not following procedures and thus when errors would be a problem.

The team created checklists and defined roles and responsibilities, including backups, to reduce handoff problems between departments. This enabled people to view their work processes as part of an overall system. To obtain further improvements, a team was chartered to find the sources of errors in the newspaper graphics, and eliminate them.

Results

In addition to reducing the errors by 65 percent, the new way of operating had other benefits, including:

- Fewer missed deadlines, including the ability to deal effectively with extremely tight deadlines.

- Improved morale at the copy desk. Copy editors were freed up to make better use of their talents and training.

- Reduced rekeying of names (rework).

- Identification of more efficient and less costly sources of information, resulting in reduced errors and less number input time (less keying of data). News assistants were freed up to do more valuable work

Fewer errors resulted in less non-value-added work and a more streamlined and effective process. Such effects are characteristic of what happens when the errors and defect levels of business processes are reduced. The processes work more effectively and efficiently, costs are reduced, employee moral improves, and customer satisfaction increases.

It is not uncommon for a project, when completed, to achieve improvements to the process that were not anticipated at the start. Six Sigma leaders should be on the lookout for these situations and make sure that all the benefits are included in the financial impact calculation of the project. It is also important that the benefits of the project be communicated widely and that the success of the project be appropriately celebrated.

We also note that two commonly applied improvement tools, FMEA and DOE, were not used in this newspaper accuracy project. This is not unusual. In any given project, some tools are not needed; in other cases, the work may have already been done in a previous project. Leaders should assess whether the proper tools were used, and provide input to the Black Belt as appropriate. Sometimes the unused tools will be needed in subsequent studies. In the newspaper accuracy case the error rate was reduced to less than 10 per day, which is not zero, the desired state. FMEA and DOE may be useful in subsequent projects intended to make further improvements.

How to Think About the Six Sigma Tools

The statistical and process improvement tools are clearly an integral part of the Six Sigma approach. As illustrated in this case study, without these powerful technical tools, Six Sigma would regress into a collection of vague concepts, slogans, and other fluff. It is the technical toolset that brings rigor to Six Sigma. The MBBs, Black Belts, and Green Belts are the resources primarily responsible for use of the tools. This raises the question, "How should leaders, such as executives, business unit leaders, and Champions think about the Six Sigma tools?"

First, it is important to understand that these leaders do not need to become professional statisticians, or even highly skilled in use of the tools. Of course, one can never have too much knowledge, but forcing leaders to become experts (as some executives have attempted to do) is a misguided approach. They simply don't need this expertise to do their job. After all, in the vast majority of projects, such as the newspaper case study, these leaders will not be the ones directly applying the tools. On the other hand, we do recommend that leaders study and learn the tools well enough to complete good Leadership Green Belt projects, as discussed in Chapter 6. During Green Belt training, leaders should actually complete their own projects, rather than relying on MBBs or Black Belts in their organizations to complete their projects for them. There is no substitute for personal experience with the tools and the overall DMAIC process.

Two extreme viewpoints that leaders should avoid are feeling they need to become experts in the tools, and refusing to study the tools at all. For example, when the topic of the technical tools comes up, some leaders will joke: "I was never good at math!" Such an attitude belittles the importance of the tools, and diminishes this leader's ability to hold meaningful project reviews.

The middle ground is for leaders to study and struggle with the tools like everyone else in the organization, and to apply them to their own projects. They should understand what the key tools are, when they should be applied, and what information each produces. This understanding will help them hold useful project and overall initiative reviews.

Leaders don't necessarily need to understand the mechanics of how each tool works, or the underlying mathematics. Rather, they need to understand how the tools fit in with the larger picture of the overall Six Sigma deployment. For example, they should understand and be able to articulate the following points:

- The statistical and process improvement tools provide the rigor in Six Sigma (as noted earlier).

- The tools themselves don't make improvements; rather it is the action taken by people based on application of the tools that generates improvement.

- The tools must be properly sequenced and integrated in a disciplined fashion to be effective.

- If the leadership aspects of Six Sigma are not in place, the tools will not have any lasting effect.

- The tools should be combined with subject matter knowledge in an iterative fashion of generating, testing, and revising hypotheses.

The Tools Themselves Don't Make Improvements

Relative to the second bullet item, notice from the case study that all improvements to the publishing process came about from actions taken by people, not from the tools. For example, implementing (and actually using) well-designed job aids significantly improved accuracy. Of course, use of the tools helped identify the root causes of inaccuracy, and determine the best countermeasures to deal with these root causes. Pareto analysis was a key tool on this project. As with most Black Belt projects, rigorously defining the appropriate metrics to be improved (CTQs), and obtaining relevant data for improvement purposes were key challenges. In this case, developing a precise definition of an accuracy error was critical for progress.

The key point here is that the tools help identify the root causes of problems and potential solutions, but for improvement to occur people have to take action based on the tools. For example, numerous investment organizations lost large sums of money when the energy conglomerate Enron collapsed in late 2001. Interestingly, many of these investment companies had tools designed to predict such corporate defaults. The typical reason many still lost money was not some inadequacy of the tools themselves, but rather the lack of prompt action based on the tools.

The Tools Must Be Properly Sequenced and Integrated

The tools must also be properly sequenced and integrated in order to be effective. Figure 8-7 illustrates how the most commonly used tools are typically sequenced and integrated by the DMAIC process during the course of Black Belt and Green Belt projects. There is a logical progression, with the input of one tool often being the output from a previously used tool.

The process map, or flowchart, is typically the first tool used. The process map sets the stage for subsequent tools by carefully documenting a common view of the process. This map enables people to see their piece of the process in the context of the bigger picture. The cause and effect (C&E) matrix naturally follows the process map. Once the team agrees on the major steps in the process, it is logical to determine which steps and process variables are most critical to achieving our CTQs. The cause and effect matrix does just this, by noting how strongly each process step and variable impacts each CTQ. The process map and cause and effect matrix also provide input to the control plan by documenting the process steps and variables that need to be included.

Once the cause and effect matrix identifies the priority steps, the team will need to ensure that it can accurately measure the key variables at these steps, utilizing a measurement system analysis (MSA). In addition, it may begin a formal FMEA to identify potential failures in the prioritized steps and variables, and begin proactive counter-measures to prevent them. Once the team is convinced that it can accurately measure the key variables, it will likely evaluate process capability using capability analysis tools. Assuming the capability is insufficient, the team can use a multi-vari analysis to identify the key process variables that are causing the bulk of the variation in the process outputs (CTQs). Formal design of experiments (DOE) provides additional power to resolve ambiguities and quantify cause-effect relationships.

A key characteristic of the Six Sigma methodology is that the output of each of these tools provides input to the control plan, by determining the most important aspects of the process that need to be controlled to maintain improvements. This approach greatly simplifies development of the control plan because much of the hard work has already been done. Statistical process control (SPC), the other commonly used tool depicted in Figure 8-7, is then utilized by the control plan to quickly identify abnormal behavior in the process so that root causes can be found. Statistical process control uses control charts to document the range of normal behavior in the process, allowing early detection of potential problems before they become major issues.

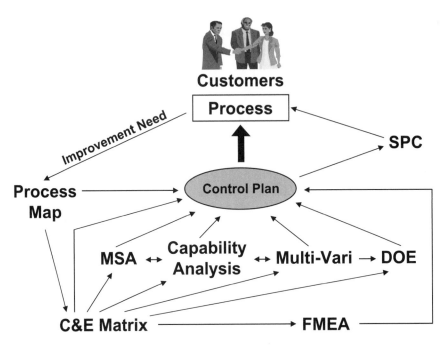

FIGURE 8-7   Six Sigma Tool Linkage

This logical integration of the tools into an overall improvement process is a major contribution of the Six Sigma methodology. Statistical and process improvement tools have been around for a long time, and have been promoted by many other initiatives, such as TQM. However, instructors have generally taught practitioners a collection of tools without providing guidance on how to properly integrate or sequence them to solve a real problem. This approach often left people confused as to how to start, or where to go next after applying one tool.

Leadership Is Still Required

We have attempted to stress throughout this book that leadership is the key to Six Sigma success. This is also true for effective use of the tools. If the leadership component is lacking, no amount of tool usage can overcome this deficiency. For example, when the job aids were originally rolled out to the newspaper organization, subsequent data revealed no improvement. Why? Because people did not think management was serious, and so they did not use the job aids. If this situation had been allowed to continue, the project would have ended in failure. Fortunately, the editor exerted leadership by directly addressing the problem, and insisting that the job aids be utilized. Errors decreased dramatically in the next few months. There is no substitute for leadership.

Leaders should be continuously looking for similar situations in their own organizations where effectiveness of tool applications is being hampered by leadership issues (bureaucracy, politics, lack of clear direction, etc.). These issues tend to be the ones the Black Belts and even MBBs are unable to address on their own, and they are one reason for having a formal Champion role. Effective use of tools should be another area of focus at both project and overall initiative reviews.

Incorporate Subject Matter Knowledge

Keep in mind that the tools work best when they are combined with good subject matter knowledge in the technical area of the project, whether it is engineering, finance, or marketing. This is why it is helpful to have Black Belts who are knowledgeable in the areas in which they are doing projects.

Subject matter knowledge provides the theory to guide initial use of the tools. The information gained from the tools then helps refine, augment, or revise the original theories. This sequence continues from phase to phase, and tool to tool, resulting in greater and greater process knowledge. This is essentially application of the scientific method to business problems. A more detailed discussion of the proper integration of data-based tools and subject matter knowledge can be found in Hoerl and Snee (2002).

In the newspaper accuracy case, it was necessary to have the editor, copy editors, graphics editors, a reporter, and supervisors on the team in order to cover all the key areas of subject matter knowledge. If such subject matter knowledge were not critical, you wouldn't need such diverse teams. For example, it would likely have been impossible to determine the costs of finding errors at various stages of the publication process without such expertise. Subject matter knowledge also helped guide the original data collection, and helped interpret the results of the data analysis. Of course, the data analysis revised the team's original theories, dispelling for example the theory that the number of absent employees was a key contributor to the accuracy problem. As is often the case, analyses of data and subject matter theory enhanced one another when properly integrated.

Leaders should ask questions about what new knowledge the organization has learned from data analyses, and how current theories about the process need to be revised based on them. In short, we should have data to validate all our theories, and theories to properly interpret all our data.

In this arena there are again extreme positions that can inhibit project success. For example, some Black Belts may become enamored of the statistical tools and feel that lots of data and analyses are a replacement for process knowledge. Such Black Belts will tend to skip over the step of interpreting the data in light of subject matter theory, resulting in invalid conclusions. Conversely, some purists may believe that all problems can be solved based on first principles (fundamental laws) of engineering, physics, or finance, and resist any data collection and analysis. Leaders must push back on both extremes, and insist on proper integration of subject matter knowledge with data analysis.

If leaders understand these key concepts about the Six Sigma tools, and can properly audit for them during project and overall initiative reviews, they will add significant value to their organization's deployment. Conversely, those who try to become professional statisticians, or totally avoid discussion of the tools by using the excuse "I was never very good at math" will significantly diminish their value-added.

Advice For Ensuring Project Success

We will now summarize some key points made throughout this book. First we focus on advice for ensuring project success, and then on success for the overall Six Sigma initiative.

Key Project Success Criteria

Improvement in Six Sigma initiatives occurs primarily project-by-project, although the resulting cultural change adds additional benefits outside formal projects. Therefore, we must ensure that these projects are successful in order for the organization to fully benefit from Six Sigma. The primary keys to project success, discussed in Chapters 4 and 5, include:

- Selection of good Six Sigma projects
- Assignment of a top talent Black Belt and Champion to the project
- Proper support, such as from functional support groups (IT, Finance, HR, Legal)
- Regular, well-structured project reviews
- Clear project close-out criteria

Chapter 4 provided suggested criteria for project selection, as well as an example of criteria used by one organization. The key points are that you should be working on important projects that are supported by management, can be completed within four to six months, and have clear measures of success. In order to obtain such projects, organizations need to develop a rigorous project identification and prioritization process. Prioritized projects are then placed into a project hopper, awaiting assignment of a Black Belt. Some pitfalls to avoid in project selection include:

- Fuzzy objectives

- Poor metrics

- No tie to financials

- Overly broad scope

- Lack of connection with strategic or annual plans

- Problem whose solution is already identified

- Projects with too many objectives

Use of top talent in Six Sigma is a theme running throughout the initiative, but is perhaps most critical in the Black Belts leading the individual projects. We have seen huge variation in success rates between projects that were led by true top talent, and projects that weren't. It is also important that projects have access as needed to resources from support groups, such as IT, Finance, or Maintenance. This often is critical in the improve phase of projects, when an identified improvement needs to be implemented. If the improvement calls for a process step to be digitized, for example, the prompt support of the IT organization will be necessary.

Well-structured project reviews serve several purposes. First, scheduling of project reviews indicates leadership's seriousness, and sets the expectation of tangible results. In addition, reviews identify issues or roadblocks hindering projects so that they can be addressed by Champions, or others in leadership roles. Projects with regular, formal reviews rarely drag on past the expected completion date. A fringe benefit is that as leaders see more and more success in Six Sigma projects firsthand, they become stronger and stronger proponents for the initiative.

Clear close-out criteria help ensure that perfectionist Black Belts do not continue on a project past the point of significant return, when there are dozens of processes in critical condition that urgently need a Black Belt. Conversely, these criteria help prevent Black Belts from prematurely jumping from one project to another before success has been assured. Well-thought-out criteria help Black Belts move crisply from one project to the next, maximizing the overall benefit to the organization.

Common Project Pitfalls to Avoid

Project pitfalls that can derail success are almost mirror images of the key success criteria; omission of each success criteria is itself a pitfall. However, some pitfalls are more common than others, so we briefly list the most common here in order of frequency, based on our experience. In each case, one or more success criteria will help address the pitfall.

- Poorly scoped projects, typically projects that attempt to boil the ocean or solve world hunger. Proper project selection and scoping are the key solutions to this pitfall. Frequent project review will also help catch the problem early.

- Lack of available data to study and improve the process. Insufficient data is generally an indication of a project that should have been weeded out before selection. A good project identification and prioritization process will minimize this pitfall.

- Failure to follow the DMAIC or DFSS process. In some cases, poorly trained or led Black Belts may attack the problem using the Six Sigma tools haphazardly, rather than following the DMAIC process in a disciplined manner. Proper training and frequent project reviews will address this pitfall.

- A weak Black Belt or Champion. Selection of Black Belts and Champions from the top talent pool will prevent this problem.

- Dysfunctional Black Belt teams. This can occur due to poorly trained Black Belts, lack of a team culture, or missing leadership support, especially intervention from the Champion. The combination of an active Six Sigma organizational structure (including functional Champions), proper training of Black Belts, and a formal project review process will help nip this problem in the bud.

Good Questions to Ask in Project Reviews

Of course, the best questions to ask in a project review are dependent on the specific project, the experience of the Black Belt, and many other factors. Therefore, we cannot provide a generic list of the correct questions that apply in all situations. However, the types of questions leaders ask in project reviews are extremely important, in that they set the tone for the projects. Here we provide sample questions that may be appropriate to ask in some reviews, particularly if the Black Belt has not already raised the subject during the review. The questions are organized according to the specific phase of the DMAIC process to which the question would most likely pertain.

Good Questions to Ask in Project Reviews

Define

- Why are we working on this project, rather than others we could be doing?
- How does this project relate to key objectives or initiatives of the organization?
- What specifically are we trying to accomplish with this project? How will you measure success?

Measure

- Can you show me a map of the process in question?
- Were these CTQs validated by customers? If not, how were they validated?
- Did you evaluate the measurement system? How? Where's the data?

Analyze

- What data do you have to corroborate that conclusion?
- Did you plot the data? May I see the graph?
- What hypothesis do you have about the process that would explain these data?

Good Questions to Ask in Project Reviews *(continued)*

Improve

- What other options for improvement did you consider? Why were they not selected?

- How do the proposed improvements relate back to the root causes found in the analyze phase?

- Have you piloted the improvements to make sure they work?

Control

- What makes you confident that this control plan will maintain improvement?

- Is the process owner comfortable with this control plan, and has he or she committed to using it going forward?

- To what extent does this control plan consider key process variables (input, controlled and uncontrolled) as well as key process outputs?

Advice for Ensuring Success of the Six Sigma Initiative

Not every organization that has launched a Six Sigma initiative has obtained the financial benefits it anticipated. Among those that have achieved significant financial benefits, some have certainly done better than others.

Key Initiative Success Criteria

In Chapter 2 we reviewed four specific companies' experiences with Six Sigma, and based on these examples we identified the key success criteria for the overall Six Sigma initiative in Chapter 3. These key success criteria were:

- Committed leadership
- Top talent
- Supporting infrastructure

Each successful deployment of Six Sigma that we are aware of has had each of these criteria. Similarly, the root causes of each less-successful deployment that we are aware of can be traced back to the lack of one or more of these three criteria. There is simply no substitute for any of them.

Committed leadership is perhaps the most critical success criteria. Remember that there is a big difference between supportive leadership and committed leadership. Committed leadership is determined to make Six Sigma deployment successful, and will spend the necessary time and take whatever actions are required to make this happen. Supportive leadership thinks it is a good idea, but is not necessarily willing to devote personal time to the deployment, or change management style to ensure success. We know of no committed leaders who have not achieved significant success.

Committed leaders must be backed up by top talent in the operational roles in Six Sigma, such as Black Belts and Champions. These are the people who will lead the individual projects that produce the tangible results; hence the organization's most talented people are needed.

Committed leaders with less talented Black Belts, MBBs, Champions, and so on, can only achieve so much since they can't do everything themselves.

One reason many initiatives are not assigned top talent is that these people are typically quite busy doing important things. It is painful and sometimes difficult to free them up from their current duties and reassign them to Six Sigma. This is why committed leadership is necessary, to take the more difficult (but also more fruitful) path, rather than the path of least resistance, which would lead to assigning whoever was available to key Six Sigma roles.

Supporting infrastructure is perhaps a subtler success factor. The supporting infrastructure is the organizational structure and systems that provide needed support to the Six Sigma initiative, as well as providing legitimacy and formality. Some of the typical elements in this infrastructure are (see Chapter 3):

- An organizational structure for Six Sigma deployment that includes overall leadership of the effort, a Six Sigma Council, and dedicated positions for key roles (MBBs, Black Belts, etc.)

- Six Sigma planning systems; that is, development and managerial review of implementation plans, budgets, human resources plans, and so forth, on at least an annual basis. This is nothing more than the routine planning done for each business unit in a major corporation, but is often overlooked for improvement initiatives

- Support from functional groups, such as Finance, HR, Quality, Engineering, Purchasing, and so on

- Project selection and review processes

- Training systems for key roles

- Modification of human resources, reward and recognition, business planning, financial, and other business systems to support Six Sigma implementation, as needed

We've previously noted that no major corporation operates its finance department without a designated leader or Finance Committee, with unclear roles, and with resources doing finance in their spare time. If such an unorganized approach doesn't work for finance, why would we expect it to work for Six Sigma? Without such an infrastructure, Champions, MBBs, Black Belts, and others have to spend considerable time and effort justifying every training class, begging for money for each project selected, trying to track down needed resources, and competing for managerial attention. This leaves little time and energy to actually complete projects that will benefit the bottom line.

A good infrastructure gives the initiative legitimacy, resolves personnel and budgetary issues at a strategic level, and provides formal mechanisms for such things as project selection and training. In other words, this infrastructure allows us to manage the effort, rather than having it just happen. Inclusion of a supporting infrastructure is one of the true enhancements Six Sigma has brought to previous improvement initiatives, such as TQM or reengineering. Contrary to popular opinion, it is possible to add organizational structure and processes without adding a lot of bureaucracy. The key to adding infrastructure without adding bureaucracy is to ensure that the focus is always on achieving the objectives of the infrastructure (tangible results), rather than on religious adherence to the infrastructure processes.

Common Overall Initiative Pitfalls to Avoid

Like project pitfalls, the vast majority of pitfalls for the overall Six Sigma initiative have root causes related to the absence of one or more of the success criteria noted earlier. We again provide the pitfalls in the order of frequency of occurrence based on our experience, and offer suggestions for avoiding them.

- Lack of true commitment from senior leadership. Unfortunately, there is no solution for this pitfall. Our recommendation is to hold off on deployment until such commitment exists, and in the meantime try to obtain this commitment through sharing of Six Sigma success stories.

- Lack of dedicated resources; that is, an attempt to do Six Sigma in people's spare time. Obviously, in today's business world who has spare time? Such an approach will retard, if not derail, deployment. The solution is to implement a proper Six Sigma organization, including full-time resources.

■ Assignment of less than top talent to key positions. This pitfall is similar to the one in the previous bullet, in that both relate to providing the required human resources to Six Sigma. We can appreciate that it is very tempting to assign resources that are available, even if they do not represent top talent in the organization. This will not only hinder current success, but may also convince top talent in the organization that Six Sigma is not for them. The solution is to ensure that only top talent is assigned to key leadership positions. This can be done by referencing annual employee evaluations, where these are relevant.

■ Ad hoc deployment of Six Sigma, without the proper supportive infrastructure. This pitfall may not become obvious until a year or two into deployment, but it will prevent Six Sigma from having lasting impact. The key to avoiding it is for the Six Sigma leadership (overall Champion or leader, Six Sigma Council, etc.) to prioritize development of the key elements of supportive infrastructure discussed in Chapters 4 and 5.

■ A bureaucratic focus for the initiative. This can occur when such things as number of Black Belts trained, number of projects completed, percent of employees Green Belt certified, and so on, become the emphasis of the organization's Six Sigma effort. In other words, the focus is on the effort itself, and not on the results it is supposed to generate. Certainly there is no problem in measuring these internal metrics, but you must always keep in mind that the purpose of implementing Six Sigma is to better satisfy customers and generate financial benefits. Therefore, the solution to this pitfall is to always make financial benefits and direct measures of customer satisfaction, such as retention and attainment of additional business, the overall measures of success.

Good Questions to Ask in Reviews of the Overall Initiative

In Chapter 6 we discussed the need to hold periodic management reviews of overall Six Sigma deployment, as well as project reviews. Project reviews help ensure success of the Black Belt projects, but are not designed to evaluate the overall initiative from a strategic perspective. This is the purpose of the reviews of the overall initiative. A key similarity with project reviews is that the questions leaders ask in the initiative reviews also help set the tone of the Six Sigma initiative; they establish expectations, determine direction, create a mindset, and so on. Therefore, it is important that leaders ask questions that create the desired tone. There is no single list of correct questions, but the list below may prove useful to set the tone needed to make Six Sigma successful. Leaders can ask the questions at any time, but they are typically most relevant in the deployment phase noted.

Good Questions to Ask in...

Launching the Initiative

- How often are the Six Sigma projects reviewed by their Champions? By you and your staff?

- What percent of your and your leadership team's time will be allocated to Six Sigma deployment over the next year?

- May we review your overall deployment plan?

Managing the Effort

- What level of incremental operating profit from Six Sigma do you feel confident committing to this year? What is your basis for this number?

- May I see your project selection criteria, and your current project hopper? Please describe your project prioritization process.

- May I review some projects in your project tracking and reporting system?

Good Questions to Ask in ... *(continued)*

Sustaining Momentum and Growing

- Will you show me your overall financials for the Six Sigma initiative so far, expenses and returns?
- Will you show me the status of each element of your Six Sigma deployment plan?
- What are your deployment plans for extending Six Sigma across your entire business unit?

The Way We Work

- How do you manage differently now versus before Six Sigma?
- What process management systems have you implemented so far? What others are planned? Can I see the details of these systems?
- How has Six Sigma been integrated with other key initiatives in your business unit?

Summary

While many companies have achieved significant financial benefits, launching a Six Sigma initiative does not guarantee significant success. The initiative must be properly led and managed in order to be successful. We believe the material in this book will help leaders do just this. As we have noted elsewhere, Six Sigma works if you follow the process. If it is not working, you are not following the process.

Certainly anything can be improved and streamlined. However, readers should beware of claims for instant success with no significant investment or effort required. Such claims should be viewed with the same skepticism as fad programs that guarantee large weight loss without dieting or exercise. The saying "no pain, no gain" is true in both weight loss and Six Sigma. Lasting Six Sigma success requires both financial and personal commitment. Committed leadership is the single most important key to success.

We have provided an overall process for Six Sigma deployment that goes from initial decision to launch through ingraining Six Sigma into the fabric and culture of the organization. Each of the major phases of this process has been described in detail in a separate chapter. While this process does not need to be followed religiously, every organization we know of that has followed this general process has achieved significant success (about 20 organizations). Leaders need to monitor success of both the set of individual Six Sigma projects, and also the overall initiative itself. We trust that readers will find the sets of questions to ask during reviews, and lists of pitfalls for both projects and the overall initiative, helpful.

Additional Six Sigma resources that readers may find helpful are given below. Finally, we provide additional information in the form of frequently asked questions about Six Sigma deployment, and our answers to them, immediately after this chapter. These questions are based on numerous leadership interactions we have held since 1995. Good luck with your deployment!

Additional Six Sigma References

General References (What Six Sigma Is)

Eckes, George. (2001). *The Six Sigma Revolution.* John Wiley and Sons, New York, NY.

Harry, M., and R. Schroeder. (2000). *Six Sigma—The Breakthrough Management Strategy Revolutionizing The World's Top Corporations.* Currency Doubleday, New York, NY.

Pande, P., R. Neuman, and R. Cavanagh. (2000) *The Six Sigma Way.* McGraw-Hill, New York, NY.

References on the Statistical and Problem-Solving Tools

CAUSE AND EFFECT MATRIX

Breyfogle, F. W. (1999). *Implementing Six Sigma—Smarter Solutions Using Statistical Methods.* John Wiley and Sons, New York, NY, Chapter 13.

CONTROL CHARTS (STATISTICAL PROCESS CONTROL)

Automotive Industry Action Group. (1995a). *Statistical Process Control Reference Manual*, 2nd ed. Available from AIAG, Suite 200, 26200 Lahser Road, Southfield, MI 48034 (313-358-3570).

Montgomery, D. C. (2001). *Statistical Quality Control*, 3rd Ed. John Wiley and Sons, New York, NY.

CONTROL PLANS

Automotive Industry Action Group. (1994). *Advanced Quality Planning and Control Plans.* Available from AIAG, Suite 200, 26200 Lahser Road, Southfield, MI 48034 (313-358-3570).

DESIGN OF EXPERIMENTS

Box, G. E. P., W. G. Hunter, and J. S. Hunter. (1978). *Statistics for Experimenters.* John Wiley and Sons, Inc., New York, NY.

Koselka, R. The New Mantra: MVT (multivariable testing) *Forbes*, March 11, 1996, 114-118.

Myers, R.H., and D. C. Montgomery. (1995). *Response Surface Methodology.* Wiley-Interscience, New York, NY.

FAILURE MODES AND EFFECTS ANALYSIS

Automotive Industry Action Group. (1995b). *Potential Failure Mode and Effects Analysis Reference Manual,* 2nd ed. Available from AIAG, Suite 200, 26200 Lahser Road, Southfield, MI 48034 (313-358-3570).

MEASUREMENT SYSTEMS ANALYSIS

Automotive Industry Action Group. (1990). *Measurement Systems Analysis Reference Manual.* Available from AIAG, Suite 200, 26200 Lahser Road, Southfield, MI 48034 (313-358-3570).

Wheeler, D.J., and R.W. Lyday. (1989). *Evaluating the Measurement Process,* 2nd ed. SPC Press, Knoxville, TN.

MULTI-VARI STUDIES

Breyfogle, F. W. (1999). *Implementing Six Sigma—Smarter Solutions Using Statistical Methods.* John Wiley and Sons, New York, NY, 277-280.

Montgomery, D.C., E. A. Peck, and G. Vining. (2001). *Introduction to Linear Regression Analysis.* John Wiley and Sons, New York, NY.

Snee, R. D. "My Process is Too Variable—Now What Do I Do?" *Quality Progress*, December 2001, 65-68.

STATISTICAL THINKING

Hoerl, R.W., and R. D. Snee. (2002). *Statistical Thinking: Improving Business Performance.* Duxbury Press Thomson Learning, Pacific Grove, CA.

Training in the Tools

Hoerl, R. W. (2001). "Six Sigma Black Belts—What Do They Need to Know? (With Discussion)," *J. Quality Technology*, Vol. 33, No. 4, 391-435 (also see references noted).

Compilation of Six Sigma Tools

Breyfogle, F. W. (1999). *Implementing Six Sigma–Smarter Solutions Using Statistical Methods*. John Wiley and Sons, New York, NY.

Pyzdek, T. (1999). *The Complete Guide to Six Sigma*. Quality Publishing, Tucson, AZ.

Rath and Strong. (2001). *Six Sigma Pocket Guide*. Rath and Strong Management Consultants, Lexington, MA.

References on Individual Companies' Experiences

English, Bill. (2001). "Implementing Six Sigma—The Iomega Story," Presented at the Conference on Six Sigma in the Pharmaceutical Industry, Philadelphia, PA, November 27-28, 2001.

"The Honeywell Edge", *Six Sigma Forum Magazine*, February 2002, 14-17.

Welch, J.F. (2001). *Jack, Straight From the Gut*. Warner Business Books, New York, NY.

Young, J. (2001). "Driving Performance Results at American Express", *Six Sigma Forum Magazine*, November 2001, 19-27.

DEPLOYMENT QUESTIONS AND ANSWERS

Throughout this book we have addressed common issues, questions, and potential pitfalls involved in Six Sigma deployment. We now integrate and document our advice on a large number of such issues. We present this advice as a series of the most common questions we've been asked about Six Sigma deployment since 1995. They represent the most critical concerns of most organizations implementing Six Sigma. Our responses are based on our experiences, both positive and negative, deploying Six Sigma with a large number of organizations. We hope these answers will guide you and help you to avoid many of the mistakes made by other organizations.

The questions are summarized in Table A-1 and have been organized into the following logical categories:

- Six Sigma in general
- MBB and Black Belt roles
- Project selection and review
- Training
- Financial benefits
- Other HR issues

TABLE A-1   Frequently Asked Six Sigma Deployment Questions

General Questions About Six Sigma
1. How is Six Sigma different from TQM?
2. How should Six Sigma fit with other existing quality systems?
3. How do I convince my leadership if they are not committed?
4. How can we speed up Six Sigma implementation?
5. How does Six Sigma apply outside of manufacturing?
6. How does Six Sigma apply to design?
7. How does Six Sigma apply to smaller companies?
8. How does Six Sigma apply to government or non-profit organizations?
9. How do I use Six Sigma to improve the top line?
10. How do I reduce the bureaucracy of Six Sigma?
11. How do I select a Six Sigma provider?

Questions Concerning MBB and BB Roles
12. How do I select good MBBs and BBs?
13. Should MBBs and BBs be line or staff jobs?
14. Should MBBs and BBs be certified?
15. How many MBBs, BBs, and GBs do I need?
16. How many projects should a Black Belt work on at one time?

Project Selection and Review Questions
17. How do I select good projects?
18. How do I properly scope a project?
19. What if my project can't be done in four to six months?
20. How do I structure project reviews?
21. How do I close out projects?

Training Questions
22. How do I design a good Six Sigma training system?
23. What training do project teams need?

Questions Concerning Financial Benefits
24. Are the published benefits of Six Sigma real?
25. How do I sustain the gains of Six Sigma?
26. How do I calculate the financial impact of a project?
27. Can Six Sigma successfully achieve non-financial objectives?

Other Human Resources Questions
28. How do I involve the entire organization in Six Sigma?
29. How should I modify the reward and recognition system to support Six Sigma?
30. How do I form effective teams?
31. How do I find the resources?

General Questions About Six Sigma

1. How is Six Sigma different from TQM?

While Six Sigma is certainly different from previous initiatives, it builds on many of the aspects of previous improvement initiatives, especially TQM. Like most of these initiatives, TQM had much to offer and was fundamentally sound technically, but often lacked a deployment process and the associated managerial and leadership components needed to drive fundamental change.

Some of the components of TQM that are found in Six Sigma are:

- A customer orientation and focus

- A process view of work

- A continuous improvement mindset

- A goal of improving all aspects and functions of the organization

- Data-based decision making

- The use of statistical tools on a broad basis

There is very little disagreement about the value of these positive aspects of TQM. So how does Six Sigma go beyond these and drive sustained tangible benefits on a massive scale, something TQM struggled to do?

In Chapter 1 we described Six Sigma as having a managerial initiative aspect and a methods and tools aspect. Most of the methods and tools listed were applied in TQM initiatives, so they are not new. Nor do they guarantee success. The most important contribution of Six Sigma in this technical area has been the introduction of a roadmap (DMAIC) that shows how to link and integrate the tools into an overall approach to improvement. This roadmap enables trained Black Belts to quickly improve virtually any process. They don't have to invent a new methodology to solve each new problem. The DMAIC roadmap has been a huge breakthrough for Six Sigma. Such an integrated approach was sorely missing in most TQM implementations.

It is on the managerial initiative aspect, however, that Six Sigma really stands out as bringing something new to the party. Specifically, Six Sigma provides the needed leadership and infrastructure to enable the methods and tools to be successfully deployed on a large scale. Leadership and infrastructure were also not part of most TQM implementations. In our experience, TQM typically suffered from the following deficiencies:

- Led by midlevel managers while senior leaders worried about the "really important stuff"
- Not directed at achieving tangible, budgeted results
- Did not obtain the services of the top talent
- Lacked formal processes for project selection and review
- Lacked financial scrutiny to budget for and validate financial savings
- Did not have well-defined roles
- Was implemented by part time resources

Fortunately, the three major success factors in Six Sigma deployment address each of these issues:

- Committed leadership
- Top talent
- Supporting infrastructure

Chapter 3 explains each of these in greater detail. If TQM had each of these success factors in place, it would also have been hugely successful. If your Six Sigma implementation looks like a rehash of TQM, it is probably accomplishing nothing more than giving Scott Adams more material for Dilbert™ cartoons. A properly deployed Six Sigma initiative that has each of the success factors noted will not look like a rehash of TQM.

Six Sigma has the best combination of technical and nontechnical aspects that we have seen, but it is certainly possible that another even better methodology exists or will be developed in the future.

2. How should Six Sigma fit with other existing quality systems?

This question is discussed at length in Chapter 7, so we will only summarize here. Six Sigma is a methodology for making breakthrough improvements. It was never intended as a system for managing quality in an ongoing manner, nor was it intended to define the proper criteria for world-class quality management. We do not do Six Sigma *instead* of ISO 9000 or Baldrige assessment. For example, many customers, especially in the European

Community, require ISO 9000 compliance. Being a Six Sigma company does not satisfy this requirement; you will still need to comply with ISO 9000.

Fortunately, there are logical linkages between these systems. For example, in Chapter 7 we discussed how to move from Six Sigma being an initiative to being the way you work. It takes a considerable amount of effort to take everything you have accomplished through Six Sigma and institutionalize it into daily operations. ISO 9000 compliance can provide considerable help here. In essence, ISO 9000 requires that you "say what you do" and "do what you say". Therefore, if you modify your ISO 9000 documentation to say what you are doing with Six Sigma, the quality audits and other ISO infrastructure that ensures compliance will also ensure that you continue to "do what you said" about Six Sigma. You can then dismantle that part of the Six Sigma infrastructure that is redundant.

Similarly, Six Sigma does not provide a template for evaluating an organization's overall quality management efforts. It does not dictate quality policy, strategies for working with suppliers on a corporate (versus an individual project) basis, quality awareness training of rank and file employees, labor relations, or structure of quality auditing. Since Six Sigma is project-oriented, there is still a need for development and deployment of overall quality policy, and ongoing quality systems to ensure you follow the quality policy. This is where the Malcolm Baldrige criteria can still play an important role. Some corporations choose to formally apply for the Baldrige Award, while many others simply use the published criteria as a benchmark to assess their own quality management efforts.

The Baldrige criteria provide one generally respected overview of the most important aspects that organizations need to consider in quality management. Six Sigma does not provide a replacement for this holistic overview. It is, however, a proven approach for succeeding in many of these Baldrige criteria, such as tangible business results. Again, there is a good linkage rather than a competition here. In summary, you should integrate Six Sigma with existing quality management systems, rather than trying to make Six Sigma something it is not.

3. How do I convince my leadership if they are not committed?

For the reasons discussed in Chapter 3, Six Sigma cannot succeed without committed leadership. Unfortunately, many business leaders will find themselves in a situation where they wish to implement Six Sigma, but their CEO is not convinced. Our advice is to proceed cautiously until top leadership is willing to truly commit. One approach to convince them is to use a partial deployment of Six Sigma, as explained in Chapter 4.

In a partial deployment, an organizational unit (division, business unit, plant, etc.) deploys Six Sigma completely within that one unit, where there is leadership commitment. Obviously, the leadership above this unit needs to be aware of the partial deployment, and agree not to interfere. Once the partial deployment has successfully improved the bottom-line, senior leadership will become convinced and willing to commit to a full deployment. Another option is to arrange for executives from Six Sigma success stories like AlliedSignal, GE, or DuPont to meet with your senior leadership.

4. How can we speed up Six Sigma implementation?

Like any major change effort, institutionalization of Six Sigma takes time. Fortunately, it pays its own way with project savings, so there isn't a long wait for tangible benefits. Nevertheless, some executives will be anxious to make the effort go even faster. First you should recognize that you speed up implementation by following the Six Sigma process. We are reminded of an AlliedSignal manager's admonishment: "Six Sigma works if you follow the process. If Six Sigma is not working you are not following the process." Taking short cuts will invariably slow the implementation down rather than speed it up. Conceptually, there is no limit to how fast you can go. If you wish to go twice as fast, you just need twice as many Black Belts and projects. This gives leaders a lot of leeway, in that they can go at whatever pace they would like. However, there are some practical constraints that limit the overall pace of the effort.

For example, you can pull only so many employees away from their existing work before operations come to a screeching halt, and you are no longer serving the needs of your customers. Someone has to keep the standard products and services going while others are focused on improvement. In addition, most organizations, including Six Sigma providers, will be limited in the number of qualified MBBs they can make available to train new Black Belts and Green Belts. More and more projects will also strain your project selection and review systems. Obviously, leaders have more to do than select and review projects. So while in theory you can go as fast as you want, there are some practical considerations that limit your speed. We don't know of anyone who has fully deployed Six Sigma in less than five years. Leaders should be impatient, but not unrealistic.

Some shortcuts that we do not recommend include:

- Making Black Belts part time so that you can have more of them

- Shortening the training, or putting large numbers of Black Belts (over 30) in each training session

- Giving the four weeks of Black Belt training consecutively without breaks between weeks

- Targeting project completion for two to three months instead of four to six months

Taking the first or last shortcut obviously doesn't actually save anything; you just have divided everything in half. The second and third shortcuts result in less learning in the classroom. These do save training time, but generally produce less benefit from each project. Anything can be improved, including Six Sigma training, but we have not seen effective Black Belt training done in significantly less than four weeks in manufacturing. In non-manufacturing areas such as finance, we have seen shorter training work because some topics do not need to be covered in as much detail, e.g., experimental design (see Hoerl [2001]).

If greater speed is desired, the first action we would recommend is to choose an experienced Six Sigma provider, who can help the organization hit the ground running. Secondly, it is possible to increase the dedicated resources (see Question 15 for typical numbers). You can do this within reason and still increase the speed of both deployment and results. Another option is to hire experienced external resources, including Black Belts, who can come in and deliver results quickly with minimal direction. External resources will not be familiar with your organization or your processes, so it will take some time for these people to build credibility with the organization as well as learn the processes you use to run your business. In summary, it is certainly possible to increase speed of deployment, but there are no shortcuts.

5. How does Six Sigma apply outside of manufacturing?

This topic was discussed in Chapter 6. We provide here some additional perspectives to complement it. In our experience, Six Sigma applies equally well to non-manufacturing and manufacturing. There are several reasons why the common misconception persists that Six Sigma primarily applies to manufacturing. First of all, Motorola pioneered Six

Sigma in electronics manufacturing. Therefore, much of the early media publications and training materials were oriented towards electronics manufacturing.

Secondly, manufacturing is perhaps the easiest place to apply the process thinking that is integral to Six Sigma. In manufacturing it is not difficult to see the process—just follow the pipes! It is much harder to "see" the closing process in accounting, or the procurement process. Thirdly, as we discussed in Chapter 6, manufacturing usually has the best measurement processes in the company. This is primarily due to the fact that you are required to keep close track of raw materials and finished goods to account for your debits and credits.

The good measurement systems have two immediate impacts that lead to easier implementation of Six Sigma. First of all, the waste and rework in manufacturing has managerial visibility. If you are losing 20% of your finished products as waste, the cost of this problem is visible to management. On the other hand, the cost of financial analysts reworking the numbers five or six times in the budgeting process until management is willing to accept them is invisible. You cannot look at standard financial reports and immediately see that you are wasting huge amounts of analysts' time (and therefore huge amounts of money) by this rework, because you are not measuring it.

The second way that better measurement systems make application easier in manufacturing is that once you begin the Six Sigma project, the data needed for analysis are more readily available. For example, in most factories a measurement system for waste is already in place for accounting purposes. This will help bring visibility of the waste problem to management, as noted above. In addition, however, once a Six Sigma project is chartered, the team will be able to hit the ground running on the project because the data they need are readily available. Conversely, if you want to work on reducing rework in your budgeting process, you must first figure out how to measure the time spent on rework, and implement a measurement system.

Implementing measurement systems is rarely easy, especially when people are involved. Often people are suspicious that Big Brother will be watching them, and managers sometimes worry that the data collected will expose the inadequacies of their operations. Without strong leadership, there will likely be stiff resistance to implementing the measurement system. Black Belts with manufacturing experience may become frustrated and suggest: "Hey, why don't we do something back in manufacturing?"

Unfortunately, overemphasis on manufacturing has several negative consequences. It certainly limits the level of tangible impact Six Sigma can have. Even in a manufacturing business, such as automobiles, a very small percentage of employees actually work on the assembly line. A much larger percentage work in non-manufacturing processes, such as design, procurement, marketing, finance, human resources, and so on. No improvements will be made in these other areas if Six Sigma is not applied there, and minimal improvements will be made if there is token application. In addition, it will be impossible to change the "genetic code" of the business, that is, to fundamentally change the culture, if only people in manufacturing have been directly involved. Without universal involvement, Six Sigma will likely be just a short-lived efficiency initiative.

Another subtler problem with "tunnel vision" on manufacturing is that it leads to a "victim mentality." Those working in manufacturing begin to feel that every improvement effort is solely focused on them. The implications of this are obvious: all your problems are in manufacturing. Finance is fine, marketing is fine, logistics is fine, everybody else is fine, but manufacturing is a mess. This perception can further sabotage the already strained relations between manufacturing and other functions. Conversely, if Six Sigma is applied across the board, then the message is that you can all improve, and indeed are expected to do so.

One suggestion for dealing with the measurement issue in non-manufacturing applications is to begin in areas where good measurement systems already exist and where the savings are immediately obvious. Accounts payable and accounts receivable are examples. In order to satisfy accounting needs there are generally good measurement systems not only on the amounts in these accounts, but also on the timing of billing and payment. Another advantage of applications in these areas is that there is usually lots of money to be made by improving the process, all of which is easily quantified because of the measurement systems.

For example, by collecting faster in accounts receivable you can benefit from the time value of money, and also avoid costly delinquencies and defaults. One Black Belt project in collections at GE (see Chapter 2) produced just under $3 million in annual savings. By paying your invoices just in time to receive early payment discounts, you are able to hold your money longer on average, but still receive all available discounts. This typically amounts to huge savings, and as previously noted, these savings are easily quantified.

Manufacturing operations have typically been the focus of previous improvement initiatives, and have often been analyzed and "tweaked" on a daily basis by engineers trained in the scientific method. Therefore, in some instances making further improvements, even with an approach as powerful as Six Sigma, requires a lot of analysis and hard work. Fortunately (or perhaps unfortunately), most non-manufacturing operations have not been subject to major improvement initiatives, and employees in these areas have usually been held accountable for conformance to standard practices (generally accepted accounting principles, or GAAP, for example) rather than for engineering-type improvement efforts. The net result is that there is typically a great deal of "low-hanging fruit" that can be quickly harvested through Six Sigma. Why any business would want to narrowly focus on manufacturing without picking up this low hanging financial fruit is not clear to us.

6. How does Six Sigma apply to design?

DFSS was discussed in Chapter 6, so we provide only a short summary of this discussion here. Six Sigma applies to both product and process design (recall the GE LightSpeed digital CT scanner mentioned in Chapter 2). Conceptually, design can be considered a process, and Six Sigma can be applied in a straightforward manner to improve this process. In most cases, however, organizations wish to apply Six Sigma to the design of a specific new product or service. Six Sigma applies here as well. What is needed is a different roadmap more tailored to design. If a team applies the DMAIC roadmap to designing a new product, it will likely stumble in the measure phase, since there is no existing process on which to take measurements.

GE developed the DMADV (define, measure, analyze, design, verify) roadmap (adopted by many others since then) to apply to design projects. The focus of each phase is as follows:

- Define—develop project charter
- Measure—determine CTQs, and ability to measure them
- Analyze—develop the high-level or conceptual design; predict CTQ performance
- Design—add details to high-level design; refine predictions; develop control plan
- Verify—pilot the design under realistic conditions to measure actual CTQ performance

This approach to DFSS maintains the key technical elements of DMAIC:

- Disciplined approach
- Use of metrics throughout the process
- Use of analytical tools
- Emphasis on variation
- Data-based decision making

One unique challenge in DFSS is estimation of financial benefits. Since you are typically avoiding problems rather than fixing them, it is much more difficult to determine an auditable savings figure. Many organizations have not attempted to report financial savings from DFSS projects.

7. How does Six Sigma apply to smaller companies?

There is nothing unique about large companies that would make Six Sigma deployment easier for them. On the contrary, in large companies the middle management layer may have their own opinions about Six Sigma, and slow the initiative barring strong senior leadership. We have found that it is generally easier to introduce radical change to smaller companies because there are fewer organizational layers between the CEO and the front line workers. To use a nautical analogy, it is easier to turn a small ship than an aircraft carrier. We believe that the main reason Six Sigma is generally associated with large companies is that firms such as Motorola, AlliedSignal, and GE have been more frequently discussed in the media.

Admittedly there are unique challenges in smaller companies. For example, small companies will lose the economies of scale when setting up MBB or Black Belt training. A small company may not have 20–30 Black Belts to put into a class together, and may have to use very small class sizes (effective for learning, but less efficient for training), or utilize public courses. Small companies operate in a lean environment with employees assigned numerous jobs. A small company may also not have the opportunity to benchmark internally that a large conglomerate like GE or DuPont has. Instituting any new formal infrastructure may be difficult in very small firms. However, the infrastructure may not need to be formal. The key point is that there must be a supporting infrastructure; for most organizations, it must be formal to work, but it is possible that a very small company can do this informally. It is important to make sure that all the infrastructure roles are being carried out.

Other unique considerations with small companies include: the typically lean organizational structure, making it harder to dedicate Black Belts; the fact that most employees do more than one job—leading to frequent distractions; and the need for Black Belts and MBBs to be experienced with this particular business. We have found that each of these concerns can be adequately addressed with proper planning. Conversely, if they are used as excuses, the initiative is not likely to succeed.

8. How does Six Sigma apply to government or non-profit organizations?

While making a profit is not the objective of government or non-profit organizations, they still need to produce tangible results subject to financial constraints. Budget issues, that is, not having enough money to do what they really want to do, are a constant concern for both government and non-profits. By eliminating waste in government agencies, public schools, and non-profit organizations, there will be money saved, meaning more for services or less of a need to raise taxes or tuition. Certainly, being able to do more with less would be of significant value to government, including state-funded universities, and non-profits.

Unfortunately, local, state, or federal governments are not generally expected to produce continuous improvement. The public has accepted as fact the supposition that to do more requires more money. For example, while many may whine about the rising cost of postage stamps, very few seriously challenge the U.S. Postal Service's need to raise prices to keep up with inflation. However, many business leaders have been asked to hold costs steady in times of inflation, or even to lower costs while enhancing services, and they have relied on improvement methods like Six Sigma to accomplish these goals. There is no reason why Six Sigma could not be used to eliminate waste and rework in the U.S. Postal Service, for example, thereby avoiding or delaying the need for price increases. We are not intending to single out the U.S. Postal Service; the same argument could be made for the Department of Defense, the Commerce Department, local and state government organizations, and so on.

On a similar note, tuition at most universities in the United States has been increasing at a rate faster than inflation for many years. While there are certainly valid reasons for additional expenditures, such as wiring classrooms and dorms for the Internet, these unavoidable increases have not been offset by savings from productivity and cost reductions. Again, there is no societal expectation for universities to reduce waste and rework in their operations, hence the increasing tuitions are met with minimal pubic outcry. However, major universities have billion-dollar budgets that have the same accounts-payable and accounts-receivable savings opportunities as businesses. In addition, Six Sigma could be used to improve the educational experience of students, as well as other non-financial measures. Recall that some Six Sigma projects will be more focused on enhanced customer satisfaction than on directly saving money.

Relative to non-profit organizations, improvement initiatives such as Six Sigma offer a potential solution to their funding gaps. By eliminating waste and rework you are able to do more with the same or less money. Roger Hoerl met with executives of the Wildwood Institute, a non-profit organization for the neurologically impaired, as part of a GE-Wildwood discussion of Six Sigma. After the interaction, Managing Director Bill Sofko Jr. noted, "Many of the concepts you introduced with regard to Six Sigma are directly applicable to our situation here at Wildwood" (personal communication). Why, one might ask? Because, Sofko noted, "…we are trying to improve the quality and cost effectiveness of current services while we pioneer new approaches as well."

GE volunteers have, in fact, completed Six Sigma projects with a number of non-profit organizations. Sofko also pointed out another benefit of quantitative approaches such as Six Sigma for non-profits: "Long-term survival in human services will necessitate that we become better able to measure our results and articulate them in terms that our multiple and varied customers understand and value." In other words, many supporters of non-profits want tangible evidence of the impact of their contributions. Again, we can consider projects focused on enhanced customer satisfaction rather than on direct cost savings.

9. How do I use Six Sigma to improve the top line?

Most of the published benefits of Six Sigma have involved bottom-line improvements—cost savings from reduced waste and rework. However, Six Sigma is also extremely valuable in improving the top line, growing sales, and market share. Top-line growth and internal savings are a powerful combination. This issue was discussed at length in Chapter 6, so we will simply highlight the key points here.

Almost all Six Sigma projects will produce intangible top line benefits by improving the products and services that customers see. Satisfied and delighted customers generally lead to more business. However, it is hard to attribute top line growth directly to a specific internal improvement project. The major means of using Six Sigma to directly increase top line growth are:

- Using Design for Six Sigma (DFSS) to create new and better products and associated services (say, handling logistics for customers)

- Increasing process capacity when the product line is sold out

- Applying Six Sigma to sales and marketing processes

- Improving the service processes that directly touch the customer, such as delivery, billing, and customer service (leading to more sales)

- Taking Six Sigma directly to the customer with "at the customer, for the customer" projects (leading to more sales)

10. How do I reduce the bureaucracy of Six Sigma?

Whenever organizations are set up, some level of bureaucracy will creep in. Since Six Sigma does indeed introduce a new infrastructure, it is susceptible to this phenomenon. A key fact to remember is that bureaucracy focuses on the letter of the law rather than on the spirit. This is why many legal institutions, which are required to follow the letter of the law, come across as very bureaucratic. The U.S. Internal Revenue Service (IRS) is one example that immediately comes to mind.

Your Six Sigma infrastructure should focus not on rigidly following rules, but rather on the results you are trying to achieve. Generally, the rules help you achieve the results and therefore should be followed. However, whenever the rules do not help but rather hinder your efforts, you should either change the rules or violate the rules, assuming there are no legal or ethical issues in doing so. It is the responsibility of Six Sigma leadership to ensure that your infrastructure is focused on delivering tangible results, not on counting the number of Black Belts, completed projects, or management reviews. Certainly, there is nothing wrong with counting such things, but these metrics are means to an end, not an end in themselves. Senior executives should be looking for signs of bureaucracy when performing audits of the overall deployment.

11. How do I select a Six Sigma provider?

Selection of a Six Sigma provider is a very personal decision, much like selecting a family doctor. The provider should have impressive credentials, but organizations should also feel that they have a good relationship built on trust with the provider. The provider that worked well with Company *X* may not be the right provider for Company *Y*. The process we recommend for selection of a provider is this:

- Develop overall company philosophy and principles relative to Six Sigma
- Develop tangible criteria for providers
- Develop a candidate list, based on research, word of mouth, and benchmarking
- Interview the candidate list of providers
- Select the most desired provider
- Negotiate with desired provider; repeat previous step if these negotiations are unsuccessful
- Announce final decision

This approach is obviously very different from the "bid" approach in which providers are asked to submit a bid for Six Sigma services, and then the company goes with the lowest bidder. The bid approach is certainly appropriate in certain situations, such as short-term needs for commodities. However, few people would want to follow the bid approach to select a family doctor! You want to go with the best doctor you can find, unless his or her price is unrealistic.

The reason we suggest starting with your overall philosophy and principles relative to Six Sigma is that consistency with these strategic values should be a primary consideration in developing the original list of candidates, and of course in interacting with them. For example, if the company wishes to become self-sufficient within a couple of years, it should look only at providers who promote this philosophy.

Of course, credentials, track record, and testimonials from existing customers are also relevant factors in the decision. You should base your specific criteria for provider selection on these values, but in more specific form. For example, if your principle is that the provider should deliver tailored training, your specific criterion might be that the provider must have experience in your industry. On the other hand, you may want a provider who is not experienced in your industry and who will bring a fresh perspective to your organization.

We strongly recommend face-to-face interviews with candidate providers. This is too critical a decision to be made via emails or conference calls; remember that the relationship with the provider is as important as the tangible qualifications it may have. Table A-2 lists potential questions to ask candidate providers. No doubt there will be other, more company-specific questions that you will add to this list. Price and terms are obviously still important, so it is possible that you will not be able to reach agreeable terms with your most desired provider. If this occurs, you move on to your second choice. However, using the existence of multiple vendors to leverage price is dangerous unless you feel comfortable with the capabilities of each of the vendors you are considering.

TABLE A-2   Questions for Evaluating the Qualifications of Six Sigma Providers

1. What percentage of your employees have served in senior management positions (CEO, COO, President, Vice-President)? In middle management positions?

2. May I see a list of companies your firm has consulted with, including a list of references that I can contact to learn more about the service you provide?

3. With what awards or honors have members of your firm been recognized by professional societies?

4. May I see a representative list of the papers, books and articles that have been published by members of your firm?

5. What national, state, and local quality awards have the members of your firm been involved with as an examiner or in some leadership position?

6. How many instructors do you use in a typical BB and GB training class?

7. Who will be the project manager for our deployment? What qualifications does this person have and what will his or her role be? May I see his or her resume?

8. What is the Six Sigma experience of your instructors for our deployment? May I see their resumes?

9. What types of Six Sigma consulting and training do you offer? For example, what do you offer by level (MBB, BB, GB, etc.) and by type (manufacturing, DFSS, business process-oriented, and so on)? May I see your training curricula with detailed agendas?

10. In what languages is your training material translated? In what languages do you offer live training? Electronic training?

11. How flexible are you in customizing your instructional material?

12. What is your approach to leadership training?

13. How do you evaluate your training programs? May I see your data from previous courses?

14. How do you integrate Six Sigma with other improvement initiatives such as Lean manufacturing, Baldrige, or ISO 9000?

15. How do you integrate Six Sigma into the entire enterprise?

Questions Concerning MBB and BB Roles

12. How do I select good MBBs and BBs?

This issue was discussed at length in Chapter 4 and rather than repeat ourselves, we'll briefly summarize here. Both MBBs and Black Belts need to have a combination of leadership skills, technical skills, and "soft" skills (communication, mentoring, and so on). Black Belts in particular should also have good subject-matter knowledge of the processes they are improving.

Some key attributes to look for in Black Belts are:

- Technical leader in the area of the project
  - Helpful for the first project
  - Less important for subsequent projects
- Respected by the organization
- Computer literate
- Analytical thinker—not afraid of numbers
- Comfortable with basic statistics
- Able to lead teams—"soft skills"
- Skilled at project management
- Positive, can-do attitude

Keep in mind that Black Belts are valued for what they can *do*, not for what they *know*. Therefore, you should look first to those who have demonstrated ability to achieve tangible results, not necessarily those who have the most extensive training in quality or statistics. MBBs need similar skills, although their technical, mentoring, and teaching skills need to be even more extensive. We suggest looking first within the company, although in some cases you will need to bring in external candidates. See Hoerl (2001), in addition to Chapter 4, for more discussion of this topic.

13. Should MBBs and BBs be line or staff jobs?

The key point here is whether the MBBs and Black Belts should continue to report to their existing chain of command, or be pulled out into a central Six Sigma organization. We have seen both approaches work. For example, AlliedSignal generally had Black Belts continue to report through their existing line organization, while GE often pulled them into a central organization. There are a couple of important principles to keep in mind when making this decision.

The most important principle is to ensure that Black Belts and MBBs are truly freed up from their regular jobs to concentrate 100% on Six Sigma. There is often concern that if Black Belts continue to report to their existing bosses, who are primarily accountable for results other than from Six Sigma, these bosses will be tempted to pull the Black Belts back into operational issues not related to their projects. If you share this concern for your organization, or you find evidence after launch that it is happening, then we would recommend you go with a central Six Sigma staff organization. Conversely, if you do not share this concern for your organization, and there is no evidence that it is occurring, then there is no problem with leaving MBBs and Black Belts in their current line organization.

A second principle is that you want to minimize bureaucracy. Certainly, there needs to be a strong infrastructure supporting Six Sigma, including an organizational structure and the required systems and processes (see chapters 5 and 6). However, you need to make sure that any additional structure or systems add significant value. Therefore, before removing MBBs or Black Belts from their line organizations and putting them into a central quality staff organization, you should make sure this will add value to your efforts.

Our general recommendation is to leave MBBs and Black Belts in their existing line organizations, *assuming* they will not be drawn back in to operational issues.

14. Should MBBs and BBs be certified?

Here too, different approaches can work. Overall, we recommend certification of MBBs, Black Belts, and Green Belts when this actually drives the desired behavior. As a counter-example, certification based on number of projects may drive the behavior of rushing through projects to get another check mark towards certification.

One of the major issues about certification is the lack of standard certification criteria. For example, recruiters will often request a "certified" MBB or Black Belt to fill a position, but this term has no meaning without specifying the certification process. Many consultants, companies, and professional societies such as the American Society for Quality (ASQ) have their own certification criteria and processes. Some stress test results, while others stress number of projects completed.

Another challenge is that you really want to certify *ability to achieve results*, rather than *knowledge of the field*. Therefore, certification criteria must include results obtained in actual projects rather than just test scores, although we do recommend testing trainees to ensure they are developing the required knowledge. See Hoerl (2001) for a more in-depth discussion of these issues.

A good certification process will carefully consider the purpose for certification in the first place. Generally the goals of certification include documenting that someone has reached a desired level of competency, and perhaps recognizing key contributors as part of the overall Six Sigma reward and recognition system (see Chapter 5). Good certification criteria will thus elicit the behaviors the organization wishes to encourage. For example, we recommend that total savings produced (either "hard" or the total of "hard" and "soft") be a key criteria. Certainly you wish to drive the behavior of achieving greater savings. Credit should also be given for DFSS projects, whose savings may be difficult to quantify, and for resolution of critical customer issues, where you may have protected business but again it is difficult to quantify the exact dollar savings.

Further, the certification process, and any benefits of certification—be they tangible or intangible—should be completely clear to the organization. A "secret" certification process will likely produce a lot of negative energy. It is important to solicit and take into account inputs from MBBs, Black Belts, and Green Belts in the design of the process. A certification process that is aligned with the strategy and desired behaviors of the organization, and that is based on the inputs of the MBBs, Black Belts, and Green Belts themselves, will likely be a successful one.

15. How many MBBs, BBs, and GBs do I need?

There is no single correct answer to this question, although we can provide some general guidance. The number of resources required is directly linked to the speed and magnitude of the organization's deployment effort. As noted above, one way to speed up implementation is to allocate more resources to it. Based on the typical savings of Black Belt projects, and the typical number of projects completed per year, you can forecast the savings that will likely be achieved. Therefore, the desired pace of improvement and bottom line savings, and your willingness to invest to achieve that pace, will largely determine the number of MBBs, Black Belts, and so on.

That said, the general rules of thumb we suggest are:

- Designate one Black Belt per 50-100 employees (total employees, not just exempt)

- Designate one MBB for every 10-15 Black Belts

- All employees should eventually be trained in the Six Sigma improvement process

Although these are only rules of thumb, consider carefully before deploying Six Sigma with MBB and Black Belt resources significantly different from these levels. With significantly fewer, it will be difficult to obtain critical mass. With significantly more, it will be difficult to properly support the effort and still maintain current operations.

16. How many projects should a Black Belt work on at one time?

Obviously, the best answer to this question depends on a number of factors, such as the experience and capability of the Black Belt, the complexity of the projects, size and experience of the teams working with the Black Belt on each project, and so on. However, we recommend that while in initial training, the Black Belt be allowed to focus on only one project. After he or she completes training and gets experience on this project, you can add another project (two total). More experienced Black Belts should be able to handle three or four projects at a time.

Project Selection and Review Questions

17. How do I select good projects?

This question was discussed at length in chapters 4 and 5, so we will only summarize the key points here. First, you want projects to be strategically chosen based on well thought out criteria, rather than selected in an ad-hoc manner. The two main focus areas should be current strategic initiatives, and in any areas in which the organization is experiencing pain, such as a serious complaint by a critical customer. Process baseline and entitlement data is very helpful here.

In general, you should be maintaining a project hopper that identifies potential projects, reviews them, and selects the most promising projects ahead of time. In this way, once a Black Belt completes a project, there will be other pre-screened projects waiting to be done. The project hopper avoids "downtime" for Black Belts, and also helps prevent the selection of poor projects, which could happen if Black Belts are rushed in selecting their next assignments. The Six Sigma organization is responsible for maintaining the project hopper. We do not recommend each Black Belt selecting his or her own projects.

Some general criteria for selecting projects are:

- Clear connection to business priorities
- Solution to problem of major importance to the organization
- Reasonable scope—doable in four to six months (if not—split up into several smaller projects)
- Clear quantitative measures of success
- Support and approval of management.

18. How do I properly scope a project?

As we've noted throughout this book, proper planning is key to the success of Six Sigma projects, and to the overall Six Sigma effort. The project scope is a critical component of the charter, your contract that also defines the problem to be addressed, goals and objectives, high-level project plan, resources, and so on. The scope specifically defines what you will and will not do. A draft of the charter, including the scope, should be developed when the project is put into the project hopper. Once the project is given to a Black Belt, this draft needs to be further refined.

A common pitfall is for Black Belt teams to overcommit and thereby fail when they might have succeeded with a more reasonable scope. In setting the scope, it is important to document what you think you can actually accomplish in four to six months. (We address projects that can't possibly be done in four to six months below.)

It is equally important to document what you will *not* accomplish. By explicitly stating what is outside your scope, you can minimize the risk of "scope creep" sabotaging your project. Scope creep occurs when you start with a reasonable scope, but gradually the scope is widened as "just one more thing" is added several times.

For example, in designing (DFSS project) a new web-based system, one manager may suggest that it would be great if the system had foreign language capability. Later, a business leader may ask for customization for one of her critical customers. Later, the Champion may point out that marketing would be delighted if you could just add one more platform to your architecture. This is a very common phenomenon, and results in a well-scoped project becoming a "boil the ocean" project destined for failure. However, if the scope explicitly excluded foreign language capability, customization, and additional architectures, saying no would be much easier.

In summary, we recommend that a high-level scope be developed when the project is put into the project hopper. The Black Belt and Champion who take this project should then refine the scope, ensuring that they can achieve meaningful results in four to six months. It is helpful to consciously think about, and document, what is outside the scope and will not be done in this project. Future projects could add to the original project, and address some of the important issues outside the current scope. In general, the scope should be "frozen" in the define or measure phase of the project.

19. What if my project can't be done in four to six months?

Isn't four to six months unrealistic? Recall that Six Sigma uses a four to six month drumbeat of projects being completed and savings being realized. Six Sigma avoids long, drawn-out projects that tend to test managers' patience. You can best handle major, multiyear projects in Six Sigma by splitting them up into several smaller, but well-coordinated, projects. Some companies refer to this approach as a multigenerational project plan when the projects are done sequentially. Each project produces a tangible deliverable in a reasonable amount of time, and this deliverable is a milestone towards a longer-term objective. Subsequent projects build on this deliverable to take it to the next level, producing their own deliverables. After several such projects, the organization reaches its desired end-state, but since it has produced tangible deliverables along the way, management's patience is not tested.

Another alternative is to have several Black Belt teams working in parallel. When this is done, someone (typically a MBB) should "own" the overall initiative and periodically bring the individual Black Belts leading each project together, to plan and coordinate the overall effort. This results in a tiered structure for the overall initiative, allowing each Black Belt to produce tangible results in a four to six month time frame while still working toward the overall objective.

20. How do I structure project reviews?

This topic was discussed in Chapter 5, so we will provide only a summary here. Similar information about reviews of the overall initiative is in Chapter 6. Management review of projects is critical for several reasons. These reviews demonstrate management's commitment, ensure that Black Belts take the projects seriously, and provide direct feedback to management as to how things are progressing.

We recommend that Champions review projects weekly, and business unit or functional managers review them monthly. The idea is to have a quick check to keep the project on track by finding out what has been accomplished in the last week, what is planned for next week, and what barriers if any need to be addressed. The Champion review is typically short, about 30 minutes, and covers topics such as the following:

- Activity this week
- Accomplishments this week
- Recommended management actions
- Help needed
- Plan for next week

The monthly management reviews are typically even shorter, about 10-15 minutes per project. A typical agenda for these reviews is:

- Project purpose
- Process and financial metrics—progress versus goals
- Accomplishments since the last review
- Plans for future work
- Key lessons and findings

Notice that this agenda is similar to that for the weekly review with the Champion. In the monthly review much more emphasis is placed on performance versus schedule, progress towards process and financial goals, and key lessons and findings. As Six Sigma grows, the number of projects may become large and reviews may require a lot of time. The review time can be reduced by rating projects as Green (on schedule), Yellow (in danger of falling behind schedule if something isn't done) and Red (behind schedule and in need of help), and reviewing only those rated Red and Yellow.

21. How do I close out projects?

Project closure was discussed at length in Chapter 5, so we will only provide a summary here. Project closure is an important part of your project identification and prioritization system, for the simple reason that Black Belts can't take on additional projects until they complete their current ones. You can't inhale unless you are able to exhale. The key participants in this decision are the Black Belt, the Champion, the finance representative, and the "process owner"—the person who has responsibility for the process being improved by the Black Belt.

The organization should have a standard set of steps to close out a project, a project closure form that is an integral part of the project tracking system, and a method for electronically archiving the project in the reporting system so the results will be available to the whole organization. This last item is important because Black Belts working in non-standard areas, such as risk management, find documentation of previous projects in this same area extremely helpful. The specific closure steps and form should be tailored to each organization, but we recommend that the following steps be required:

- Successful completion of each phase of the DMAIC (or DFSS) process
- Finance sign-off on the savings claimed
- Control plan in place and in use by process owner
- Needed training implemented
- Final Champion and management reviews

Training Questions

22. How do I design a good Six Sigma training system?

As noted in Chapter 6, it is critically important that you design and implement a training system, as opposed to holding a wave of mass training. A training system is built around the ongoing needs of the entire organization. It takes into account the different curricula that need to be available for different roles, the need for specialized or tailored training, periodic refreshers, training new hires, and so on. The Six Sigma training system should be integrated into the existing training system (assuming there is one), and become a permanent part of your supporting infrastructure.

Someone (often a MBB) should "own" the training system before and after it is integrated into the existing training system.

The Six Sigma training system should be designed by those who understand adult learning and behavioral science, as well as those knowledgeable in Six Sigma. In other words, it will likely be a team effort. The design team should begin first with the development needs of the organization, now and in the immediate future, and then determine what curricula is required to satisfy these needs. Other important design considerations include:

- Who will teach each course? How will instructors be qualified and evaluated?

- What materials will be developed for each course? Who will maintain and update these materials?

- Who needs to take each course? Are some courses mandatory? Do some have prerequisites?

- Will exams be given? If so, how will they be developed and graded?

- Will digital (web-based) training be used? How about digital exams?

- What system will be used to track who has taken which courses and which exams, and identify those in need of training?

- Who will handle the logistics (arranging for rooms, obtaining and delivering materials, refreshments, and so on)? Will this be done centrally, or on a class-by-class basis?

Clearly, a true training system that addresses each of the issues noted above is much more complex than a wave of mass training. The system basically answers the questions of Who?, What?, When?, Where?, and How? The needs of the organization answer the question Why? The training system should be dynamic, changing over time to meet the evolving needs of the organization.

23. What training do project teams need?

It is generally accepted that every member on a Black Belt team does not have to be trained as a Black Belt. Our recommendation is that eventually everyone in the organization should be trained in the Six Sigma improvement process, but starting out this will certainly not be the case. As a new Black Belt team is formed, it may turn out that several members of the team, who were selected because of subject matter knowledge, have little or no Six Sigma training. What training do they need in order to function effectively on the team?

In general, we do not recommend that everyone be trained in everything. Therefore, we do not suggest that the team members must all be trained as Green Belts at the time they join the project. This will come, but if you insist on doing it now, it will delay the completion of the project. Instead, we recommend more of a just-in-time approach. The Black Belt should first provide training on Six Sigma awareness to the team. This will help them understand the big picture, and follow where they are in the project at any point in time. Typically, awareness training takes about a half day.

Once the awareness training has been completed, the Black Belt should take the responsibility to develop the team's ability to apply whatever tool is needed at that time.

Questions Concerning Financial Benefits

24. Are the published benefits of Six Sigma real?

We cannot comment on all published Six Sigma benefit claims, since we have not been privy to all of these. However, we do have evidence that the majority of published claims from major corporations are completely valid. At GE, AlliedSignal, and W. R. Grace for example, there have been rigorous financial controls and audits to validate the published benefits. In addition, many of the intangible benefits, such as preventing rather than fixing a problem—through Design for Six Sigma for example—have not been included in published benefit figures.

Therefore, it is highly probable that the true benefits of Six Sigma exceed the published figures. We believe that this is true for most companies appropriately deploying Six Sigma. Of course, it is certainly possible that some companies that have received less media scrutiny have "massaged the numbers." Certainly companies claiming huge benefits should provide external analysts with some degree of "transparency" to the savings, so that others can see the specific sources of savings. Also, bottom line profitability should show improvement to the level claimed as Six Sigma benefits.

Part of the reason for skepticism about published financial benefits is that people simply cannot believe such huge savings are possible. Many people in the business world have gotten so used to historic levels of scrap, rework, wasted effort, and ineffectiveness, that they honestly believe such waste is an inherent part of business. Studies have shown for years that waste and rework costs in US businesses are typically 20–30% or more of sales revenue. This is a huge figure, typically much larger than gross profit! The potential for radical improvement has always been there, but the leadership, will, and a scientific, disciplined methodology have often not been present.

25. How do I sustain the gains of Six Sigma?

As explained in Chapter 6, you sustain the gains of Six Sigma in three major ways. First, you sustain the gains of individual projects that have been completed through the individual project control plan (proactive), and through periodic reviews of previously completed projects (reactive).

Second, step back from individual projects and look at maintaining the gains of the overall initiative. This can be done by developing a good implementation plan (proactive), and also by conducting periodic leadership reviews of the overall initiative (reactive).

Third, you ensure permanent benefit from Six Sigma by institutionalizing it into your culture and managerial processes, as outlined in Chapter 7.

26. How do I calculate the financial impact of a project?

This question is discussed in Chapter 5, so we will only summarize here. Members of the finance organization should be primarily responsible for calculation of financial benefits. This is their area of specialization, and they form an objective third party for projects outside Finance. Financial benefits should be segregated into hard dollars, those savings that will directly hit the bottom line, and soft dollars, savings that will hit the bottom line indirectly.

For example, reducing wasted materials by 10% is a direct savings that will show up in lower procurement costs. However, saving the time of financial analysts by improving the closing or budgeting processes will not directly hit the bottom line and is a "soft dollar savings" unless there is a headcount reduction. Note that some projects may be focused on customer or employee satisfaction, with no quantifiable financial benefit anticipated. Also, some projects may focus on top line growth rather than bottom line savings, but the same principles apply relative to hard and soft dollars.

27. Can Six Sigma successfully achieve non-financial objectives?

Absolutely! Six Sigma has most often been applied to improve the bottom line through financial savings from reduced scrap and rework. However, it is a generic improvement methodology; it can be applied to improving virtually anything. For example, Six Sigma has frequently been applied to improving relationships with customers by attacking sources of customer frustration, whether or not they directly lead to financial benefits.

Similarly, many charitable or not-for-profit organizations are implementing Six Sigma to better achieve their objectives, which are obviously not financial in nature. Examples include measuring the impact of exposing inner city children to fine arts, providing services to the disabled, or offering education and mentoring to at-risk youth. Since 9/11/2001, Six Sigma has been applied to countering terrorism, among other government applications. As previously noted, educational organizations from kindergarten through college are prime opportunities for Six Sigma improvement.

Other Human Resources Questions

28. How do I involve the entire organization in Six Sigma?

The best way is eventually to have all employees trained in Six Sigma thinking and improvement methods. This goal requires too much training and project activity to do all at once, but it should be a long-term objective with a specific action plan, as part of the overall deployment plan. In addition, you should be involving large numbers of employees in Black Belt teams, the project identification system, the project reporting system, and so on, even before they become Green Belts.

29. How should I modify the reward and recognition system to support Six Sigma?

This subject was discussed at length in chapters 4 and 5, so we will only summarize here. First of all, we prefer that Black Belts and others become actively involved in Six Sigma because they truly believe in it, that is, because of intrinsic motivation. However, we understand that to attract top talent management must provide incentives to demonstrate that a Six

Sigma assignment will help rather than hurt one's career. Perhaps even more important, management must ensure that the reward and recognition system actually reinforces the desired behavior. A common failure of leadership is to ask for one type of behavior while tangibly rewarding the opposite behavior.

Obviously, financial benefits are one type of reward. Many companies have used salary increases, special bonuses, and stock options to provide tangible financial rewards. Another type is career progression. If Black Belts and MBBs rotating out of their Six Sigma assignments obtain promotions or highly desired positions, this reward sends a clear signal to the entire organization. There are also non-financial rewards, such as peer recognition, opportunities to present projects to senior executives, participation in limited-attendance annual business meetings, and attendance at external Six Sigma conferences.

30. How do I form effective teams?

Teams are critical to the success of Six Sigma, and they should be formed carefully. The overall leadership team was discussed at length in Chapter 4, so we focus here on project teams, that is, Black Belt teams. (Green Belts often complete their projects individually.) The project team is formed to help the Black Belt successfully complete the project. Obviously, if the Black Belt can complete the project on his or her own, this is fine. You don't want teams for the sake of having teams.

Generally, the Black Belt brings the Six Sigma improvement methodology and some subject matter expertise, and the project team members bring additional subject matter expertise in the area being improved. For example, in manufacturing the project team will likely be made up of engineers and operators. In Finance, it will likely be financial analysts or accountants, in education it might include students, administrators, and teachers, and so on. Part of the work of developing the project charter is determining what specific skills will be needed on the project, and who has them. Of course, the make-up of the team may change over time as the project progresses.

Each project is unique, but in general we recommend project teams of 4-6 members. Larger teams often struggle to maintain team cohesiveness, or even to meet at the same time. If more members are needed, it may be wise to split the project into two smaller projects. Team members should be able to commit at least 25 percent of their time to the team. If they are too busy to commit to this level, others should be selected in their places. You may still be able to use the original people as ad-hoc technical advisors, but not as team members.

Effective team functioning is an extensive field in its own right, so we will give a couple of references for more detailed guidance. Two are Appendix A in Hoerl and Snee (2002), and Snee, Kelleher, and Reynard (1998), as well as the references listed in each of them.

31. How do I find the resources?

This question was discussed in Chapter 4, so we will only summarize here. There are two major options: go out or stay home. You can:

- Hire additional resources, typically experienced Quality Leaders, Champions, MBBs, or Black Belts, or use resources from a Six Sigma provider. When utilizing a Six Sigma provider, the provider's resources are gradually phased out, and internal resources that have gained experience begin to take over.

- Use the second and more common approach, which is to utilize existing internal resources. Internal resources can be freed up from their current work in a number of ways, including:

  - Utilizing Six Sigma to attack problems they would have worked on anyway (new approach but no new resources)

  - Reprioritizing work and dropping or postponing some existing work

  - Delegating work to subordinates. Our experience is that in many companies managers spend a great deal of time "micromanaging" work that should really be done by their direct reports, rather than by them

  - Backfilling for some of the resources dedicated to Six Sigma (headcount increase)

We do not recommend using part-time MBBs and Black Belts.

References

Hoerl, R.W. (2001). "Six Sigma Black Belts, What Do They Need to Know?" (With Discussion), *Journal of Quality Technology*, 33, 4, 391-434.

Hoerl, R.W., and R. D. Snee. (2002). *Statistical Thinking: Improving Business Performance*. Duxbury Press/Thomson Learning, Pacific Grove, CA.

Snee, R. D., K. H. Kelleher, and S. Reynard. (1998). "Improving Team Effectiveness," *Quality Progress*, May, 43-48.

APPENDIX

SIX SIGMA DEPLOYMENT PLAN—AN EXAMPLE

"Failing to plan is planning to fail"

—John Wooden

This is an example of a deployment plan that was developed for an organization in the Six Sigma Executive workshop. The organization is small, being a business unit of a company. It represents early thinking of the organization and will be refined as needed as the Six Sigma deployment progresses. This is an example of what one group has done and is not presented as what all organizations should do. Keep in mind that the deployment plan is organization-specific. What is good for one organization is not necessarily good for another.

Contents

- Introduction
- Deployment Elements
- Lessons Learned
- Key Issues
- Action Plan

Introduction

- The Six Sigma Initiative is better understood following Champion Training.
- Six Sigma will facilitate breakthrough process improvements as well as quality or management improvements.
- The purpose is to eliminate undesirable variation from our key processes affecting key customer outputs.
  - This is accomplished by deploying our best people (process experts) who will be highly trained in process improvement and advanced statistical methods.
- Six Sigma is unique in that it utilizes 8 key tools to arrive at, and control and optimize critical-to-quality process parameters affecting customer expectations and requirements.
- The Six Sigma initiative will be monitored quarterly for effectiveness and improvement by the Management Team.
- Twelve key elements make up the deployment effort.

Deployment Plan Elements

- Strategy and Goals
- Process Performance Metrics
- Project Selection Criteria
- Project List (Hopper)
- Champions List

- Black Belt/Green Belt List
- Training Plan
- Roles and Responsibilities
- Project Reporting and Tracking
- Reward and Recognition
- Communication Plan/Process
- Management Review

Strategy

- Deploy Six Sigma first in manufacturing and then move to administrative and transactional processes.
- Begin with Black Belt training and follow with Green Belt training in about 9 months.
- Select the top performing Black Belt to be trained as a MBB.

Goal for Six Sigma

- Six million in productivity improvements reaching the bottom line in 2000

Process Performance Metrics

- Process Performance Metrics will be used to measure organizational process performance.
- Process Performance Metrics include:
  - Defects (DPU, PPM)
  - On-time Performance
  - Parts/Labor Hour
  - Safety
  - Cost of Poor Quality
  - Scrap

Project Selection Criteria

- Project selection criteria will be used to select opportunities for breakthrough improvements.
- The Management Team will select and prioritize projects.
- The criteria selected include:
  - Customer Complaints
  - Reduce Downtime
  - Capacity Improvement
  - 50% Scrap/PPM Reduction
  - >$250,000 Cost Reduction

Project List (Hopper)

- Potential projects will reside in a project hopper.
- The project hopper will include a list of approved and prioritized opportunities assigned by the Management Team.
- An initial project hopper was established in training; however, it must be chartered and validated by accounting for potential savings.

PROJECT HOPPER LIST

- Commercialize Containers
- FG Optimization
- CC-1 Optimization
- Compression Molding Optimization
- 2007 Tooling—Downtime Reduction 60%
- Manufacturing Expansion
- Setup/Downtime Improvement by 20%
- New Product Introduction
- Field Sales Activity
- Company Staffing Model
- Tool Room Throughput

Champions List

- All individuals scheduled for champion training are potential champions.
- The champions are catalysts for institutionalizing change. They—
  - Communicate Six Sigma initiatives
  - Facilitate selecting projects
  - Track ongoing projects weekly
  - Break down barriers for Black Belts and Green Belts

Black Belt List

- The right Black Belt is assigned as projects are selected.
- Black Belts are change agents for institutionalizing the Six Sigma strategy. They—
  - Lead high impact process improvement projects
  - Master advanced quality tools/statistics
  - Deploy Six Sigma throughout the organization

Gren Belt List

- Green Belts build additional Six Sigma capability in their own area of work by—
  - Leading important process improvement teams
  - Being proficient in basic and advanced quality tools
  - Leading, training, coaching on Six Sigma tools and process analysis

Training Plan

- Training the organization in Six Sigma is key to sustaining the process.
- Champion Training—Complete
- Black Belt Training—50% complete
- Black Belt (2000)—15 June 00, AS, JF, RH
- Green Belt Manufacturing Training—15 Dec. 99, AS, JF, RH

- Green Belt Admin.—15 June 00, AS, JF, RH
- Yellow Belt Training—TBD, AS, SJ
- Design for Six Sigma— TBD, AS, JM
- Awareness Training—(all associates) AS, SJ

Roles and Responsibilities

- Roles and responsibilities were defined for—
  - Management Team, Champions, Black Belts, and Functional Support Groups
- Two areas were defined for each role—
  - Expected Role and Leading Behaviors

BLACK BELT (ROLE)

- Maintain Six Sigma Body of Knowledge
- Dedicated to project work 40-60%
- Teach Body of Knowledge to Green Belts
- Communicate project status/needs to Champions weekly
- Mentor, support Green Belts
- Informal resource to other BB, GB, Organization
- Project deliverables

BLACK BELT (LEADING BEHAVIORS)

- Provide technical leadership
- Analytical thinker
- Positive attitude —"Can-Do"
- Self starter
- Provide team leadership
- Demonstrate dedication to Six Sigma methodology—"walk the talk"
- Promote safety at all times

CHAMPION (ROLE)

- Eliminate Roadblocks
- Review Black Belt project status weekly
- Do Black Belt work when applicable
- Develop Black Belt/Green Belt charters
- Report to Management Team project status
- Keep projects focused on task
- Provide resources as required
- Reprioritize project opportunities as needed

CHAMPION (LEADING BEHAVIORS)

- Visible leader
- Motivator
- Positive reinforcement
- Supportive
- Good listener

MANAGEMENT TEAM (ROLE)

- Commitment to Six Sigma Initiative
- Provide capital as required
- Provide strategic direction
- Internal promotion
- Macro resource allocation
- Coordination of business processes
- Interface with Corporate
- Select/prioritize project list
- Select Black Belts
- Reward and Recognition

MANAGEMENT TEAM (LEADING BEHAVIORS)

- Enthusiastic
- Firm, fair, fun
- Challenge (positively)
- Be consistent
- Open acknowledgement
- Responsive
- Open door (time)
- Promote safety

FUNCTIONAL SUPPORT TEAM (ROLE)

- Functional support
- Data
- Financial/funding
- Specific research data
- Recognition
- Resources
- Project guidance
- Education, training
- Discretionary spending
- Audit safety

FUNCTIONAL SUPPORT TEAM (LEADING BEHAVIORS)

- Responsiveness
- Motivation
- Available
- Teacher/Coach
- Approachable
- Positive
- Open minded
- Follow up

Project Reporting and Tracking

- Six Sigma Flash reports to Division and Sector Directors monthly. Includes—
  - Performance metrics/dollars saved
  - Projects status
  - Champion input to projects
  - Miscellaneous
- Champions to review projects with Black Belts weekly
- Project completion presentations to Management Team

Reward and Recognition

- President and HR to establish reward and recognition for accomplishments. Options:
  - Gift certificates
  - Use of laptop computers
  - Time off
  - Special business cards
  - Pictures posted in hallway
  - Team-of-year recognition
  - Certificate/trophies
  - Dinner and awards ceremony

Communications Plan

- Communications is essential to promote and report Six Sigma progress.
- This plan has not been formalized. Current communication includes monthly Flash reports, monthly meetings. Flash reports were sent to all associates on email.
- Other mechanisms include—
  - Visual work places where projects are under way
  - Elevator speeches
  - Bulletin boards showing project status

Management Review

- The Management Team will evaluate the effectiveness of the Six Sigma Initiative on a quarterly basis.
- All 12 elements of the deployment plan will be assessed.
- To sustain the gains of Six Sigma, the following success factors were noted to assure Six Sigma projects and the initiative are successful. See the following—

SUSTAINING GAINS OF SIX SIGMA PROJECTS

- Effective control plans. (ISO 9000 quality management system is infrastructure)
- Structured project reviews
- Maintain metrics
- Training
- Audit system (projects, metrics, financial)
- Share best practices
- Library of documented projects
- Access to project information by others
- Results are measurable and visible
- Six Sigma yearbook

SUSTAINING GAINS OF SIX SIGMA INITIATIVE

- Initiative tailored for divisional culture
- Quarterly management review
- Planned training (self sustaining)
- Retain trained talent
- Projects are successful and deliver savings
- Reward and recognition (review periodically)
- Good communication (local, sector levels)
- Continue new teams/projects
- Solicit project ideas from all levels of the organization, i.e., the suggestion team
- Six Sigma results part of performance appraisal
- Promotion of high potential candidates

Lessons Learned

- The Management Team and Champions select projects for Six Sigma.

- Projects must be approved and chartered prior to making the project hopper.

- Roles and responsibilities are defined.

- Six Sigma is a second job for those involved.

- Projects should be short and focused.

- Successful projects involve 40-60% Black Belt support.

Key Issues

- Project Selection—Assure the right projects are selected and are measurable and supported.

- Time—Black Belts must be able to spend at least 50% of their time on projects. Reprioritization of work should be part of project charter (last line of charter).

- Savings are measurable—Projects savings are hard to measure per existing accounting and financial reporting system.

- Organizational Support—Where will the additional staffing capacity to sustain projects come from?

Action Plan

- Flash Report—Champions to provide input to flash report.   Ongoing

- Resolve capacity definition   S.J. 9/30/99

- Project Hopper   S.J. Ongoing

- Short Term Charters   B.S. and T.F. 9/27/99

- Establish Design for Six Sigma   A.S and J.G. TBD

- Establish Management Team   Sr. Staff TBD

- Quarterly Review Schedule   A.S. TBD

GLOSSARY

BASELINE: The level of process performance when a project is initiated.

BLACK BELT: A process improvement project team leader who is trained in the Six Sigma methodology and tools and who is responsible for project execution.

CAPABILITY: The total range of inherent variation in a stable process. It is typically determined using data from control charts.

CAPABILITY INDEX: A calculated value used to compare process variation to a specification. Examples are Cp and Cpk. Can also be used to compare processes.

CAUSE AND EFFECT (C&E): A prioritization matrix or diagram that enables you to select those process input variables (Xs) that have the greatest effect on the process output variables (Ys).

CONTROL PLAN: A process control document that describes the system for controlling processes and maintaining improvements.

COST OF POOR QUALITY: Cost associated with poor quality products or services. Examples: product inspection, sorting, scrap, rework, and field complaints.

CRITICAL TO QUALITY CHARACTERISTIC (CTQ): A characteristic of a product, service, or information that is important to the customer. CTQs must be measurable in either a "quantitative" manner (i.e. 3 mg) or "qualitative" manner (i.e., correct or incorrect).

DEFECT: Any characteristic that deviates outside of specification limits or customer requirements.

DESIGN OF EXPERIMENTS (DOE): An efficient method of experimentation which identifies, with minimum testing, those factors (key process input variables) and their optimum settings that affect the mean and variation of the outputs.

ENTITLEMENT: The best level of performance a process can be expected to produce.

FAILURE MODES AND EFFECTS ANALYSIS (FMEA): Analytical approach for preventing defects by prioritizing potential problems and their resolution.

GAGE REPEATABILITY: The variation in measurements obtained with one measurement instrument when used several times by one analyst while measuring the identical characteristic on the same part.

GAGE REPRODUCIBILITY: The variation in the average of the measurements made by different analysts using the same measuring instrument when measuring the identical characteristic on the same part.

HIDDEN FACTORY: The part of the process that handles defective product by reworking as appropriate and scrapping what cannot be reworked to meet specification.

MEASUREMENT SYSTEM: The complete process used to obtain measurements. It consists of the collection of operations, procedures, gages and other equipment, software, and personnel used to assign a number or value to the characteristic being measured.

MEASUREMENT SYSTEM ANALYSIS: Study of the measurement system typically using Gage R&R or nested variance component studies to measure the quality (repeatability and reproducibility) of the measurement produced by the system.

MINITAB™: Statistical analysis software package. Widely used in Six Sigma projects.

MULTI-VARI STUDY: A statistical study that samples the process as it operates, and through statistical and graphical analysis, identifies the important controlled and uncontrolled (noise) variables.

PARETO CHART: A way to display data graphically which quantifies problems from most to least important so that the "vital few" can be identified. Named after Vilfredo Pareto, an Italian economist.

PROCESS: The combination of people, equipment, materials, measurements, methods, and environment that produce a given product or service. It is the particular way of doing something.

PROCESS MAP: A step-by-step pictorial sequence of a process showing process inputs, process outputs, and processing steps.

PROCESS VARIATION: The extent to which the distribution of individual values of the process characteristic (input or output variable) vary; often shown as the process average plus and minus some number of standard deviations. Other related measures of spread include the range and variance.

MASTER BLACK BELT (MBB): A person who is "expert" in Six Sigma techniques and project implementation. MBBs play a key role in training and coaching Black Belts.

SIX SIGMA CHAMPION: A business leader who facilitates the leadership, implementation, and deployment of the Six Sigma initiative and philosophies, and provides support to Black Belts and Green Belts and their projects.

SPECIFICATION: The engineering requirement or customer requirement for judging acceptability of a particular characteristic.

STANDARD DEVIATION: A measure of the spread of a process characteristic (width of the distribution).

Xs (INPUT VARIABLES): An independent material or element, with descriptive characteristic(s), that is either an object (going into) or a parameter of a process (step), and has a significant effect on the output of the process.

Ys (OUTPUT VARIABLES): A dependent material or element, with descriptive characteristic(s), that is the result of a process (step) and either is, or significantly affects, the customer's CTQ.

ACRONYMS

ACFC: "At the customer, for the customer" projects

ANOVA: Analysis of Variance

AOP: Annual Operating Plan

ASQ: American Society for Quality

BB: Black Belt

C&E: Cause and Effect

CEO: Chief Executive Officer

CFO: Chief Financial Officer

CIO: Chief Information Officer

CQ: Commercial Quality (non-manufacturing)

CTQ: Critical to Quality metrics

DFSS: Design for Six Sigma

DMAIC: Define, Measure, Analyze, Improve, Control

DMADV: Define, Measure, Analyze, Design, Verify

DOE: Design of Experiments

FMEA: Failure Modes and Effect Analysis

GB: Green Belt

GE: General Electric Corporation

GR&R: Gage Repeatability and Reproducibility

HR: Human Resources

ISO: International Standards Organization

IT: Information Technology

MBB: Master Black Belt

MSA: Measurement System Analysis

PPM: Parts Per Million

QFD: Quality Function Deployment

R&D: Research and Development

R&R: Reward and Recognition

RSM: Response Surface Methodology

SIPOC: Process map identifying Suppliers, Inputs, Process steps, Outputs, and Customers

SOP: Standard Operating Procedure

SPC: Statistical Process Control

VOC: Voice of the Customer

YB: Yellow Belt

INDEX

8 reasons why you should read the Financial Times for 4 weeks RISK-FREE!

To help you stay current with significant
developments in the world economy ...
and to assist you to make informed business
decisions — the Financial Times brings you:

❶ Fast, meaningful overviews of international affairs ... plus daily briefings on major world news.

❷ Perceptive coverage of economic, business, financial and political developments with special focus on emerging markets.

❸ More international business news than any other publication.

❹ Sophisticated financial analysis and commentary on world market activity plus stock quotes from over 30 countries.

❺ Reports on international companies and a section on global investing.

❻ Specialized pages on management, marketing, advertising and technological innovations from all parts of the world.

❼ Highly valued single-topic special reports (over 200 annually) on countries, industries, investment opportunities, technology and more.

❽ The Saturday Weekend FT section — a globetrotter's guide to leisure-time activities around the world: the arts, fine dining, travel, sports and more.

FT FINANCIAL TIMES
World business newspaper

The *Financial Times* delivers a world of business news.

Use the Risk-Free Trial Voucher below!

To stay ahead in today's business world you need to be well-informed on a daily basis. And not just on the national level. You need a news source that closely monitors the entire world of business, and then delivers it in a concise, quick-read format.

With the *Financial Times* you get the major stories from every region of the world. Reports found nowhere else. You get business, management, politics, economics, technology and more.

Now you can try the *Financial Times* for 4 weeks, absolutely risk free. And better yet, if you wish to continue receiving the *Financial Times* you'll get great savings off the regular subscription rate. Just use the voucher below.

---

4 Week Risk-Free Trial Voucher

Yes! Please send me the *Financial Times* for 4 weeks (Monday through Saturday) Risk-Free, and details of special subscription rates in my country.

Name _____

Company _____

Address _____ ❑ Business or ❑ Home Address

Apt./Suite/Floor _____ City _____ State/Province_____

Zip/Postal Code_____ Country _____

Phone (optional) _____ E-mail (optional)_____

Limited time offer good for new subscribers in FT delivery areas only.

To order contact Financial Times Customer Service in your area (mention offer SAB01A).

The Americas: Tel 800-628-8088 Fax 845-566-8220 E-mail: uscirculation@ft.com

Europe: Tel 44 20 7873 4200 Fax 44 20 7873 3428 E-mail: fte.subs@ft.com

Japan: Tel 0120 341-468 Fax 0120 593-146 E-mail: circulation.fttokyo@ft.com

Korea: E-mail: sungho.yang@ft.com

S.E. Asia: Tel 852 2905 5555 Fax 852 2905 5590 E-mail: subseasia@ft.com

www.ft.com

FT FINANCIAL TIMES
World business newspaper